6106

culinary
BOOT CAMP

culinary

BOOT CAMP

Five Days of Basic Training at The Culinary Institute of America

THE CULINARY INSTITUTE OF AMERICA
and MARTHA ROSE SHULMAN

JOHN WILEY & SONS, INC.

The Culinary Institute of America
PRESIDENT Dr. Tim Ryan
VICE-PRESIDENT, CONTINUING EDUCATION Mark Erickson
DIRECTOR OF INTELLECTUAL PROPERTY Nathalie Fischer
MANAGING EDITOR Kate McBride
EDITORIAL PROJECT MANAGER Mary Donovan
EDITORIAL ASSISTANT Margaret Otterstrom
PRODUCTION ASSISTANT Patrick Decker

This book is printed on acid-free paper.

Published by John Wiley & Sons, Inc., Hoboken, New Jersey
Published simultaneously in Canada

Limit of Liability/Disclaimer of Warranty: While the publisher and the author have used their best efforts in preparing this book, they make no representations or warranties with respect to the accuracy or completeness of the contents of this book and specifically disclaim any implied warranties of merchantability or fitness for a particular purpose. No warranty may be created or extended by sales representatives or written sales materials. The advice and strategies contained herein may not be suitable for your situation. You should consult with a professional where appropriate. Neither the publisher nor the author shall be liable for any loss of profit or any other commercial damages, including but not limited to special, incidental, consequential, or other damages.

For general information about our other products and services, please contact our Customer Care Department within the United States at (800) 762-2974, outside the United States at (317) 572-3993 or fax (317) 572-4002.

Wiley also publishes its books in a variety of electronic formats. Some content that appears in print may not be available in electronic books. For more information about Wiley products, visit our web site at www.wiley.com.

LIBRARY OF CONGRESS CATALOGING-IN-PUBLICATION DATA:
Shulman, Martha Rose.
  Culinary boot camp : five days of basic training with the Culinary Institute of America / Martha Rose Shulman.
     p. cm.
  Includes bibliographical references and index.
  ISBN-13: 978-0-7645-7278-4 (alk. paper : cloth)
  ISBN-10: 0-7645-7278-4 (alk. paper : cloth)
  1. Cookery. 2. Culinary Institute of America. I. Culinary Institute of America. II. Title.
  TX652.S5373 2006
  641.5--dc22

                          2005007860

PRINTED IN THE UNITED STATES OF AMERICA

Photographs by Ben Fink
Cover and interior design by Vertigo Design, NYC

10 9 8 7 6 5 4 3 2 1

To Mary Shulman, my first cooking teacher

This book was both a cook's and writer's dream project, and I have Angela Miller and Pam Chirls to thank for giving me the opportunity. Also hearty thanks to Mary Donovan and to Chefs John DeShetler and Hinnerk von Bargen. Bill gets a thank you for getting up at 6 every day while I was away at Boot Camp to get Liam to the bus, and Liam always gets a thank you for being such a good eater.

Contents

Preface ix
Introduction x

Day 1
INTO THE KITCHEN: STOCKS AND SAUTÉS 2
Into the Kitchen 5
Our Space 9
Stocks 12
Sauces 15
Sautés 16
Knife Skills and Mise en Place 23
Thickeners 24
Dinner at St. Andrew's Café 27

Day 2
SOUP PRODUCTION AND FRYING TECHNIQUES 30
The Final 32
Soups 34
Cooking with Fats 39
Stir Frying 39
Pan-Frying 40
Deep Frying 47
The Underbelly of the CIA 49
Dinner at the Escoffier Restaurant 53

Day 3
DRY HEAT COOKING METHODS 56
Roasting 59
Broiling and Grilling 65
Introduction to Wines 72
Dinner at American Bounty Restaurant 77

Day 4
MOIST HEAT COOKING METHODS 80
Combination Methods 84
Steaming 91
Poaching 91
Simmering and Boiling 97
Developing a Menu 98
Turning Skills into Recipes, from Basic to "Stepped Up" 100
Dinner at Ristorante Caterina de' Medici 103

Day 5
OUR FINAL EXAM 106
Into the Kitchen, for the Last Time 108
Production 114
Show Time 119
Graduation 120
Postscript 120

Mise en Place and Knife Skills 122
Mise en Place 125
Our Knife Kits 126
Basic Cuts 128
How to Cut 131

Additional Boot Camp Recipes 138
Stocks and Sauces 140
Appetizers and Soups 150
Entrées 170
Side Dishes 190

Reflections on Culinary French 229
Index 235
Benefactors Acknowledgments 242

Preface

When we first had the idea of creating boot camps at our Hyde Park campus, we knew that we wanted to keep learning at the forefront of a great experience. We examined the way the basic curriculum for the CIA's students ran. We were also determined to be sure that our "campers" not only learned impeccable foundation techniques, but that we also exposed them to our entire campus—from the public restaurants to student dining, from the classroom to the kitchen, from the library to the recreation center.

Over the years, the number of boot camp courses we've offered has grown from one to ten. Nearly one thousand people have graduated from these courses. Many people have come back after completing one boot camp to try something new. Today, you can find boot camps that focus on healthy cooking, big flavor cooking, gourmet meals you can make in minutes, and Italian cuisine.

Of course, the point of all that cooking is to make great meals to share with family and friends. One of the most important (and enjoyable) parts of any boot camp are the meals the campers share in our restaurants. Afternoon lectures that cover topics like food science and food and wine pairings, as well as excursions into the Institute's storeroom, give our students a whole new appreciation for dining in restaurants and creating menus.

Boot camps aren't demonstration classes, and our boot camp graduates will tell you that they felt real pressure to produce, just as a restaurant chef does. Whether producing their own lunch and having it ready at a very specific time or creating a menu based on selections from a mystery basket of ingredients, they have to accomplish the same things we expect of any full-fledged culinary professional.

As instructors for these boot camps, we are in a privileged position. We get to bring the art and craft of cooking to life. We get to debunk the myths that sometimes get in the way of great cooking. And we get to share our passion for the culinary arts with the wonderful students who come to Hyde Park, New York.

We hope to see you at a boot camp soon!

JOHN DESHETLER
HINNERK VON BARGEN

Introduction

In the predawn of a below-zero January day, as I crunched through snow from the parking lot of The Culinary Institute of America to a venerable building called Roth Hall, it became clear to me: I am living my life in reverse. When the children of my friends were busy filling out college applications, I was having a baby, my first and only. As my friends settled into their empty nests, I was putting Liam on the bus to go to kindergarten. I had begun my career in my early 20s, published a cookbook before I was 30, lived in Paris for 12 years. And now, having been a culinary professional for 30 years, I was finally going to cooking school.

Actually, it was cooking *camp*, a week-long intensive course called Culinary Boot Camp that The Culinary Institute of America in upstate New York offers in its continuing education department. I love camp. I spent 8 happy weeks at sleep-away camp every summer between the ages of 9 and 14. One of the few things that my husband Bill doesn't understand about me is this nostalgia and enthusiasm. "I've been to camp (scout camp)," he says in a sour sort of way, "I've dug latrines." Unlike our six-year-old son, Bill doesn't care to listen to my Forest Acres camp songs and spirited cheers, which I still remember word for word, or my stories about color war, the night the skunk got into Cabin 21, and Friendship Circle. He will tolerate my reminiscences about winning the swimming cup two years in a row and placing second in the riding cup. Although he

rolls his eyes, he will listen to me talk about how much my fellow campers and I cried at the end of each summer. He does, though, appreciate the camp friends that I am still close to after all these years.

Not that I expected sing-alongs and campfires at Culinary Boot Camp. I just liked the idea that the week-long course I was flying off to take was called camp. "I'll be away next week," I'd say to my friends, "I'm going to cooking camp!" A few weeks before I left I was thrilled to get a call from the CIA, inquiring about my uniform size. I'd get to wear the Institute's standard-issue houndstooth checkered pants and a crisp white chef's jacket, with necktie, apron, side towels, and chef's hat. And I'd carry a black canvas knife case that held a 9-inch chef's knife, an 11-inch slicer, a 3 1/2-inch paring knife, a wooden spoon, a large rubber scraper, a 10-inch whip and measuring spoons; a y-peeler, a plastic bowl scraper, a bench scraper, a 10-inch offset spatula, and tongs. I already had chef's jackets and pants, and all of these tools in a blue knife kit at home, but there was something extra-special about my new CIA gear. For a week, I would look like somebody who was becoming a chef.

A self-taught cook, I'd taken cooking classes when I wanted to learn about a particular thing like ravioli or puff pastry, and I'd taught many as well. I had toyed with going to cooking school, particularly during my first years in Paris. I looked into Anne Willan's popular school La Varenne, where many of my assistants went and developed first-rate skills. But I was a vegetarian then, and I didn't really want to cook—let alone eat—most of the dishes you learn to make when you receive a classical French culinary education. Believe me, nothing was better for my cooking than living, eating, and work-ing in France for 12 years. But the skills I developed were honed making the kind of food I am known for, which is healthy home cooking with a decidedly Mediterranean (and sometimes Mexican) focus.

As the years went by, I crept slowly up the food chain. In Paris I began to work with

The Martha Berns Reading Room, Conrad N. Hilton Library

fish and to eat and prepare poultry and rabbit. By the time I moved to California in the early '90s, I'd stopped defining myself as a vegetarian, though that was and still is largely the way I cook and eat at home.

I began to take on projects that required more range. Always the autodidactic, I learned a lot by doing. Over the course of several years I wrote a book called *The Foodlover's Atlas of the World*, for which I tested signature recipes from every country in the world. I delved into cuisines that I'd never explored, and I cooked many classical dishes that had heretofore been far from my repertoire. Although I never stopped until I was satisfied with a recipe, sometimes I felt that I was cooking in the dark.

I also began helping chefs with their cookbooks, not only with the writing but also with the recipe testing. Home cooking is so utterly different from restaurant cooking, and I felt strongly that all of the recipes in the books that I worked on had to be worked out and tested in a home kitchen. This was a new challenge for me, and a lot of fun, as again I was branching out, stretching my wings, making dishes I'd never done before. Now dinner might just as well be a beautifully plated Wolfgang Puck recipe, such as Rack of Lamb with Mint Vinaigrette or Pan-Seared Beef Filets with Port-Dijon Sauce, as the more rustic type of Mediterranean fare that my family was used to.

* * *

The CIA's Boot Camp course description reads as follows:

In Culinary Boot Camp, you will become well versed in the fundamentals of cooking, including knife skills, kitchen terminology, dry-heat cooking methods, and moist-heat cooking methods. You will also participate in a Practical Exam at the end of the course to enable you to use the new or improved skills presented in the class.

The video center in the Conrad N. Hilton Library

When the chance to attend came my way, I jumped at the opportunity. I always learn something new when I take a cooking class, and here was a chance to spend a week mastering some basic culinary concepts that had passed me by during my 30-year career.

What I didn't know that first day was just how profoundly the experience would affect the range of my kitchen skills. After my first Boot Camp (I went twice) I would return home to work intensely on a book with the California star chef Wolfgang Puck.

Boot Camp had given me the basic training I needed for this project. I could test several recipes in a day, because my freshly honed skills made me more efficient. And I knew more. Now when I seared Wolfgang's pork chops that would be served with a hoisin-based sauce and dried cranberries, I understood exactly what those pork chops were supposed to look and feel like. I "cooked to color," as my chef/instructor John DeShetler had taught me to do, the words forever implanted in my brain. I could press

The natatorium, Student Recreation Center

on the chops lightly with my fingertip and know they were done, then quickly make a pan sauce while I kept the chops warm. I would have been able to test all of these recipes had I not gone to Culinary Boot Camp, but now I had much more confidence about what I was doing.

My cooking life changed in other, smaller ways. Take blanching or parboiling vegetables: before I worked with Chef Hinnerk von Bargen, who taught the second Boot Camp I attended, I never thought about tasting the cooking water. By way of explaining how much salt to add to the boiling water, Chef Hinnerk stressed, in his emphatic, accented, baritone voice, that the water must taste "like the Atlantic Ocean," otherwise the green beans or the snap peas or the greens would be under-seasoned. How would I know unless I tasted? Pasta water, on the other hand, was to taste like a well-seasoned stock; if you salted it too generously the pasta would be too salty. Or stock: now when I make chicken stock I bring the water to a gentle simmer only, and watch the bubbles "breaking lazily at the surface" over many hours. I keep the pot partially off the burner so that it's easier to skim; and my stock is the better for it. Today I truss my chicken before I roast it; I never bothered to before. And the skin is more uniformly crisp.

Post Boot Camp, I understand things that I'd taken for granted for years—or not known at all. That you heat a pan before you add the oil so that the oil doesn't overheat before the pan gets hot enough. That you add cool or warm, but not simmering, liquid to a roux when you make a sauce because the roux needs time to disperse in the liquid before it comes to a boil, or lumps will form. Knowing things like this doesn't transform me into a chef who can mince 40 carrots in 5 minutes, or flip food neatly in a heavy skillet, or grill 20 duck breasts perfectly to order on a line. But it does make me a better cook. And that was why I and my fellow students—cooking enthusiasts and even some noncooks—had left jobs and home and family for a week to come and cook in the teaching kitchens of The Culinary Institute of America.

Day 1

INTO THE KITCHEN:
STOCKS AND SAUTÉS

In upstate New York in the middle of January, it's still dark at 5:30 in the morning. But when I awake on the first morning of my course, I can see that snow is falling, and the radio tells me that the temperature is somewhere below 20°F. I put on long silk underwear under my new starched houndstooth chef pants and white jacket, don warm hiking boots, and drive the icy 6 miles up Route 9 to the CIA, arriving just before dawn with many other bleary-eyed, knife-kit-toting students.

I make my way through new snow and over old ice to Roth Hall, the CIA's main building, and find the student dining room. This is not like the student dining halls I remember from college. It's a grand, sweeping room, at one time the chapel of the Jesuit seminary that this building used to be, with vaulted ceilings and stained-glass windows recently restored under the supervision of the same architect who was in charge of refurbishing Grand Central Station in New York City. Once called Alumni Hall, this imposing room now bears the name of the donor who paid for the renovation, Farquharson.

The food is also not what I remember from college. This is one of the many proving grounds for CIA students, and the production is impressive. A line of hungry students has been forming outside the kitchen since 5:45 a.m. The cooks have been there since 3 a.m. One team takes and shouts the orders to the cooks. There are omelets and eggs any way you want them, bacon and sausage, pancakes and waffles and French toast, a different hot cereal every day, a selection of pastries from the CIA pastry kitchens, yogurt, cold cereal, fruit smoothies, juice, and fruit salad. The line moves quickly, and I am soon seated with my fellow Boot Campers with a very necessary cup of coffee and a hot, welcome bowl of cream of rice topped with a delicious dried-fruit compote.

INTO THE KITCHEN

We take our places at desks in Lecture Hall 1. Chef John DeShetler comes into the room and writes his name on the board. He's a short guy with a round face and a round girth, red-blond hair that is just beginning to gray. He wears the CIA staff jacket (gold and green stripes around the collar, knotted cloth buttons) a green name badge, and the chef's kerchief around his neck, which he later shows us how to tie. "YOU ARE MINE!" he says with a sly smile on his face, and we know that he's going to give us the guidance we need. He'll be strict, but kind.

When I go to Boot Camp again, the following September, our instructor Hinnerk von Bargen, at 6 foot 8 inches Chef John's physical polar opposite, will stride in and say

something similar, if not a little more earthy: "Now your butts are mine, you little maggots." It's a stock first-day line we've all seen acted out by drill sergeants in movies and on TV, and it's probably in the Boot Camp instructor training manual. Chef Hinnerk's tone when he says this, like Chef John's, is not menacing. Indeed, he sees Boot Camp as a wonderful opportunity to "learn about cooking in a non-threatening environment."

The chef divides the class into five teams of three people each. These teams will work together in the kitchen throughout the week preparing designated menus, each designed to illustrate that day's cooking techniques. "Culinary Boot Camp is a six-month cooking course that is taught in a week," Chef John begins. "You'll learn everything you can without dropping over. Today each

team is going to work on the same entrée, but different stocks and side dishes. Then you're going to get progressively busier until the last day, when each team will compose and execute its own menu. By then you'll be very busy," he says with an impish smile. "I will be the drill sergeant in the kitchen, challenging you on time management. You're going to learn how to get your act together and master what you can do in advance, your mise en place." Mise en place, as we all will come to know, is the basic principle of getting yourself ready to work.

Each Boot Camp chef instructor is different, and I will be lucky enough to have two instructors with complementary approaches to the course. In this January session, Chef John, while teaching us everything there is to know about the different cooking techniques, emphasizes kitchen management; he makes

Basic Flavoring Agents (clockwise from left): Tomato paste, mirepoix, oîgnon brûlé, bouquet garni, sachet d'épices.

sure we keep our eye on the clock and our stations clean. Before he begins his first lecture, he outlines what he calls "housekeeping issues."

In September, Chef Hinnerk is more conceptual in his approach. He sees Boot Camp as a way to enlighten us about the principles of cooking—sautéing, braising, roasting, and so on. "Master the fundamentals of cooking first; the fancy-schmancy stuff comes later." He likes to say, "Welcome to the culinary arts, the world of uncertainty." Not surprising, given that most of his answers to our questions begin with "That depends."

"I hope you will ask me many questions, but you will see that many of your questions won't have one simple answer," Chef Hinnerk explains. "Cooking is an art, not a science, although there are many scientific reasons why things happen the way they do in cooking." (He's excellent at explaining the science, by the way.) "The answers to some questions depend on what you're looking for, and what the variables are. There is always more than one way to do something. The recipes you will get here are only vehicles for teaching you the basic culinary concepts. I want you to learn to cook without recipes. There are many things that a recipe doesn't know. It doesn't know how many BTUs of heat are coming out of

HOUSEKEEPING ISSUES

Keep your individual stations clean and organized.
Work as a team, organize trays, clean as you go along: clean, cut; clean, cut.
Place your dirty pots, pans, cutting boards, and the like on the rolling cart after use.
Wash all small stainless-steel equipment as you go along.
Return all food to proper areas.
Assist in the breakdown and closing of the kitchen.
Clean and put away your knives before lunch.
Remember, mise en place.

your burners. It doesn't know the size or the weight of your pan or what ingredients were available to you at the supermarket. But when you understand the concepts of cooking, you won't need to rely on recipes. You'll be able to buy anything at the market and know what to do with it."

Whatever his teaching style and focus, once the Boot Camp chef introduces the course and we introduce ourselves, he launches into the subject of the first day's "learning objectives." Between the Power-Point lectures, the loose-leaf Culinary Boot Camp manual, and our reading and video assignments (for which I never have time), there is no shortage of information.

Our lecture this first day introduces some basic culinary preparations: stocks and sauces. We are also going to master a basic technique: sautéing. The instructor goes through key terms such as *sachet d'épices, bou-*

Farquharson Hall

quet garni, *mirepoix, oignon brulé,* and *tomato concassé,* and explains why the terms are mostly French: because they standardize and provide a common culinary language. Historically, French chefs were regarded as the most skilled. After the French Revolution, many of the chefs in France who had worked in the houses of the royals and nobles left France and traveled throughout the world. Their culinary organization, and language, became the common thread for all cooks and chefs.

Chef Hinnerk discusses some of the recipes with us before we go into the kitchen. He makes changes wherever he sees fit, both in ingredients and in method. If he thinks there is a better way of executing a recipe, he won't hesitate to make the change. And he always explains techniques that are embedded in the text. Most significantly, after he does his demos and before we get to work in the kitchen on the first day, Chef Hinnerk emphasizes the importance of tasting: "You taste, adjust seasonings, and taste again." He makes us raise our right hand and repeat after him: "I solemnly pledge to taste the food before I serve it." And with that we get to work.

OUR SPACE

Skills Kitchens I and II are in a huge open space divided in the middle by a row of stainless-steel work/serving tables that extend under adjustable heat lamps. Our chefs do their demonstrations here at the beginning of each class, and sometimes while we're busy with our production the chef yells, "Demo!" and we stop our activity to go and watch him.

Two back-to-back commercial ranges dominate our kitchen, each with twelve burners and two wide ovens. They barely suffice at times, but there's another big range around the corner next to the grill and the deep fryer, where the chef does his demos.

CONTINUING EDUCATION AT THE CIA

We share kitchen space with students taking another course with a different chef. During my January Boot Camp, the other group of students is wearing black uniforms, which I find puzzling at first. It turns out they are all from the military — they've gone to real boot camp. One group is from Camp David, the other is stationed in Europe, and they are here at the CIA (but is this the right CIA?) for training. This isn't unusual; just the week before a large group from the Navy came.

In addition to the Boot Camps and other programs offered for enthusiasts such as myself, there are a number of other options available, from professional certification courses to intensive studies in wine. Courses (both hands on and Web-based), conferences devoted to topics such as world cuisines, and international travel programs are offered through both the Hyde Park, New York, campus and the campus at Greystone, located in St. Helena, California.

Stainless-steel tables and counters provide enough room for each team member to have a station, consisting of a large cutting board (set on damp paper towels to keep it steady) and two disposable aluminum pans, one for recyclable scraps, one for trash, as well as a container of water and detergent for wiping down our cutting boards. We're given sturdy cookbook racks for our notebooks, and the chef urges us to put plastic over the recipe pages so they don't get splattered. By the door are three large trash bins: a blue one for compostable food scraps, a yellow one for recyclables, and a gray one for garbage. Huge stainless-steel refrigerators line the wall at one end of the room, and under the counters on either side of the ranges are half-refrigerators for each team. This is where we find our meat or fish, portioned ("fabricated" is the culinary term) in the CIA meat and fish kitchens and brought up by the able Boot Camp assistants.

There are three sets of deep double sinks—one for food, one for pots and pans, and one for rinsing utensils that we'll reuse—plus a small pedal-operated sink for hand washing, which we use often. A large cooler with glass doors houses dairy products and other oft-used perishables such as tomato paste and condiments. Flour and salt are in large rolling bins. Onions, garlic, shallots, and potatoes are in bins under the demo table. Two immense baker's racks house scores of sauté pans (sautoirs and sauteuses), pots, bowls, measures, chinois, scales, food processors, and blenders. Shelving beneath work tables houses sheet pans and hotel pans. Big

sliding drawers are marked for various utensils—spoons and whisks, spiders, spatulas and ladles, dry measures and measuring spoons, mixers, and food processor attachments. A section of one of the drawers is used for Band-Aids and finger guards, and a nurse is just down the hall. This is a good thing.

DAY 1 TEAM PRODUCTION ASSIGNMENTS

All Students
Chicken Breast Provençal*

Team 1
Chicken Stock (page 142)
Buttered Sugar Snap Peas (page 194)

Team 2
Fish Stock (page 143)
Sautéed Mushrooms (page 218)

Team 3
Vegetable Stock (page 144)
Sautéed Zucchini (page 219)

Team 4
Chicken Broth (page 162)
Braised Red Cabbage (page 193)

Team 5
Brown Veal Stock (page 140)
Glazed Carrots (page 200)

Supplemental Starches
Basic Rice Pilaf (page 190)
Potato Puree (page 215)

*Recipe and photographs on pages 20–23.

STOCKS

Many tens of gallons of stock are produced daily at the Culinary Institute. It's strained and sealed airtight in heavy plastic bags, then refrigerated for use in the next day's classes. Stock is the backbone of much of what is cooked at the CIA.

We make veal stock, chicken stock, vegetable stock, fish stock, and chicken broth on our first morning. No, we won't spend 6 to 8 hours in the kitchen waiting for our stock to be done. Our heroic assistants take care of this. They roast the bones we'll need for our veal stock, and then chill and strain it when it is done. We will be in the kitchen long enough, however, to see our chicken stock and broth, fish stock, and vegetable stock through. We'll use these stocks the following day for our soups.

The CIA defines stock as a flavorful liquid produced by simmering bones, meat, and/or vegetables along with aromatics in clear water. The basic ratio is 6 quarts water for 8 pounds bones with 1 pound mirepoix (and 3 to 6 ounces of tomato product for brown stocks). Chef Hinnerk simplifies this further by telling us that 1 pound of bones should make 1 pint of stock, with the bones barely submerged in the water.

Stocks are used to flavor other dishes (soups and sauces, braises and stews, roasts) and as a cooking medium for grains, pasta, and vegetables. Chef Hinnerk emphasizes that while a stock can taste bland to the untrained palate, it is an essential foundation for classical cooking—indeed, in French it is called a *fond de cuisine* or simply *fond,* a foundation of cooking. It should add background flavor to a dish. As he puts it, "You don't invite your neighbors to see the foundation of your new house, but the inspector needs to look at it." In Japan, a chef is judged by the quality of his dashi, which is the simplest of stocks, made only with water, kombu, and bonito flakes.

A good stock is clear and should taste like the main ingredient—chicken, beef, vegetables, or fish. It should be nearly fat free and should have some structure and body. "A stock has more structure than hot water," says Chef Hinnerk, "because of the soft proteins from the meat." What else makes a stock good? Its flavor and aroma, which are impacted by its components, beginning with water. The water should taste good; filter it if it's chlorinated. The bones should be fresh. Supporting flavor is provided by aromatics, mirepoix, and in the case of brown stocks a tomato product, usually tomato paste, all of which are added during the last hour of cooking. Aromatics traditionally include peppercorns, thyme, parsley stems, and bay leaves; mirepoix is composed of 50 percent onions, 25 percent carrots, and 25 percent celery. Tomato paste is roasted first to caramelize its sugars and break down its acids. Chef Hinnerk comments that tomatoes are essential for vegetable stocks because of their high glutamic acid content, which is a flavor enhancer (think MSG). Mushrooms also are high in glutamic acid.

The size of your ingredients matters. The bigger the meat or food, the longer your

SIMMERING TIMES FOR THE VARIOUS STOCKS		
Beef:	8 hours	Add aromatics after 7 hours
Veal:	6 hours	Add aromatics after 5 hours
Poultry:	3 to 5 hours	Add aromatics after 2 hours
Vegetable:	20 to 40 minutes	Add aromatics at start
Fish:	30 to 45 minutes	Add aromatics at start

stock needs to simmer (which also means that if you want to make a quick stock, you can do so by grinding up the ingredients). However, it's important that you not cook stocks for too long, because overcooking liberates sulfuric acids in vegetables. That's why you add the mirepoix only during the last hour of cooking. Once you get the flavor out of the ingredients, you should be done with them.

Brown stocks get their color from roasting the bones and aromatics. They're made from beef or veal bones (you can also make a brown chicken stock by browning the chicken bones and aromatics in a heavy pan). They have a stronger flavor than the more delicate chicken and vegetable stocks and are used when a brown-colored sauce or soup is desired. Chicken stock or broth is used for light-colored soups or sauces.

The difference between a broth and a stock is that broths are made with meat and bones, whereas stocks are made with bones only (both include aromatics). Broths do not simmer as long as stocks; they're done when the meat is done. The timing for a chicken broth will depend on the age of the chicken. Hens are much tougher birds than fryers and will consequently give you a more aromatic broth than a younger bird, because the meat must simmer for a longer time before it is tender.

Two special types of stocks, fumets and essences, have a special place in the kitchen. A fumet is made by gently cooking fish bones with some wine and aromatic ingredients. This results in a stock that is less clear but more flavorful. An essence is made by simmering intensely flavored, aromatic ingredients like celery or mushrooms in a little liquid to make a broth.

Stock Maintenance

The water in your stock pot should cover the bones by no more than 2 inches. Bring it slowly to a simmer. As the water heats, blood and other impurities will be released into the water and will coagulate and rise to the surface as scum and foam. This should be removed because, as Chef Hinnerk says, "it tastes nasty." It also clouds the stock. The clearer the stock, the longer its shelf life.

The culinary term for the skimming process is the French word *dépouiller,* which means "to skin." If possible, you should skim the impurities from your stock before it actually reaches the boiling point. The more you skim, the clearer your stock will be. If you agitate the mixture by stirring before it comes to a simmer, you will encourage the scum to rise. Once it is simmering, try not to agitate it too much. One trick for getting the fat and scum off is to simmer the pot slightly off-center on the burner. Impurities and fat will rise to the surface and collect along the edge of the pot away from the heat, as if they too did not want to be there. Use a skimmer to remove the impurities. Use a ladle to degrease: working in a circular motion, start in the center and move toward the outside of the pot, removing the fat from the top of the stock as it collects along the edge. Of course, if you have time, the easiest way to remove

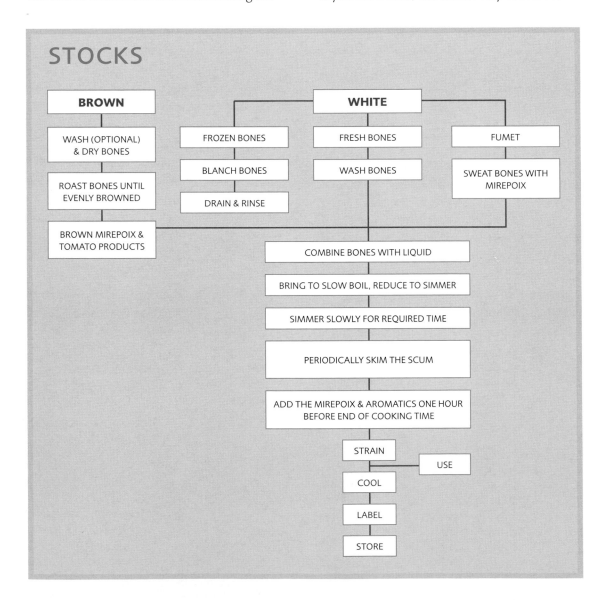

fat from stock is to chill the stock after straining it through a fine chinois or cheese-cloth-lined strainer. Then the fat will congeal on the surface and can be lifted off easily.

Stocks should be made in pots that are taller than they are wide, to minimize evaporation during simmering. You should taste them regularly as they simmer, so that you can ascertain the point at which they've achieved their peak flavor. If you continue to cook stocks after this, their flavors will become flat. It's best to taste stocks for final seasoning while they're still warm. They should smell and taste like the main ingredient. When you taste them, try to hit all of the areas of your tongue. This will also help you to ascertain the stock's body. If you are going to be reducing the stock, it should be left unsalted or very lightly salted. Otherwise, season to taste.

To strain the stock, set a fine wire-mesh sieve, or a colander or sieve lined with moistened cheesecloth, over a metal bowl or another pot and carefully ladle in the stock. Try not to disturb the solid ingredients. Place the bowl or pot in an ice bath to cool if not using right away. Refrigerate or freeze, and when ready to use, lift off any fat that has hardened on the surface.

SAUCES

Our chef defines a sauce as a flavorful liquid served to complement the main item in a dish. It adds flavor and sometimes reintroduces liquids lost in cooking. Sauces can also add color and texture to a dish.

The Grand Sauces

We learned about the five "grand sauces" as delineated by Auguste Escoffier. Escoffier was one of the world's most famous and influential chefs in the early 1900s. He was often referred to as "the king of chefs and the chef of kings." Chefs today still read and adhere to his basic principles of simplicity and organization. These roux-thickened or emulsified sauces, which can be made in large batches and stored, are Béchamel, Espagnole (which is the basis for demiglace), Tomato Sauce (a creamy one, not marinara sauce), Hollandaise, and Velouté.

The grand sauces and their many derivatives date from the seventeenth century and represent the old style of cooking, which is laborious and time-consuming but has unique and complex results. A Sauce Espagnole, for example, requires the cook to make a brown sauce from veal stock, additional bones, and aromatics, then thicken it with a roux, a process that takes 2 to 4 hours from start to finish (not counting the amount of time it took to make the veal stock, the quality of which will determine the success of the sauce). Demiglace is made by combining Sauce Espagnole and brown stock and reducing by half, which requires another hour or two, with constant and careful skimming. When a reduced brown sauce is thickened with a pure starch slurry, it is called a jus lié.

Grand sauces are often referred to as "mother sauces" because they're the basis for many other sauces. Add a red wine reduction and poached marrow to demiglace and you have Sauce Bordelaise. Add mushrooms, shallots, white wine, and tomato concassé (peeled, seeded, and chopped tomatoes) and you have Sauce Chasseur. Add cheese and mustard to Béchamel and you have Sauce Mornay. A Hollandaise to which you've added blood orange juice is a Sauce Maltaise; add whipped cream and it becomes a Mousseline Sauce. Add onions to Béchamel and you have Soubise. And so on and so forth. Many of these sauces—there are hundreds of them—are now considered old-fashioned, but they are a fundamental aspect of classical French cuisine.

Though our Boot Camp curriculum is firmly rooted in the classics, I'm happy to report that the CIA has kept up with modern times when it comes to sauces. We don't have to make brown sauce, Sauce Espagnole, or demiglace. Chef John is pretty clear about how he feels about demiglace: "You spend 8 hours making it and end up with half a cup of sauce that disappears in a few minutes!" We did make—and observe the chefs make—Velouté and Béchamel, but these mother sauces are far less laborious than brown sauce. Nonetheless, some of us, myself included, choose to use brown sauce in the final exam, when we create our own menus.

Contemporary Sauces

Contemporary sauces include purees and coulis (Chef Hinnerk defines these two aptly as "sauces thickened with their main ingredient"); emulsions such as mayonnaise, vinaigrette, and beurre blanc; chutneys and catsups, relishes and salsas; flavored butters; and pan sauces made from the fond left over from a sauté. They're quicker to produce and require less labor than the grand sauces. Some are arguably sounder nutritionally—though I certainly wouldn't call the beurre blanc we made with 12 ounces of butter healthy (just delicious). These sauces are made in smaller batches and can be culturally diverse, with big, bold flavors derived from regional and seasonal ingredients. If a contemporary sauce is to be thickened, it is not likely to be thickened with a roux; instead these sauces tend to be thickened by reduction, emulsion, a puree, or a pure starch slurry.

SAUTÉS

We all sauté chicken breast suprêmes on our first day in the Boot Camp kitchen, and with this exercise, dressed as we are in our uniforms, we all feel a little like chefs. There's something about the physicality of sautéing—the high heat, the sound of the sizzle, the way you move the pan, the speed with which the food is cooked and a sauce produced in the same pan—that evokes the ethos of a professional kitchen.

Sautéing is a method of cooking foods at high temperature in a small amount of fat. Typically, a sauce is made after the food is cooked by deglazing the juices and the solids left on the bottom of the pan.

Sautéing is a quick cooking method, but how quick depends on the thickness of the meat. For example, a thick steak is best seared first over high heat, than sautéed for a longer time at a slightly lower temperature than, say, a chicken breast. Generally, though, this method is quick enough to require a perfect mise en place. Everything should be prepped and ready to go before you begin to cook: the items to be sautéed should be seasoned and floured if necessary, the seasonings and sauce ingredients measured and close at hand.

The types of meats that are suitable for sautéing are the naturally tender parts, such as the loin, rib, tenderloin, and breast—the part of the animal that doesn't move much (Chef Hinnerk calls them "low-motion animal parts"). Seafood, particularly shellfish and sturdy fish such as swordfish and tuna, is also suitable. More delicate fish such as sole or flounder might fall apart when sautéed. Other candidates for sautéing are high-mois-

ture vegetables including peppers and zucchini. Vegetables that have been precooked or parboiled can be sautéed as a means of finishing or reheating them before service. No matter what the food, it should be portion-size or cut into small pieces.

Pans used for sautéing are called sauteuses or sautoirs. The sauteuse is a wide, shallow pan with gently sloping sides, and the sautoir is a wide, shallow pan with straight sides. The sloping sides of the sauteuse allow moisture to escape; this is important because if moisture is trapped in the pan, it causes the food to steam instead of sauté—you will not be able to achieve the proper browning and the meat will be tough. We will use the straight-sided sautoir the next day for pan-frying. The size of the pan in relation to the amount of food you are cooking is also important. If you crowd the pan,

A sauteuse (left) has sloped sides; a sautoir (right) has straight sides.

so there is not sufficient space between the items to allow steam to escape, the food will not brown and the trapped steam will toughen meat fibers.

We learned the term *cook to color*. White meats should be cooked to a golden brown, and red meats to a dark brown. When you remove your sautéed meat from the pan, the browned proteins that are left on the bottom, called the *fond*, provide the base for a sauce. You deglaze them by introducing a liquid to a pan, stirring up the solids from the bottom with a wooden spoon, and cooking the sauce until it coats the back of a spoon like cream (sometimes a starch slurry is used to further thicken the pan sauce). The term *nappé* describes this creamy viscosity. Once the sauce is done, it is spooned onto the serving plate and the food is placed on top to showcase the skin or the surface of the food. You wouldn't want to cover the food with the sauce, because part of the appeal of sautéing is the color of the finished product.

The Sauté Demo

Keeping the skin on helps to keep the breast juicy, and it looks very nice when it browns. The chef seasons the chicken breast generously with kosher salt and pepper. Chef

---

TESTING DONENESS "BY HAND"

To approximate what meat should feel like at various stages of doneness, press together your thumb and forefinger and feel the flesh on your palm, right below your thumb, with the index finger of your other hand: that's rare. Now, press together your thumb and your middle finger, then your thumb and your ring finger, and finally, your thumb and pinky. As you change fingers, you will be able to feel that the flesh is tightening. These changes represent an increasing degree of doneness, all the way from rare (your forefinger) to well-done (the pinky).

Hinnerk uses pepper on the flesh side only, because the skin side is the presentation side and he doesn't think the pepper looks nice.

The pan is first heated, then oil is added, and not too much of it. You don't pour the oil in the pan until after you've heated it, because otherwise the oil will become too hot and smoke before the pan is hot enough.

"Do you sear to lock in the juices?" Hinnerk asks us.

We all answer, "Yes."

"Wrong. Searing, contrary to popular belief, does not lock in juices. You sear for color and flavor."

Humbled, we watch as the chef cooks to color, turns the chicken breast over, cooks to color again, then places the pan in a 350°F oven for about 5 minutes to finish cooking it through. The cooking time is determined by the way the breast feels. Press gently on it; it should not be too soft. Listen for a slow sizzle in the oven. When it's ready, the chef removes it from the pan and lets it rest on a rack above a sheet pan. He admonishes us not to drain on paper towels, or the skin will get soggy. Meanwhile, he makes the sauce while the chicken rests, releasing juices (which run clear, another indicator that it is done) into the pan underneath.

Making the Pan Sauce

"First," Chef Hinnerk tells us, "evaluate the amount of fat in the pan in which you cooked the chicken. If it appears to be too much, pour some off. If you want, you can add some shallot or garlic to the pan." For this dish, the chef adds just tomato concassé, as there is already enough moisture. He stirs to loosen the fond, then he adds some white wine, brings it to a boil, and reduces it to concentrate the flavors. "The white wine also contributes to the color. The sugar in the white wine will help caramelize the tomatoes, and the acid will tighten the fibers; you don't want the tomatoes to fall apart."

The pan deglazed, he adds a little chicken stock and finally lots of butter. He swirls the pan constantly, as the motion emulsifies the butter. "It can come to a boil, but if too much of the liquid evaporates, the sauce will curdle. If you see this beginning to happen, you add a little water to the pan." He pours the juices from the chicken back into the sauce, tastes it and adjusts the seasoning, and spoons some onto a plate.

After our first morning in the kitchen, lunch, and cleanup, we go back to our classroom and have a short discussion about the day's work. The chef asks us to make a list of words associated with sautéing. The words come out willy-nilly, but then we number them so that the list reflects a certain order in the procedure.

PROCEDURE FOR SAUTÉ

1. Prepare food items for sautéing (e.g., marinate, flour, prepare mise en place, etc.).

2. Heat pan first.

3. Add fat and heat.

4. Sear items, show side first.

5. Reduce heat and finish larger items covered on stovetop or uncovered in an oven. Light meats are cooked golden brown; red meats are browned thoroughly.

6. Remove items from the pan and reserve, keeping warm.

7. Degrease the pan.

8. If you plan to make a sauce, deglaze the pan.

9. Make sauce and thicken the liquid.

10. Spoon sauce onto plate and top with main item.

1. The chef's sautéed chicken breast demo is the first demo of the week. The breast is a suprême, meaning the lower part of the wing bone is still attached. This looks nice and makes the chicken more flavorful. First the chef trims the breast and then frenches the wing bone—he scrapes the meat all the way down after trimming the end, then trims off the edges. The exposed bone is handy for handling the chicken breast. I don't always do this at home; it's much easier to buy boneless breasts. I leave the skin on to protect the chicken as it cooks even if I don't plan to eat it.

2. The chicken breast is lightly floured (although some chefs prefer not to flour) and placed in the pan show side down. "Do not move it for the first few minutes," the chef warns us, "or you will tear the meat." The meat sticks at first, then it loosens, and that's when you can shake the pan. Sear to a golden brown, then turn. There are some additional clues we learned to look for before turning the meat. The edges of the cut will start to change color. The upper surface of a skinless piece of chicken will appear moist and slick when it is time to turn it.

3. Capturing all of the flavorful juices from the ingredients in a sauce is delicious, but it's also very practical—if you don't use them to make a sauce, they're just wasted. The first step, known as deglazing, is dramatic, as a small amount of an aromatic ingredient, such as wine, hits the hot pan and instantly turns into billows of steam. Be sure to stir well and scrape the pan so that every last bit of the flavorful fond is dissolved into the pan sauce.

4. For presentation, the suprême is cut crosswise into 3 or 5 pieces (always an odd number) that are arranged over the sauce at a slant, in the order in which they were cut (this is called *sequencing*). We added a bed of potatoes to our heated plates and leaned the slices against it to give the dish a bit of height. The sauce was pooled around the food, directly on the plate, to act as a frame for the entire dish. In addition to our sauté lesson, we have just had our first lesson in plating.

CHICKEN BREAST PROVENÇAL

This is the first dish we make on Day 1 in Skills Kitchen 1, and we do it to put our new knowledge of sautéing to the test. The chef demos everything first—frenching the wing bone, sautéing the chicken, making the tomato concassée, and preparing the sauce. When Chef Hinnerk makes this dish, he lightly flours the chicken breast, as he thinks it adds color and also retains moisture. Other chefs don't flour; the choice is up to you.

The term Provençal *refers to the sauce, which contains garlic, anchovies, olives, and tomatoes. This is the approach to the sauce and garnish suggested by Escoffier, although I've never actually eaten anything exactly like it in my many years in Provence. Though the recipes from the CIA specify either clarified butter or olive oil for sautéing, when we cooked it in class we used olive oil, and that would certainly be my choice.*

SERVES 6

Things to watch

- Don't burn the garlic.

- Don't season the sauce until the end. The anchovies and olives are salty.

6 half chicken breasts, boneless or semi-boneless, skinned if desired

Salt and freshly ground pepper

About 3 tablespoons all-purpose flour

About ¼ cup olive or vegetable oil (enough to lightly coat the surface of your sauté pan)

1 teaspoon minced garlic (1 medium clove)

½ cup dry white wine

2 medium tomatoes, peeled, seeded, and diced

2 tablespoons sliced or julienned imported black olives

1 anchovy, mashed to a paste

1 cup Chicken Stock (page 142)

2 tablespoons butter, softened

1 teaspoon slivered basil

1. Preheat the oven to 350°F. Season the chicken breast with salt and pepper. Dredge lightly in the flour and shake off the excess.

2. Heat a large, heavy sauté pan over medium-high heat. When it is hot, add enough oil to lightly coat the surface. When the surface is just rippling and the pan feels hot when you place your hand above it, place the chicken breasts in it, skin or rounded side (presentation side) down. If your pan is not large enough to hold all of the chicken breasts without crowding, sauté the chicken in batches. Let the meat cook undisturbed for a few minutes. It will stick at first, and if you move it during this time, it will tear. Once the meat loosens from the surface of the pan, shake the pan. Sear to a golden brown, about 3 to 4 minutes, then turn the breasts over and cook on the other side until golden brown, about 3 to 4 minutes. Place the pan in the oven and allow the chicken to sizzle slowly for 5 minutes, or until the breasts are cooked through. They should feel firm but not hard when you press on them. Remove the chicken breasts from the pan and transfer to a rack set over a pan. If you wish, place in a warm oven while you make the sauce.

3. Evaluate the amount of fat left in the pan. If there appears to be more than you would like in your sauce, pour some or most of it off and discard. Add the garlic to the pan and stir for only a few seconds, being careful not to let it brown. Add the wine and stir to deglaze the pan, making sure to scrape up all the drippings from the bottom. Add the tomatoes, olives, anchovy paste, and chicken stock. Stir together and bring to a boil. Turn down the heat and simmer until fragrant and cooked down to a creamy consistency, 5 to 10 minutes. Taste and adjust seasonings. Stir in the butter, swirling the pan constantly. The sauce should be glossy. Add any juices that have accumulated under the chicken to the sauce, stir well, taste again, and adjust seasonings. Spoon the sauce onto warm serving plates and place the chicken on top. Garnish with the slivered basil and serve.

Note: If you don't have the oven on when you are sautéing, try this approach to quickly warm the cooked chicken: Just after you've adjusted the seasoning of the sauce, return the chicken pieces to the pan and turn to coat them in the

What the recipe doesn't know

` The size of your pan. Most likely you will have to cook the chicken in batches. Or you may have to use more or less oil than the recipe calls for. Use only enough oil to lightly coat the bottom of the pan.

` The availability of chicken breast suprêmes. You can do this with boneless chicken breasts, and even with boneless, skinless breasts.

warm sauce before you slice and serve them. This is especially effective if you are using boneless, skinless chicken breast pieces to give them an attractive, glossy sheen and a bit of added moisture.

KNIFE SKILLS AND MISE EN PLACE

Our first Boot Camp afternoon is devoted to a lecture on knife skills, which includes information on types of knives and their care and sharpening, different ways of holding a knife, the various cuts, and how to cut specific fruits and vegetables. The chef describes basic vegetable cuts—brunoise, various sizes of dice, julienne, bâtonnet, and paysanne—and explains how each type of cut impacts cooking time and presentation. Although this constitutes our first lecture, the actual lessons in mise en place and knife skills will keep coming all day, every day. (I've gathered those lessons together in a later chapter, pages 125–137.) The hours of prep work we do over the course of the week, with our brand-new chef's knives, paring knives, and swivel peelers, really do help to hone our skills. By the end of the week, all of us are better with a knife than we've ever been. And that appears to be the heart of knife skills: practice, practice, practice!

THICKENERS

Chefs use thickeners to change a liquid into one with some body, an important part of making sauces and soups. Chefs today use a variety of ingredients, techniques, and preparations to thicken a sauce, ranging from the classic butter-and-flour mixture known as roux to a puree of fruits or vegetables. They might use potatoes or rice to thicken a liquid. Other ways to thicken a soup include reduction, adding a liaison or beurre manié, or adding a pure starch slurry.

> *Liaison* A mixture of 1 part egg yolks and 3 parts heavy cream, added after being tempered with the hot soup at the end of cooking.

> *Beurre manié* A mixture of equal parts butter and flour, kneaded together and added at the end of cooking. Chef Hinnerk describes this

as "less pleasant than other thickeners" because the flour has a raw taste.

Roux Cream soups and veloutés are usually thickened with a roux, a cooked paste made from flour and fat (usually clarified butter, but it can also be regular butter or oil).

Slurry Made by blending a pure starch (arrowroot, cornstarch, potato starch, or rice starch) to a cold liquid. This is stirred into a boiling sauce at the end of cooking time.

Making and Using Roux

The ratio of fat to all-purpose flour is typically 40 to 60 percent by weight, or 1 part fat to 2½ parts flour by volume. A proper roux, say all the chefs and the CIA textbook, should look and feel "like wet sand at low tide."

The roux can be cooked several ways: until it smells very slightly toasty but has not yet begun to brown (for white roux), until it looks and smells moderately toasty (for pale or blond roux), or until it is brown (for brown roux). It is then added to a liquid—or a liquid is added to it—and stirred in as the liquid comes to a simmer. The roux needs to simmer in the liquid for at least 20 minutes in order to be properly dispersed and reach its maximum viscosity. If you add liquid that is too hot to a roux, the mixture will boil before the roux has been properly dispersed in the liquid, and you'll get lumps.

As a rule of thumb, 4 ounces of white or pale roux will thicken 1 quart of liquid. The basic ratio for cream soups is 1 quart of

Thickeners (clockwise from top): beurre manié, roux, slurry.

velouté, 1 pound of the main ingredient (usually a vegetable), and ½ to 1 cup of cream. White roux, which has the greatest thickening power, and pale roux, which has moderate thickening power, are used for cream and velouté sauces and soups. Brown roux is the least effective thickener, so more of it is required. It's used in brown sauces and gumbos, to which it contributes flavor and color as well as viscosity.

Making and Using Slurries

A slurry is made by combining a pure starch with a small amount of cold liquid. This mixture should have the consistency of heavy cream. Slurries have two times the thickening power of flour, but they don't have the velvety aspect of a roux, nor do they have the stability. For this reason they're added to a boiling liquid near the end of cooking. If you continue to cook a slurry-thickened sauce or soup, eventually it will break down.

Arrowroot, cornstarch, and potato starch are pure starches that are used for slurries. The clarity, gel strength, and thickening ability of the slurry vary depending on which starch is used. Chef Hinnerk demos all of them by thickening a chicken stock with each one, then having us taste it and comment on the texture. This is fascinating.

First he mixes up cornstarch and water. "This should resemble heavy cream. It must be mixed into your soup or sauce while it is dispersed in the liquid, so if you mix it up, then wait and it settles, be sure to mix it up again." Cornstarch settles because it doesn't dissolve in liquid; the heat of the liquid swells the granules, which is what gives it its thickening power. That's also why cornstarch will cloud and become gelatinous when the food cools—which is the reason we use it to thicken the filling in fruit pies. For sauces, you add the cornstarch slurry to the boiling liquid, stirring constantly, and bring it back to a boil. Then it's done. The thickened mixture will be clearer than a roux-thickened velouté.

Potato starch makes a stiffer, less creamy slurry than cornstarch. When the chef thickens the chicken stock with it, the liquid is clearer, but its texture isn't as appealing; it has a more mucus-like aspect to it.

The thickener with the smoothest viscosity and the most agreeable texture is arrowroot. This is a good choice, but it is also the least stable of the pure starches, so you must be sure to serve your soup right after it thickens and not let it continue to boil. In restaurants, where soups must be continually reheated, arrowroot can be a problem, as eventually it loses its thickening power.

Clarifying Butter

Clarified butter is whole butter, cooked long enough to separate the milk solids and water from the pure butterfat. To make clarified butter, cut unsalted butter into pieces. Put them in a heavy-gauge pan or pot over low heat. Once the butter is completely melted, increase the heat a little. As the butter continues to cook it will change. Some foam will rise to the top of the butter; use a flat spoon to skim it away. The milk solids, or proteins, in the butter will fall to the bottom of the pan, which is just exactly where you want them. The butterfat will become very clear. Once the foam is removed and the butterfat clear, you can carefully pour the butterfat out of the pan and into a clean container. Decant the butter carefully so the milk solids and liquids remain at the bottom of the pan. You now have clarified butter. Store any unused clarified butter in the refrigerator in a clean, covered jar.

DINNER AT ST. ANDREW'S CAFÉ

Part of the Culinary Boot Camp package is a nightly dinner in one of the four CIA restaurants on campus, fine dining establishments known among the students as "restaurant row." This is where students spend their last four blocks of the CIA curriculum, working both the front and the back of the house. The restaurants are well regarded, and at least on weekends are fully booked. The dining rooms are spacious and comfortable, with open kitchens and a warm atmosphere even in the dead of winter. Their menus are sophisticated, contemporary, and interesting, and they are pricey. Even so, dinner can be hit or miss. Students, after all, are your waiters, and students are working the lines in the kitchen. Sometimes service can be uneven, sometimes excellent. You just have to remind yourself that you, as a paying customer, are participating in the education of one of the future chefs of America.

At St. Andrew's Café, the first restaurant on our schedule, the table I sit at has the misfortune of having nervous waiters. It doesn't help that one of our entrees has to be replaced, which means that one member of our party has to wait for at least 30 minutes after the rest of us have been served our main dish.

But it's the food that we have come for, and now that we've cooked for a day and know all about knife cuts, we're curious to see how this knowledge has been put to work. I want to order at least one dish that's sautéed, because that's what I've learned about and done today.

St. Andrew's Café was conceived as a restaurant that would focus on healthy food, but they soon found that by defining themselves that way, they were not drawing enough customers. In fact, they are committed to healthfully prepared food, but their scope is wider than this. They like to present a range of cuisines on their menu, so along with contemporary California-style pizzas such as Thai-Style Barbecue Chicken Pizza there will be a classic Pizza Margherita. There is an Asian inflection to the menu, with Steamed Shrimp Wontons, Seared Tuna Cake, and Chicken Yakitori among the starters on this night, and Grilled Marinated Tuna with Soba Noodles and Braised Korean-Style Short Ribs with Kimchee and Snow Peas as entrées. Nestled in with these are comforting dishes such as Tuscan White Bean Soup with Sweet Italian Sausage and Grilled Chicken Breast with Spicy Apple Chutney and Multi-Grain Cake.

That multi-grain cake points to the restaurant's commitment to healthy cooking, and indeed, they do not pile on the butter as most restaurants do. Their Pan-Seared Salmon and Shrimp with Saffron Papardelle, for example, is finished with a saffron shrimp broth whose intense flavor is a result of reducing the stock, not whisking in lots of butter at the end.

By the time I get to my table on this freezing cold night, Marty, a former junior high school math teacher from Massachusetts who's now teaching at Smith College, has already ordered a St. Andrew's aperitif: a glass of Veuve Clicquot with a little grape-

St. Andrew's dining room

fruit liqueur. It sounds good to me—I'll never say no to a glass of Veuve Clicquot, with or without the added liqueur. We sip and peruse the menu, and as we do so the waiter brings us all an amuse-gueule, compliments of the chef. It's a slice of a California-style pizza—I guess that it's Thai-style barbecue pizza— with rounds of jalapeño, cilantro, and maybe even some pineapple. Never my cup of tea, these fusion pizzas, but it's well executed.

I choose, as planned, something sautéed for my appetizer, and as it turns out, I've chosen well: a seared tuna cake. This is nothing like a crab cake. Instead, tuna, perfectly diced, is formed into cakes, breaded, and quickly seared, so that the outside is crispy and golden, but the inside is raw like sushi. Accordingly, the cakes are garnished with pickled ginger, soy sauce, and a seaweed salad. They are beautifully plated (we'll learn a lot about plating at Boot Camp), with the oval plate diagonally bifurcated by a wall of thin, half-moon shaped cucumber slices standing on their cut side.

Sticking with the day's cooking themes (sauté method, stocks), I order Pan-Seared Salmon and Shrimp with Saffron Pappardelle and Wilted Spinach, Saffron Shrimp Broth, and Feta Cheese as my entrée—quite a mouthful on the menu, but typical of many American menus today. The salmon is seared on both sides, so that the surface is beautifully browned but the fish still moist, just pulling apart when I stick my fork into it. There are just a few shrimp, plump and juicy, cooked in a hot pan in minutes. A seafood stock has been reduced and doused with saffron, which gives it and the saffron noodles that are tossed in it a heady flavor and gorgeous yellow hue. Spinach is the perfect vegetable with this, and a classic accompaniment to salmon. Feta is an original touch, and superfluous, I think—but it adds a Mediterranean twist, as pan-cooked shrimp with feta is a classic Greek dish.

I do have dessert: chocolate cake. It tastes rich, and I wonder if there is anything healthy about it. Not that I care. I've had an active day in the kitchen and a swim at the student recreation center, and now I'm ready for sleep and another 5:30 a.m. wake-up call.

Day 2
SOUP PRODUCTION AND FRYING TECHNIQUES

The entertainment business has always been a familiar one to me; my father, a writer, worked in Hollywood, and I live in Los Angeles now. When I began my cooking career—I was a caterer before I began writing books—I couldn't help drawing parallels between show business and the world of the professional chef. Today in particular, a chef can attain movie star status. Restaurants and catered events are like theater: the curtain goes up when the first guests arrive and doesn't come down until the last customers go home. Then the set must be struck and everything put back into place so that the show can go on again the next day. The kitchen is behind the scenes, and much goes on there that the audience doesn't know about.

In a professional kitchen, cooking is referred to as "production," just like making a movie. And so on our second day of Boot Camp, we learn about soup production. We already have the stocks we made the day before to work with. We'll learn about thick soups and all the different ways to thicken them, clear soups and regional soups, fruit soups and chilled soups. We'll learn how to clarify a consommé by "building a raft," and I will make my first lobster bisque, which entails cooking my first lobster.

THE FINAL

The first thing we hear about in our Day 2 lecture is the menu development assignment for our "final exam" on the last day of Boot Camp. Each team will create a restaurant-style hot appetizer and entrée, designed around "proteins" (i.e., meat, fish, or poultry) that the chef assigns each team. Our entrées will consist of the assigned protein plus sauce and garnish, a starch, and one or two vegetables; the appetizer plate will be an entrée in miniature. We are to build on the

different cooking techniques we are learning, and use the library to research recipes.

In the first phase of this assignment, the cooks on each team get together and develop their menus. Chef Hinnerk urges us to keep it simple and to take advantage of both the Internet and the cookbook collection in the library for ideas. "You can find recipes and follow them blindly, or you can use recipes for inspiration and be creative. However you go about it, you can make marvelous food using simple ingredients. Your learning experience will not benefit from you ordering truffles and foie gras." In each Boot Camp session the chef makes it very clear that he is available for consultation, and indeed, he guides our group with much-needed expertise in both the conception and planning of our menus.

For further inspiration we are given a tour of the CIA storerooms and walk-ins in the afternoon. This tour of the CIA underbelly is one of the high points in my week. It opens up a whole universe of possibilities for the vegetables, sauces, and starches that will accompany our fish, meat, and poultry.

The second phase of the assignment will involve making supplemental food order lists, so that the chef can order our ingredients. The third phase will be the cooking. The teams will have three hours to make their meals, which will include a presentation plate for the appetizer and the main dish; the remaining five portions will be set out in hotel pans for others to taste. We will be discussing presentation in our final morning lecture before getting to work in the kitchen.

As Chef Hinnerk hands out protein assignments, he imagines out loud what we might do with them. "Team 1, you will have ground veal and pork for your appetizer. Maybe you'll make a meat loaf and use a salad dressing as a sauce." (They make pot stickers.) "Your entrée will be salmon," he tells them.

"Team 2, you have shrimp for your appetizer. Maybe you'll make dumplings? Or tempura? Or how about a nice gumbo?" (They grill them on skewers with lemon wedges and serve them with a mâche salad.) "You have chicken breasts for your entrée; mmm, you could make a nice pot pie." (They don't.)

And so on with Team 3, which has sole and beef tenderloin. Team 4 gets pork loin for the entrée ("Be sure not to overcook it"), quail for the appetizer ("How about stuffing them with dried cherries soaked in port, then smoking them and serving them with a green peppercorn and cherry sauce?" which is exactly what they do). Team 5 is to use pork tenderloin in their appetizer and turkey breast in their main dish. My team is assigned scallops and beef tenderloin. We want to begin brainstorming at once, but that will have to wait until our coffee break. Now it's time to learn about the day's production.

SOUPS

The Boot Camp course breaks down soups into two main categories: thickened and clear. Thickened soups include cream soups and veloutés (contemporary chefs use these two terms interchangeably), purées and bisques, specialty soups (meaning regional and international soups), and many cold soups. Clear soups include consommés, broths or bouillons, clear vegetable soups such as minestrone, some cold soups, and the Japanese broth dashi.

Most soups have three major entities: the main ingredient, which is often the name-giving ingredient; the aromatics (onion, mirepoix, vegetables, spices, herbs); and the liquid. The liquid can be stock, water, fumet, vegetable essence, or even fruit and vegetable juices. Most often it is stock or water, and there is sometimes milk or cream added to the mix.

Soups should be cooked at a simmer. Boiling can curdle a soup if there are thickeners, and cloud a clear soup. It will overcook vegetables before their maximum flavor is drawn out, and it will overcook and toughen meat. As your soup simmers, you should taste it at various stages, to ascertain the doneness of vegetables and to check how the flavors are developing. Seasonings should be adjusted as necessary. Of course we know that we should taste our soups: we pledged to taste all of our food.

Thick Soups

The primary flavoring ingredient in a thickened soup is usually the name-giving ingredient; think cream of mushroom soup, black bean soup, split pea soup. The thickener can be a puree of the flavoring ingredient, a roux, or potatoes or rice.

Clear Soups

Any doubts that anyone in our group might have about the value of Boot Camp should be dispelled after watching the consommé demo. Consommé is the king of the clear soups. It is made by clarifying a stock or broth until it is crystal clear and completely fat free. Consommés are light, yet they have an intense, pure, full flavor, a rich body, and a deep amber to golden brown color. Though we will be serving our consommé with a simple garnish of cooked diced vegetables, the soup can be served with special garnishes such as quenelles.

Other clear soups include bouillons or broths, and vegetable soups other than cream soups. Bouillons or broths are translucent soups made from flavorful meats, poultry, fish, or vegetables. Flavorful meats are usually mature ones, which is why stewing hens or fowl make good bouillons. Beef cuts from the neck or shank, the more muscular parts of the animal, will also yield a flavorful broth. Broths are amber to golden brown in color and should have a rich, well-balanced flavor. They're served hot, often with spoon-sized cuts of the meats from which the bouillon was made, and/or with diced cooked vegetables, and sometimes with pasta or grains such as barley (think Scotch Broth) or rice.

Vegetable soups can include meat or not. They can be made from stock or broth, with vegetables simmered until tender, or they can be made with water. They aren't clear like a bouillon or consommé, but they aren't thickened either. A minestrone is a good example of a clear vegetable soup. The Amish-Style Chicken and Corn Soup that we make (page 163) is a good example of a clear vegetable soup that contains some meat.

DAY 2 TEAM PRODUCTION ASSIGNMENTS

Team 1

Pan-Fried Breast of Chicken with Prosciutto and Mozzarella (page 179)

Cream of Mushroom Soup (page 167)

Braised Greens (page 192)

Team 2

Deep-Fried Flounder with Tomato Coulis (page 182)

Amish-Style Chicken and Corn Soup (page 163)

Boiled or Steamed Potatoes with Parsley (page 191)

Team 3

Pan-Fried Pork Loin with Herb Sauce*

Lobster Bisque*

Spaetzle (page 223)

Team 4

Rainbow Beef (page 176)

Chicken Consommé (page 164)

Steamed Rice (page 222)

Team 5

Pan-Fried Buttermilk Chicken with Country-Style Gravy (page 180)

Santa Fe Chili Soup (page 168)

Sautéed Zucchini (page 219)

*Recipes and photographs on pages 44–47 and 36–38

1. Bisques are unique among soups in that they are flavored with both the flesh and the shells of crustaceans. Not only that, the shells are actually pureed right into the soup before it is strained. Getting the meat out of a lobster is extremely difficult if the lobster is uncooked, so we very briefly blanch the lobsters, just enough to make it easier to separate the shell from the flesh. Chef John tells us that long ago, chefs would store shells from lobsters, shrimps, or crayfish in a warm place in the kitchen, often on a shelf above the stove. Once the shells were dry, they would be pulverized to use in seafood soups such as this one, or seafood sauces.

2. Every time we start working on a recipe, Chef John or Chef Hinnerk stresses the importance of developing flavor. We learn that this is an ongoing process, not just adding salt and pepper to taste when the dish has finished cooking. The technique we use for the lobster is something my teachers refer to as *pinçage*. Essentially, it means that you carefully cook aromatic vegetables—onions, carrots, celery, garlic, and tomatoes—until the mixture has a deep brick-red color and a sweet aroma. The sherry and the brandy are added and cooked down (reduced) to give the dish a deep, complex flavor profile.

3. A traditional bisque is thickened with crushed bread added to the soup as it simmers. Another classic approach to making bisque calls for rice to be added to the soup; it cooks long enough to fall apart in the soup and thicken it. We are going to add an arrowroot slurry as the thickener at the end of cooking time. While the soup simmers, we keep an eye on it, skimming the surface every once in a while so that the finished bisque will have a very fine texture and color. Like other soups that include starchy thickeners such as roux or rice, we have to be concerned that the soup might stick to the pot and burn so we stir and skim frequently.

4. Bisques are a type of cream soup. Chef Hinnerk describes the proper consistency as being similar to heavy cream. He also says that one of the greatest problems with thick soups is keeping them from getting too thick while they simmer. And if you cool the soup down to store for another day, you have to be very careful to heat the soup up gently so it won't scorch (now that it has a thickener in it). Chef John tells us to use stock or even water to thin a soup that seems too thick after you reheat it; adding more cream would mask the taste of the lobster. A final garnish of lobster tail, and you really can't tell our bisque from a bisque served at a classic French restaurant.

LOBSTER BISQUE

I have the good fortune to have a Massachusetts woman on my team, who really knows about shellfish. When we are assigned this soup on Day 2 of Boot Camp, I am thrilled, as I've never even cooked a lobster, let alone made a bisque. Christine teaches me how to handle the lobsters, and once they're cooked, she intrepidly breaks them apart and shows me how to extract as much meat as possible.

SERVES 4 TO 5

> 2 live lobsters, about 1 pound each
>
> 2 tablespoons olive oil
>
> 1 onion, sliced
>
> 1 large celery stalk, sliced
>
> 1 small carrot, sliced
>
> 1 head of garlic, cut in half crosswise
>
> 1 large fresh tomato, sliced
>
> ¼ cup tomato paste
>
> 2 tablespoons chopped fresh tarragon
>
> 2 tablespoons chopped fresh thyme
>
> 2 bay leaves
>
> 8 whole black peppercorns
>
> ½ cup brandy
>
> ½ cup dry sherry
>
> 1 quart Fish Stock (page 143) or bottled
>   clam juice
>
> ½ cup heavy cream
>
> Salt to taste
>
> 2 teaspoons cornstarch
>
> 1 tablespoon water

1. Bring a large pot of water to a boil. Leave the bands on the lobsters' claws and lower them into the water by the tail. Boil 8 minutes, until the lobsters are bright red. Using tongs, transfer the cooked lobsters to a large bowl and allow to cool. Reserve 2 cups of the cooking liquid and drain the rest.

2. When the lobsters are cool enough to handle, cut off their tails and claws. Crack the tails and claws and remove the meat, working over the bowl to catch the juices. Coarsely chop the meat, place it in a bowl, cover, and chill. Coarsely chop the shells and bodies.

3. Heat the oil in a large, heavy pot over high heat and sear the lobster shells and bodies until they begin to brown. Add the onion, celery, carrot, tomato, tomato paste, herbs, and peppercorns. Reduce the heat slightly and cook, stirring, until the tomato paste takes on a deep rust color (see page 141 for a description of pincé).

4. Stir in the brandy and sherry and boil until most of the liquid has evaporated. Add the fish stock, the reserved lobster cooking liquid, and the lobster juices. Bring to a boil, reduce the heat, cover and simmer for 1 hour. Transfer the soup to a food processor or blender and puree until the shells are coarsely ground.

5. Place a sieve over another large pot and strain the soup, pressing on the solids to extract as much flavor as possible. Discard the solids and bring the soup to a boil. Reduce to 1 quart.

6. Stir the cream into the soup and bring to a simmer. Add salt to taste. Dissolve the cornstarch in the water and add to the soup. Boil until slightly thickened. Stir the reserved lobster meat into the soup, heat through, and serve.

COOKING WITH FATS

If I have one thing to learn at Boot Camp, it is how to cook with fats. My sautéing lessons certainly gave me a good start, but that method requires relatively little fat. Not so with pan-frying, stir-frying (although the amount of fat required for stir-frying is closer to sautéing), and deep-frying. I have devoted the better part of my career to healthy cooking. I've worked hard to develop methods of cooking that yield tasty, sensuous results with a minimum or moderate amount of fat. Oh, I can follow a recipe, and can do what I have to in order to test doughnut and beignet recipes for pastry chef Sherry Yard, or homemade potato chips and deep-fried panko-crusted scallops for Wolfgang Puck. I've developed and tested delicious crab cakes for my Food Atlas and for magazines, and I can make a good potato latke. I've done my fair share of stir-frying, especially in my early vegetarian days. But I've never been very comfortable around (or successful with) lots of hot oil in a pan. Here at Boot Camp, though, that is about to change.

STIR FRYING

Both Chef John and Chef Hinnerk have a lot to say about stir-frying. Chef John taught Chinese cooking at the Institute for a while and has worked with Chinese chefs. Chef Hinnerk has been chef de cuisine at a large hotel restaurant in Beijing, where he met his wife, who is Chinese.

The stir-fry method requires a relatively small amount of fat, like sautéing, but the heat is very high and the food is kept moving constantly. Stir-frying is usually done in a wok, a bowl-shaped pan that should be made of spun steel, a very efficient heat conductor. Steel woks must be seasoned, then maintained. Wok utensils include a spatula, to push and scoop food, and a ladle, to catch and transfer food.

In the Asian Kitchen at the Culinary Institute, the woks are so hot that the surface of the stove where they nestle must be cooled with a constant water bath. Because the heat is so high, it's important to use oil that has a high smoke point, the temperature at which fats break down and become unstable. Peanut oil is traditional, but soybean and vegetable oils are also suitable.

Foods that are stir-fried are cut into small pieces (bite-sized or smaller) so that they'll cook quickly. Beef, pork, and poultry are traditional candidates, but veal and lamb are also suitable. Meat is sometimes marinated in egg whites, because egg whites have a pH of about 8, and the alkalinity breaks down the protein in less tender meats. Shellfish stands up to quick stir-frying, but delicate fish such as sole will fall apart. Vegetables of all kinds are good candidates, but the harder ones should be blanched or parboiled first. It's important to cook vegetables quickly so that they retain a crisp-tender texture.

Perfect mise en place is essential for stir-frying. There is a lot of chopping and precutting of ingredients involved, but once you begin cooking, the process is over in a matter of minutes. Not only must your ingredients be cut and measured out, but they should be placed within reach in the order in which they'll be used. These will include the main ingredient or ingredients (which have already been blanched and shocked if that is called for), the sauce ingredients, and the aromatics—usually garlic and ginger, onion or green onion, and spices. Sometimes herbs such as cilantro are added at the end of cooking. There are "dry" stir-fries, but most are "wet": they have a sauce, which is thickened with a slurry, either cornstarch or arrowroot, sometimes rice flour. The liquid ingredients almost always include soy sauce, often a fortified wine such as sherry, and stock or water. Other ingredients such as vinegar, chile sauce, bean paste, sesame oil, and sugar often go into a stir-fry sauce.

> ## BASIC PROCEDURE FOR STIR-FRYING
>
> 1. Heat the oil in a wok or a large sauté or stir-fry pan. Add the flavorings and stir just for a few seconds. (In my sautéing lessons I learned to "cook to color." In my stir-fry lecture I learn to "cook to aroma." That's as far as you cook the flavorings, ginger and garlic, before you add the main item.)
>
> 2. Add the main item and stir-fry for a few minutes, until cooked through, keeping the food in constant motion. Remove the main item with the flavorings (so they don't burn) and set aside.
>
> 3. Add the additional ingredients in the proper sequence (longest-cooking in first, shortest-cooking in last).
>
> 4. Add the liquid for the sauce. Add the slurry. Stir the main item back into the sauce and heat through, stirring until the items are glazed. Serve immediately.

PAN-FRYING

Pan-frying is a cooking method in which items are partially submerged in fat or oil; thus it requires much more oil than stir-frying, enough to cover the bottom quarter to half of the food. "This is not a method for the American Heart Association," Chef Hinnerk replies when I ask him how much of that fat is actually absorbed by the food (the answer is 6 to 10 percent).

Only tender foods are used for pan-frying. Meats include white meats such as chicken breasts, veal, and pork loin or pork tenderloin. Beef isn't usually pan-fried, although there is one notable exception: chicken-fried steak that's been pounded and floured. Seafood, some vegetables such as eggplant, and starches such as potatoes can be pan-fried, as well as previously prepared items such as crab cakes and fritters.

The items, which should be portion-sized or smaller, are first breaded or battered, which serves a few purposes. The coating plays the important role of providing armor against the hot oil, which should be at about 325°F. The meat (or fish) doesn't get exposed to this high heat, but cooks in its own juices while the crust gets fried. What results is the pleasant texture contrast of a crispy crust against tender meat or fish. The food can be completely cooked during the frying process or finished in the oven.

Because you don't want to detract from the flavors of the coating and the item being pan-fried, you should use a neutral fat with a relatively high smoke point: canola, corn, or safflower. Sometimes rendered fats are used, and occasionally clarified butter is specified for a special flavor.

"Don't waste your extra-virgin olive oil on pan-frying," Chef Hinnerk admonishes. And when one of the women in our group, a Southerner, asks him about shortening, he goes into a very informative tirade about why shortening is bad. He draws diagrams of fatty acids on the board and shows us how the fatty acid chain is manipulated to artificially saturate it. This makes a very stable fat that is semisolid or solid at room temperature with a high smoke point. However, this hydroge-

nization process changes more than the fat's physical structure; it also results in substances known as trans fats. "The resulting trans fats are known to be more harmful to your health than saturated fatty acids. But just as important," he says, "they taste nasty…use oil." And that is that.

Straight-sided sautoirs are excellent choices for pan-frying. They should be large enough so that you are not crowding the items, but not so large that the oil doesn't cover the bottom quarter to half of the food. Use tongs or a spatula to turn the food, and have a rack set over a pan ready for draining the cooked items. Although the CIA course

BASIC PROCEDURE FOR STANDARD BREADING

Chefs have a system for breading. It makes the cooking move along efficiently, and—very important—it also minimizes the risk of cross-contamination and food poisoning. The steps that I learn turn out to be incredibly helpful to me when I go back to my small kitchen.

Standard breading ingredients and mise en place:
Product to be breaded

Flour for dredging

Egg wash (2 whole eggs beaten with ¼ cup milk for 6 pieces)

Breading agent as needed (about 1 cup for 6 pieces of meat or fish)*

Empty pan for finished product

*Dry or fresh bread crumbs, nuts, seeds, shredded coconut, panko, corn flakes, grated cheese, or chopped herbs, alone or in combination

materials instruct us to drain the items briefly on paper towels, Chef Hinnerk feels that food drained on paper towels is likely to become soggy, and so he always uses a rack. Chef John uses paper towels but cautions us to remove the food very quickly from the paper once drained. "If you leave the food on the paper too long, its flavor and juices will leach out. Leave it only long enough to absorb excess fat." In either case, food that is pan-fried should be cooked as close to serving time as possible. If it's held, the coating becomes soggy and the item dries out. Anyone who has ever eaten steam-table cutlets knows this.

The sauces for pan-fried items are made and served separately, unlike in sautéing, where the sauce is usually made in the pan the item was cooked in, and served on the plate. That's because when an item is pan-fried, there is no fond left in the pan for deglazing, and there are bound to be burned bits of coating that would make a sauce taste bitter. You serve the sauce separately so that you don't compromise the crispiness of the pan-fried food. The exception to this rule is southern fried chicken, which sometimes has a gravy that is made in the same pan, but if this is the case, it's very important to discard the fat with the burned food particles.

The type of cooking fat you choose for pan frying or deep-fat frying is important to the success of your dish, but unless you care for your cooking fat properly, you could end up disappointed. These are the pointers that we got from the chefs concerning the selection, care, and maintenance of frying fats.

- Choose an oil with a neutral flavor, in most cases. Very flavorful oils like nut oils or extra-virgin olive oils will lose their flavor when they get very hot, so it isn't worth the extra money you'd spend on these oils to use them for frying.

- Choose a cooking pot that is non-reactive (stainless steel, cast iron, enameled cast iron, or anodized aluminum).

- Make sure that your pan or pot has a heavy, flat bottom.

- Heat the oil over medium heat to a good frying temperature.

- Test the temperature of the oil with a thermometer or with a cube of bread. If you use the bread test, remember that a 1-inch cube of bread will brown nicely in about 30 seconds when the oil is at about 350°F.

- Add foods to the oil only after it has reached the right temperature.

- Do not salt foods directly over the frying oil.

- If you are cooking more than one batch, use a slotted spoon, skimmer, or spider to remove any particles that are left in the oil after you take out the cooked foods. Give the oil enough time to return to the correct frying temperature before you add the next batch.

- Let the oil cool completely before you either discard it or strain it. (You can sometimes reuse oil once or twice, but if it gets smoky or has an off odor as you heat it up, use fresh oil.)

1. Blot the food dry with paper towels and season generously with salt and pepper. Hold the food in one hand (your "dry hand") and dip it into the flour. Shake off any excess flour and transfer the food to your other hand (your "wet hand"). Dip the food into the container of egg wash and turn it to coat on all sides. Transfer to the container of bread crumbs. Use your dry hand to pack the crumbs evenly around the food, so that you don't moisten the bread crumbs and get them lumpy. Shake off any excess, then transfer to a rack set over a sheet tray. Discard any unused egg wash, flour, and bread crumbs.

2. Heat the pan over high or medium-high heat, then add the oil once the pan is heated. When the oil reaches the appropriate temperature, you will see a faint haze or a slight shimmer. If the oil is too hot, the coating will burn or come loose from the food, so be careful. Add the breaded item to the pan in a single layer, presentation side down. Turn the heat down to medium. You want the food to sizzle when you add it to the pan. It shouldn't cook too fast or it will burn before the food is cooked through. You are looking for a golden brown color (cook to color).

3. Turn the food over and cook until nicely browned on the other side, which, if the item is thin enough, should correspond to its being done. A good way to ascertain doneness is to check the color of the surrounding loose breading particles, which will always be a little darker. When they are very dark, the golden-brown cutlet should be done. If it is not, remove to another pan and finish in a 350°F oven. Remove from the pan and drain on a rack or very briefly on absorbent paper, then transfer to a rack or directly to a serving plate or platter.

4. Since you've worked so hard to create a crisp coating, you'll want to preserve its crunch by serving the sauce underneath it. One of the variations on a basic breaded cutlet that Chef Hinnerk showed us was a classic Wiener Schnitzel. After frying a veal cutlet that he had pounded out to about the size of a dinner plate, he made a quick butter sauce by cooking whole butter until it smelled nutty, drizzling in some lemon juice, and adding a bit of parsley. If you wish, you can pour the fat off from the pan, add butter to the pan, and when it browns, add lemon juice. Spoon this over the cutlet or serve it separately.

PAN-FRIED PORK LOIN WITH HERB SAUCE

This is one of my assignments during my first Boot Camp session. I'm not entirely successful with it, either, because some of the breading comes off. That's because my oil isn't quite hot enough. The second time I come to Boot Camp, Chef Hinnerk demonstrates pan-frying with the pork loin. It looks so elegant and easy as he dips the pounded slice of pork loin first into the flour, then into the egg, and then into the bread crumbs, turning the cutlet to coat. He pan-fries it to a perfect golden-brown color and drains it on a rack. "Not on paper towels," he tells us. "The food will steam and the breading will get soggy on paper towels!"

SERVES 6

What the recipe doesn't know

` How thin your pork cutlet is. This is why it's important to use your eyes and cook to color. When the color is right, the cutlet is done if it's thin. If it's not so thin, you might have to finish it off in the oven.

` How heavy your pan is and how high your heat is. Again, this determines cooking time.

FOR THE PORK LOIN:

Twelve 3-ounce or six 6-ounce pieces of trimmed pork loin

1 teaspoon salt (or to taste)

¼ teaspoon freshly ground pepper

¾ cup all-purpose flour

2 eggs

¼ cup milk

2 cups fresh bread crumbs or panko

Vegetable oil as needed

FOR THE SAUCE:

2 tablespoons vegetable oil or clarified butter

3 tablespoons finely minced shallots

½ cup dry white wine, such as Sauvignon Blanc

2 teaspoons minced fresh herbs, such as basil, tarragon, chervil, chives, or parsley

2 cups Brown Veal Stock (page 140)

1½ cups Tomato Concassé, fresh (page 148) or canned

1 teaspoon cornstarch dissolved in 1 table-spoon water (optional)

4 to 6 tablespoons (½ to ¾ stick) butter, to taste

Salt and freshly ground pepper to taste

1. Place the pork between pieces of plastic wrap and pound to an even thickness. Season generously on both sides with salt and pepper.

2. Dredge the pork pieces in flour, tap to remove excess flour, dip into the beaten egg, and coat with bread crumbs, following the standard breading procedure on page 44. Place on a parchment-covered baking sheet in a single layer, or between layers of parchment on the baking sheet if you cannot fit all the pieces in a single layer.

Things to watch

- Make sure the oil is hot enough (but not too hot) before adding the breaded pork.

- Don't overcook the pork or it will be dry.

3. Heat a large, heavy skillet over medium-high heat and add about ⅛ inch of oil. When it begins to ripple, add the pork cutlets, presentation side down, being careful not to crowd the pan (you'll probably cook these in batches). Cook until golden, about 2 to 3 minutes, and turn over. Cook on the second side until golden, another 2 to 3 minutes. Transfer to a rack set over a sheet pan and keep warm in the oven while you make the sauce.

4. Heat the oil or clarified butter over medium-high heat in a sauté pan and add the shallots. Sauté until golden and add the white wine. Stir and scrape the bottom of the pan to deglaze, and add the herbs and the stock. Bring to a boil and reduce until the sauce coats the front and back of a spoon (this is known as nappé consistency). Add the tomatoes and heat through. If you want a thicker sauce, stir in the cornstarch slurry. Whisk in the butter, a little at a time. The sauce should be velvety. Taste, adjust seasoning, and transfer to a sauce boat. Cut the pork cutlets in half on a diagonal and serve, either with the sauce on the side or with some spooned onto each plate and the meat placed on top.

DEEP FRYING

I cherish the opportunity that Boot Camp gives me to make french fries. I've never made them, have never wanted to make them, and probably will never make them again. But when I speak with my son at the end of Day 2, I tell him what I've made, and he sounds very excited. "I wish you could bring one home," he says. I wish I could have, too; they're the best french fries I've ever eaten.

Of course, the deep-frying setup in Skills Kitchen 1 is a professional one, with a large two-basket, thermostatically controlled industrial fryer. I have only one friend who has a deep fryer. Home cooks must rely on deep pans or woks and digital thermometers. You can get perfectly good results at home, but then you are faced with the leftover oil and a bit of a mess to clean up. Even while I am savoring my perfect french fries, I know that I probably won't be making them at home for my son.

When food is deep-fried, it is completely submerged in hot fat or oil. The temperature of the oil should be between 350°F and 375°F. The food is almost always given a protective coating—either a breading, a dry coating such as flour, or a batter. The exception is starchy foods such as potatoes, which form their own starch coating when they are blanched in hot oil (see recipe, page 198).

There are two methods commonly used for deep frying. The basket method is used for a quantity of smaller unbattered items such as french fries (though it can be breaded or floured). The food is placed in a basket, which is lowered into the hot oil and stays there until the food is cooked. Larger items and food that has been battered are deep-fried using the swimming method. These items are slowly lowered into the oil, where they swim freely until they are done. Then they're lifted out of the oil with a spider or skimmer. When items are deep-fried using the swimming method, they must be agitated or turned during the cooking so that they will brown evenly.

Items that are deep-fried should be relatively tender and small enough so that they're completely cooked by the time the coating is properly browned. Harder items such as potatoes are blanched first in hot oil (275°F). This cooks the interior starch, which moves to the outside of the item and forms a protective crust. Then the food can be deep-fried at 350°F to cook it on the outside. If it isn't blanched first, it will burn on the outside or become saturated with oil before the inside is properly cooked.

The type of oil used for deep frying should have a high smoke point and a neutral flavor. When you lower the food into the oil, the temperature will drop momentarily, then come back up to the desired temperature. The time it takes the oil to regain its temperature is called the recovery time. If you try to cook too much food at the same time, you will lower the fat temperature too much and slow the recovery time, resulting in oil-saturated food. When you deep-fry several batches, you must make sure that the oil comes back up to temperature between each batch. If you try to deep-fry food in oil that isn't hot enough, your results will be limp and soggy.

Oil maintenance is crucial during deep frying, both for your own health and safety

BASIC PROCEDURE FOR DEEP-FAT FRYING

1. Heat the oil to the proper temperature (275°F if blanching first, 350°F for deep-fat frying).

2. Coat the food with the desired coating (optional). Breaded and floured items may be coated in advance (see the standard breading procedure, page 44) and held. Battered items that are floured before being dipped into batter may be floured and held, but they are battered just before cooking. The food is seasoned, lightly floured, dipped into the batter, removed from the batter with tongs or a fork, and lowered into the hot oil.

3. Add the food to the hot fat using the basket method or the swimming method.

4. Turn the items during frying if necessary.

5. Remove the item and finish in the oven if necessary. If necessary, blot briefly with absorbent paper toweling.

6. Season while hot and serve with the appropriate sauce.

and for successful cooking results. If the oil gets too hot, it will break down, releasing free radicals (molecules that are very unstable). "The health hazards of broken-down oil are even greater than those of hydrogenated fats," Chef Hinnerk tells us, and we know how he feels about hydrogenated fats. If the oil is throwing a lot of dark smoke, you should immediately lower the temperature and avoid touching the pan, because motion can cause fire (this is called *molecular splashover*). Once the oil has cooled, drain it and discard.

Fire can also result if salt or water gets into very hot oil. For this reason, you should never salt your food above the fryer. It's important to salt items such as french fries immediately after frying, so that the salt adheres to the food, but do this away from your oil. Other enemies of fat include prolonged heating (turn down the heat if your fryer is not in heavy use), certain metals such as iron and aluminum, and exposure to air (the fatty acids react with the oxygen in the air). Food particles will also contribute to the breaking down of hot oil, so it is very important to filter the fat frequently, cover your fryer between uses, and keep it clean.

There are a number of ways to tell if your oil has broken down. If it gets very dark, starts to smoke before it reaches the right frying temperature, begins to foam, has an unpleasant odor, or fries foods that are too dark on the outside but not fully cooked on the inside, chances are that the oil needs to be replaced.

THE UNDERBELLY OF THE CIA

All of the food that is cooked in the CIA's 48 kitchens comes up from fabrication rooms, walk-ins, and storerooms located on the basement level of Roth Hall. The amount of food that is received and processed is mind-boggling. Take butter: the CIA goes through 1,500 to 2,000 pounds of it in a week, along with 15,000 eggs. In one day the students in the meat room will fabricate (cut up) 3,000 pounds of meat.

Our second afternoon at Boot Camp is devoted to touring this underbelly. The tour is partly meant to help inspire us with our final-exam menus, and how can it not? It's as if, here in this maze of storage and fabrication rooms, the contents of every great souk and food market in the world have been assembled, arranged, and made accessible to us.

Chef Hinnerk, interested as he is in everything, takes us through the teaching kitchens as well as the fabrication and storage rooms. Our first stop is Kitchen 9, where Cuisines of Asia is taught. One wall is lined with an elaborate, water-cooled row of woks. The huge woks are set above burners that pump out 100,000 BTUs of flame, so hot that the unit must be cooled by a constant stream of water. The kitchen also houses a tandoori oven. This is where culinary students at the CIA do their three-week-long rotation in Cuisines of Asia.

Our next stop is the very cold Seafood ID & Fabrication Kitchen, where the instruc-

tor has laid out one of each type of fish that the supply room is currently stocking in preparation for her students, who are at present having a lecture next door. She apologizes for the relatively small number of fish, though I would love it if my local fishmonger had such a varied supply, and proceeds to give us a quick lecture on the distinguishing features of each one. There's farm-raised Atlantic salmon (huge) and wild king salmon, Atlantic cod and dogfish (dogfish is bled at sea because it has no bones, I learn), daurade and mahi (mahi bones are not good for stock because the fish has high acidity, I learn), gray sole and turbot. The chef tells us about "left-eyed" and "right-eyed" flatfish, which has to do with whether the eyes end up on the dark or light side of the fish. They're not born with both eyes on the same side, I learn, but as they grow, one eye migrates across the skull so that they have a blind side. That's the side with white skin. Who knew? The students at the CIA have to know all of this.

In the walk-in are 40-pound wheels of swordfish, vats of whole fish on ice, hotel pans filled with oysters, trays of octopus, boxes of mussels and clams, trays of salted cod and precut sushi-grade tuna, and vats of bones for fish stock. Everything is fresh and inviting, with the sea-like smell that a good fishmonger's place should have.

We move back into the chilly, noisy underground hallway, which echoes with the sound of wheels moving over tiles as students pick up orders for their afternoon classes. Every night the requisitions from the 48 CIA kitchens, which must be sent in three days in advance, are packed down here. Meat is left in lockers assigned to each class. The place is most chaotic early in the morning and after lunch, when students from the morning and afternoon classes, which start at 7 a.m. and 2 p.m., respectively, are picking up their orders. Then there's a momentary calm until students begin to rush down for supplemental requisitions.

Shivering, we proceed to a slightly warmer storage area for dry goods. The walls are lined floor to ceiling with bags of legumes, dried fruits, grains, flours, condiments of every imaginable kind, oils and shortenings, vinegars, sugars, syrups, jams, jellies, and pastes (such as guava paste). At one end of the room are refrigerated cases for butter, eggs, and other dairy products. Orders are placed in big plastic boxes. One entire room houses spices and bottled and canned condiments. I've never seen so much soy sauce, Asian chili sauce, salsa, and peanut oil—all this in a training ground for classical French chefs.

The walk-in refrigerator is next. Here we encounter piles of gallon bags filled with stock. Each Skills Development class at the CIA produces 30 gallons of stock a day, which is then sealed in plastic bags and sold to the supply room. Beyond the stock, it's a vegetable lover's paradise. In addition to the squashes, peppers, green beans, lettuces and other greens, broccoli, leeks, carrots, turnips, and cauliflower that you'd expect to find in a produce section, there's an abundance of more exotic items—lotus roots and lemongrass, curry leaves and yuca, fresh galangal and salsify, sunchokes and celeriac, and every fresh herb you can think of. There are gallon jars filled with peeled garlic and shallots, and in an adjacent cellar-temperature room are potatoes of all kinds and colors, onions, bulbs of garlic, shallots, winter squash, and mushrooms (both cultivated and wild). Items that should not be refrigerated—heirloom tomatoes by the crate, along with local peppers and gooseberries—line the hall.

We walk past the loading dock to our last destination, the meat room, where three busy students are cutting up beef and pork. They're fabricating steaks from long strip loins, and 7-pound roasts and tenderloins from pork loins. Each piece is weighed and vacuum-packed. This room is not for the squeamish. Nor is the walk-in meat refrigerator, where four goats are hanging, waiting to be jerked, Jamaican style, in the Cuisines of the Americas class. Shelves are stacked with tied tenderloins and flank steaks, veal racks

and duck breasts, bone-in pork loins, legs of lamb and trimmed lamb loin, strip loin and skirt steaks, beef chuck, short ribs, cases of free-range chickens and ducklings, and on and on. Outside the walk-in, in the fabrication room, a student squares off lamb shanks with a band saw.

Years ago, when I added a fish chapter to a second edition of my book *Fast Vegetarian Feasts*, I received an angry letter from a strict vegetarian who had, up until that point, been a fan. "Now that you have strayed from the cause," she wrote, she was forsaking me. *Oy,* I think. *If only she could see me now...*

Our tour is over, and we walk out onto the loading dock, into the light. There are people employed by the CIA who spend their working lives down there in the underbelly. I'm glad not to be one of them. But with all that I've seen, I'm ready to cook. I can't wait to get to work on my menu assignment.

DINNER AT THE ESCOFFIER RESTAURANT

The Escoffier Restaurant, housed beyond etched-glass doors at one end of Roth Hall, is the Culinary Institute's fancy French restaurant. Waiters learn a kind of formal French service here that, outside of Michelin-starred restaurants, is rarely even practiced in France anymore. It's the kind of service that enthralled me on my first culinary trip to France, in 1977. Nouvelle cuisine was in its heyday then, and, inspired by what I'd read about the new generation of three-star chefs, I wrote to a number of them and asked them to prepare vegetarian meals for me, which I would then write about in a magazine article.

I can remember almost everything I ate at those meals—a boiled egg that was topped with the finest caviar, served from a porcelain egg cup set under a silver dome. A feuilleté filled with a buttery wild mushroom ragoût. A starter of delicate marinated vegetables à la Grecque, which gave me an indelible taste memory of cracked coriander seeds and preserved lemon.

But what is equally vivid is the table service. Waiters with gloved hands would swoop domed plates in front of us and with great fanfare simultaneously lift the heavy silver lids off each diner's plate. Sometimes they would finish a dish tableside in a copper pan. A whole fish might be presented in the pan, then deftly filleted and served with a beurre blanc. This choreography accompanied every two- and three-star meal I ate.

The Escoffier Restaurant aspires to that level of cuisine and service. Sometimes it works and sometimes it doesn't. Most of the waiters are a bit tentative as they lift the silver domes from our plates. The young woman who graciously takes our orders and brings our food admits, as she makes Bananas Foster over a tableside burner, that as many times as she's made this dish, flaming the bananas always makes her nervous. Not so for the buff male waiter across the room, whom I observe flaming and flipping bananas with great bravado.

Still, on this night our table of four is much luckier than we were yesterday evening at St. Andrew's Café. The most noticeable problem for our table is the filet mignon that was ordered rare but arrives at the table well done. It is replaced by a properly cooked piece of meat, and we settle down to quite a good meal.

The chef sends out a tiny hard-boiled quail egg on a square of toasted brioche as an amuse-gueule while we peruse the menu. All the items are written first in French, with italicized English translations underneath. They all look good, and everything I order is beautifully composed and executed, beginning with the house aperitif, a glass of Prosecco that is doused with a bit of the melon-flavored liqueur Midori. I find the green cast a bit odd, but the flavor is as delicate as springtime.

Of course I have to order the Consommé de Volaille "Paul Bocuse," a chicken consommé with truffle and vegetables. After tackling consommé in class, I want to taste one that comes out of a professional French kitchen. The fact that it's garnished with truffles makes it all the more appealing, and I am not disappointed.

All of the cold appetizers look good. I am drawn to the Salade de Homard "Arlequin," which is described as a salad of lobster, avocado, mango, and beets with mango dressing. The dressing strikes me as having more of a cilantro flavor, but I'm not quibbling. Here is a thick, juicy slice of mango set atop a salad of diced lobster, mango, beets, and avocado, seasoned with the zesty salsa-like dressing and molded into a hockey-puck-shaped disk. On top of the mango slice is a whole, succulent shelled lobster claw. My glass of Vouvray couldn't be more perfect with it.

All of the appetizers, in fact, look good. The Tartare de Saumon aux Lentilles Vertes is a modern take on a classic French main dish. The local Hudson Valley Foie Gras that my fellow diners order comes with a beautiful garnish of baby mâche and looks as good as any French foie gras I've tasted. The Warm Goat Cheese in Crust (served with caramelized spaghetti squash, olive oil, and balsamic dressing) reminds me of the goat cheese in filo hors d'oeuvre we made at my first Boot Camp.

Having tasted a memorable rendition of today's consommé lesson, I choose a review of yesterday's material for my entrée: a beautifully seared fillet of halibut set over a mound of spinach and served with an herb beurre blanc. The line cooks certainly have learned what they need to about getting the pan hot and searing the fish: it is lightly caramelized on both sides, cooked through to shiny perfection and not a moment too long. The sparkling spinach makes a colorful, deeply vegetal contrast, and the rich, velvety beurre blanc makes my mouth very happy.

I can see most of what is happening in the bright and busy open kitchen from my ringside seat. We watch students tournéing potatoes, and wonder out loud if the tournés are going to have the requisite seven sides. Those who have them with their entrée—they are served with the rack of lamb—don't hesitate to count. Some do, some don't, but they do all look like little footballs. They are certainly better than those I attempt in class!

This being a French restaurant, I choose to have the cheese course in lieu of dessert. My waiter doesn't have very good French pronunciation, but he can tell us about each cheese, and I make a selection of three—a goat cheese from the Loire Valley, a mountain cheese from the center of France, and a Camembert. I sip a glass of red, fruity Côtes du Rhône with it and am very happy to forgo the Bananas Foster that our waitress executes at our tableside, perhaps a bit tentatively but without error.

The Rose Room in the Escoffier Restaurant

Day 3

DRY HEAT COOKING METHODS

I grew up in a meat-eating family, where no expense was spared on quality cuts. When I learned to cook, I learned to make dishes such as standing rib roast with Yorkshire pudding and broiled two-inch-thick lamb chops. We grilled prime sirloins that were so thick that one steak would feed our mostly male family of six, and thick, juicy, seasoned hamburgers that my father christened "gourmet delight." I often said, when I became a vegetarian at the age of 21, that it was because I had simply eaten my quota of meat.

I never really understood much about cooking meat, even when I was making those big roasts, though the results were always excellent. When it came to the cooking, I simply followed my mother's instructions. If it was a standing rib roast, I started the meat at high heat, then turned the oven down and cooked it 14 or 15 minutes per pound. My roast always came out rare, the way we liked it. As for steaks and lamb chops, my mother told me to cook them for so many minutes on each side; I did so, and they were good to go. I never used my fingertips to ascertain doneness, nor did we have anything like digital thermometers. I just trusted my mother, or the cookbook she told me to use. Then I forgot about learning much about meat for a very long time, until Boot Camp.

DAY 3 TEAM PRODUCTION ASSIGNMENTS

Team 1

Roast Sirloin of Beef with Jus Lié (page 184)

Broccoli Rabe with Garlic and Olive Oil (page 194)

Grilled Yellow Squash (page 207)

Pommes Duchesse (page 214)

Team 2

Grilled Pork Chops with Pommery Mustard Beurre Blanc (page 187)

Glazed Sweet Potatoes (page 201)

Green Beans and Walnuts (page 204)

Parsnip and Pear Puree (page 212)

Team 3

Roast Chicken with Pan Gravy*

French-Fried Potatoes (page 198)

Tournéed Zucchini and Carrots (page 222)

Team 4

Grilled Salmon with Caraway Orange Glaze*

Basic Rice Pilaf (page 190)

Spinach with Bacon and Pine Nuts (page 226)

Sautéed Mushrooms (page 218)

Team 5

Pork Ribs with Asian-Style Barbecue Sauce (page 185)

Warm Coleslaw (page 226)

Corn Bread (page 196)

*Recipes and photographs on pages 62–64 and 68–70

ROASTING

If there is one cooking method that is truly about meat, it's roasting. When a food is roasted (or broiled, for that matter), it is cooked only by radiant heat. "It's the oldest cooking method," Chef Hinnerk tells us. "It all started, I suppose, when a bunch of cavemen were sitting around high on something and a piece of meat fell into the fire. 'Hey, that's good,' they realized. And over time there were refinements."

Roasting, broiling, and grilling are dry-heat cooking methods. Fat can be used, but its purpose is to lubricate the meat and to enhance flavor—it is not a cooking medium. Because so little fat is used, if any, the main danger is drying out the food.

To demonstrate how meat can dry out when it's roasted, broiled, or grilled, Chef Hinnerk gives us an ingenious presentation about what happens to proteins when they're exposed to heat. First he asks a question: "What contributes to juicy or dry meat?" Then he answers it before any of us can hazard a guess: "Intramuscular fat. As it melts it lubricates the proteins in the muscles and inhibits protein-to-protein bonding. Let me show you what I mean."

With that the chef has four students come to the front of the class and hold hands, spacing themselves about a foot apart. He tells the people to squat down. "Now you are globular proteins as they occur in raw meat.

"Okay, now the meat is being cooked, which denatures the proteins so that they

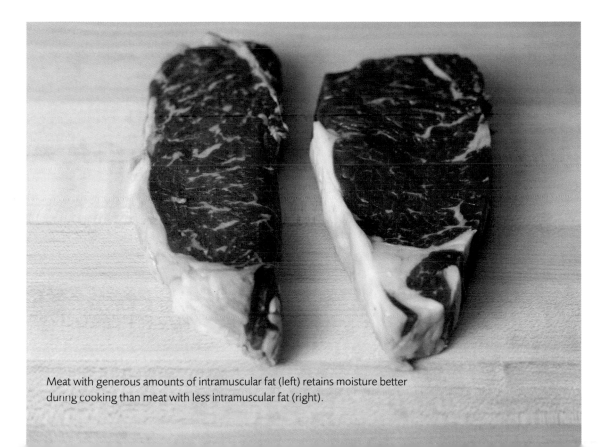

Meat with generous amounts of intramuscular fat (left) retains moisture better during cooking than meat with less intramuscular fat (right).

uncoil and form new bonds." He has the group stand up, spread out, then slowly pull closer together, still holding hands to represent the bonds. Eventually all of the people are squeezed up against each other like sardines.

"As the proteins bunch together, water is squeezed out. But if there is fat in between the proteins, all of the water can't be squeezed out. The meat will remain juicy." This is why you should choose tender and well-marbled cuts of beef for roasting, such as strip sirloin or tenderloin. Other foods that are suitable for roasting are veal, lamb, pork, game, poultry, certain types of fish, and vegetables. The cuts of meat and fish that you roast are larger than a single portion.

All of us think we know why meats that are going to be roasted or grilled are sometimes marinated first—to tenderize them. "Wrong," the chefs tell us. Marinades contribute to the flavor and color of the meat, but they don't tenderize. A brine, however, can help to moisturize naturally dry meat such as turkey or today's pork, which is much leaner than the pork that some of us grew up eating.

Sometimes the meat is seared first; the size of the cut determines whether or not to sear. Large cuts of meat don't need it because of the long cooking time, which will permit the meat to brown. The browning of meat at high temperatures is also called the Maillard reaction (in scientific terms, Chef Hinnerk explains, this is the reduction of sugars in the presence of amino acids). Dryer meats such as turkey benefit from being basted with the fat drippings that collect in the pan.

When foods are properly roasted, they develop a rich roasted aroma, a well-browned and highly flavored exterior, and a moist interior. Even when a meat is roasted until it's well done, the interior should not be dry. Meat shouldn't be roasted at temperatures that are too high, because this causes exces-

FDA RECOMMENDATIONS FOR MINIMUM FINISHED INTERNAL TEMPERATURES

Item	Description of Doneness	Safe Final Internal Temperature
Beef, venison, and lamb roasts	Rare	130°F
Beef, venison, and lamb roasts	Medium Rare	140°F
Beef, venison, and lamb roasts	Medium	145°F
Ground beef, lamb, pork, or game	Medium	145°F
Pork	Medium	145°F
Veal	Medium well	145°F
Fish and seafood	Cooked through	145°F
Poultry and stuffed meats	Well done	165°F (thigh)

sive shrinkage and drying. However, roasts—both meat and poultry—are sometimes begun at high temperatures, which sears the outside, resulting in a nice color, and in the case of poultry a crisp skin. Then the heat is turned to medium, usually about 325°F to 375°F. Large cuts of beef and lamb can be roasted over a long period at low temperatures; but a slow roast isn't suitable for poultry or small pieces of meat, because the meat will dry out before the skin is crisp; when the meat reaches the proper temperature, the skin will be gooey.

One of the most important terms for dry heat cooking is *carryover cooking.* This refers to the fact that heat penetrates meat from the outside to the inside, and when you remove it from the oven, the meat will continue to cook ("the outside is cooking the inside," Chef Hinnerk explains). The degree of carryover cooking is influenced by the oven temperature and the size of the meat. The internal temperature of a large piece of meat can rise 10 to 15 degrees after it's removed from the oven, so it should be taken out 10 degrees before it reaches the desired tem-

perature. That's why meat must rest for a minimum of 15 minutes, during which time the carryover cooking continues, the temperature equalizes, and juices are redistributed throughout the meat. (This doesn't apply to slow-cooked meat, however, which won't have much carryover.)

You can use an instant-read thermometer or, even better, a digital probe that can be kept in the meat as it roasts and will inform you by means of an alarm when the meat has reached the desired temperature.

EIGHT STEPS TO ACHIEVE A GOOD ROAST

1. Preheat the oven. You can use a conventional or a convection oven, but you have to watch the meat closely in a convection oven, as the added air circulation can dry out the food.

2. Season the food. Be generous with seasoning. It should be rubbed into all surfaces of the food.

3. Elevate the item to be roasted.

4. Roast meats uncovered. Covering meat causes steaming and toughens fibers.

5. Add mirepoix for flavoring.

6. Allow the meat to rest—*very* important.

7. Prepare a sauce from the meat juices (jus) or drippings (pan gravy).

8. Always carve across the grain.

9. Spoon the pan sauce over the meat and serve immediately.

1. Elevating a roast is important, and it's one of those facts I chose not to pay much attention to before coming to Boot Camp. "Racking" the food, they call it. The rack doesn't have to be a V-rack or a wire rack; it can be a bed of vegetables—mirepoix is typical—or bones. The important things are that the food does not sit in its own fat and that hot air can reach all of its sides.

2. Add flavorings and aromatics such as mirepoix during the last 20 to 30 minutes of roasting (which means, if you're making a roast that will be done in 20 to 30 minutes, you add it when you put the roast into the oven). There are a few ways to gauge doneness, the key to successful roasting. Time and experience come into it, and the way a piece of meat yields to finger pressure is another (see page 18). But by far the best method is to use a thermometer to determine the internal temperature of the meat.

3. When you take a roast out of the oven (and after grilling or broiling any meat), *leave it alone*. If you poke it with a knife or cut it, you will lose valuable juices. You need to let the meat rest. Chefs feel very passionate about this. If you do let your roast rest, more of the juices will stay in the roast when you carve your roasts into portions or slices, rather than spilling all over your carving board.

4. The sauce you use to accompany your roast can be as simple as the juices released by the meat during roasting, served just as they are (au jus) or thickened (jus lié). A jus lié is usually thickened with a cornstarch or arrowroot slurry. You can also make a pan gravy by preparing a roux, using flour mixed with some of the fat released by the meat or poultry, and adding a stock to it. This is usually done right in the roasting pan while the meat is resting.

ROAST CHICKEN WITH PAN GRAVY

My roast chicken was good even before I came to Boot Camp, but what I'm learning here will make it even better. Now I know that trussing and using a rack make a difference. As always, the quality of your bird matters. Try to find a good, free-range chicken for this. It does make a difference.

SERVES 6

Two 3½- to 4-pound chickens
Salt and freshly ground pepper to taste
2 tablespoons butter or olive oil (optional)
⅓ cup diced onion
¼ cup diced carrot
½ tablespoon tomato paste
¼ cup diced celery
3 tablespoons all-purpose flour
1 quart Chicken Stock (page 142)
2 teaspoons chopped fresh rosemary
2 garlic cloves, crushed
2 bay leaves
6 chervil sprigs for garnish (optional)

Things to watch

` Don't overcook the chicken. The carryover cooking will bring the temperature up from 160°F to 165°F.

` Don't use too much mirepoix (onion, carrots, and celery). You want the gravy to taste like chicken, not vegetables.

` Don't burn the flour when you make the roux.

1. Preheat the oven (or ovens) to 450°F.* Place a rack in a roasting pan large enough for both chickens, or prepare two roasting pans with racks. Season the chickens inside and out with salt and pepper (our chef only puts pepper on the inside, but I always pepper the skin too). Rub the skins with butter or oil if desired, and truss with twine (see page 137). Place on the rack(s) breast side up. Insert an instant-read thermometer into the thick part of the thigh where it meets the breast, being careful not to touch the bone.

2. Place the chickens in the hot oven and set the timer for 20 minutes. After 20 minutes, turn the oven down to 325°F. When the chicken's internal temperature registers 140°F, add the onions, carrots, and celery to the pan.

3. Roast until the thigh meat registers an internal temperature of 160°F. Remove from the oven and allow to rest while you make the gravy.

4. Discard all but about 3 tablespoons of the fat from the roasting pan. Add the tomato paste and flour and cook on top of the stove over medium-low heat to form a blond roux. When the roux smells fragrant, whisk in the stock and the herbs, and whisk until smooth. Simmer the gravy until it is thick and fragrant. Degrease thoroughly; this will be easiest if you simmer the sauce partway off the burner, so that the fat gathers to one side of the pan.

5. Strain the gravy through a fine strainer and season to taste with salt and pepper. Transfer to a gravy boat, carve the chicken, and serve.

*If you have a convection oven, you can cook the chicken at 375°F for the entire time.

BROILING AND GRILLING

All of the dry heat cooking rules that we learned about roasting also apply to grilling and broiling. Grilling and broiling are quicker cooking methods than roasting, so they generally involve individual portion sizes of meat, poultry, or fish. The cuts are lean or well marbled, and the cook must know how to gauge the exact point at which the foods are perfectly cooked. When foods are properly grilled and broiled, they will have a highly flavored exterior, smoky and slightly charred, and a moist, juicy interior.

The main difference between broiling and grilling is that in grilling the heat source is below the food, and in broiling it's above. Broiling is more suitable for delicate pieces such as sole fillets, which will not need to be turned when they're broiled.

Whereas with roasting the food is cooked by radiant heat only, when you grill, the heat is provided both by conduction from the grill rods and by radiant heat from the heat source (when you broil there is limited conduction from the heat of the grids). Chef Hinnerk empha-sized that the grill must be cast iron or another heavy material, but not stainless steel, which doesn't hold the heat. He also stressed the importance of cleaning the grid and brushing it with oil so that the food doesn't stick.

Broilers can be conventional gas or electric. In today's household stoves, the broiler is often electric even if the burners are gas. Grills can use gas burners, charcoal, or hardwood, or a mixture of the last two. Some chefs, including Chef John, insist that the term *barbecue* refers to a "slow-and-low" method of cooking done over charcoal or wood so the food cooks in the presence of smoke. Chef Hinnerk, on the other hand, equates the term *barbecue* with all outdoor grilling.

BASIC PROCEDURE FOR GRILLING AND BROILING

1. Thoroughly clean the grill. Brush it clean, wipe the grid dry with a cloth, and oil the grid.

2. Marinate or season the item to be grilled or broiled.

3. Preheat the grill or broiler.

4. Brush the item to be grilled with oil if necessary to prevent sticking, and place on the grill. Use a hand grill for delicate foods, such as some cuts of fish.

5. Turn the food 45° to produce cross-hatch marks if desired.

6. Turn the item over to complete cooking to the desired done-ness.

7. Serve the grilled item with its accompaniments.

Marinades

As Chef Hinnerk had emphatically told us, the purpose of a marinade is not to tenderize, but to add flavor and some moisture to foods.

Marinades can be dry or liquid. The components of a liquid marinade are usually an oil, an acid, and aromatics. Oils lubricate and protect the foods, both during the time they marinate and while they're cooking. Acids, such as vinegar, yogurt, wine, and citrus juices, add flavor and change the food's texture, as acids will break down proteins. Aromatic options include herbs, whole or ground spices, onions, garlic, citrus zest, or mustards.

Dry marinades, also known as rubs, are made from a mixture of salt, crushed or chopped herbs, spices, and occasionally other aromatics such as citrus zest. Sometimes just enough oil or another liquid is mixed with the dry rub to make a marinade known as a paste.

Dry marinades or pastes are rubbed over and into the food and the food is left to stand in the refrigerator to absorb the marinade's flavors. When a dry marinade contains a generous amount of salt and the food is meant to stand for some time once it is rubbed, the salt will be omitted so that it doesn't draw moisture out of the food. It will be rubbed in closer to the cooking time. Liquid marinades are poured over the food that you hold either in a covered pan or in a zip-close plastic bag. If a liquid marinade doesn't completely coat the food, turn it from time to time while the food marinates.

Sauces

Grilled and broiled foods are incredibly versatile when it comes to sauces. Those that make good matches include salsas, coulis, relishes, flavored mayonnaises such as aïoli, and other emulsion sauces such as béarnaise and beurre blanc. We make a delicious mustard beurre blanc (page 147) to go with grilled pork chops (page 187), serve beef satay with a Thai peanut sauce, and dress up fennel and chicken skewers with a tomato and red pepper coulis. Then, of course, there's barbecue sauce, with all of its regional variations. The thing that all of these have in common is that they are made quite separately from the food that is being cooked; they can even be made before the food is cooked, as they rely on neither fond, jus, nor drippings.

ADDITIONAL GRILLING AND BROILING TIPS

Thin items should be cooked quickly at high heat.

Medium-thick items are started at high heat and can be finished on a cooler area of the grill or broiler.

Thick items are started at high heat and can be finished on a cooler area of the grill or in the oven.

Foods should be broiled at the last possible moment.

Keep the broiler clean at all times.

Never pierce meat with a fork or knife during or right after cooking. Carryover cooking applies to grilling and broiling as it does to roasting.

1. There are plenty of options when it comes to a sauce for grilled foods. One of the simplest to make (and easiest to keep on hand) is something known as a compound butter. But for this recipe, we were going to make a glaze to brush on the fish as it grills and to serve with the fish as a sauce. It is flavored with orange juice concentrate (for a more intense flavor and more sugar than fresh) and caraway seeds. Here we learn a great trick: to chop the small amount of caraway for the glaze, mix it with ½ tablespoon of the butter, then chop. That way the seeds don't go flying.

2. Those appealing cross-hatch grill marks we like to see on grilled foods are achieved by placing the food on the hot grids of a preheated grill at an angle, say at 10 o'clock. You grill them for a few minutes, until grill marks appear, then shift them to 2 o'clock and grill them until the grill marks appear in the other direction. The food is usually marked on the presentation side only, then cooked until done on the other side. In professional kitchens where there is a lot of volume, food is sometimes marked off ahead of time, then finished to order.

3. You can control the cooking speed and temperature on a grill by establishing what chefs refer to as "zones." Basically, that means that you know which parts of your grill are hotter than the others. Then you can move something from the hot part of the grill to a cooler part so that it doesn't dry out or over-cook. In restaurants, chefs also use zones to keep foods separated that might otherwise transfer a strong flavor to another food. And when there are requests for a variety of done-nesses, they use zones to help them keep track of which item needs to cook for the longest (or shortest) amount of time.

4. Grilled foods should be served almost as soon as they come from the grill, unless you need to slice or carve them. We are reminded to get our plates hot so that the food will stay hot on its way to the table, something chefs do as a matter of course when they set up their stations in the restaurant. They even have spe-cial equipment to keep the plates hot.

GRILLED SALMON WITH CARAWAY ORANGE GLAZE

Chef Hinnerk's ideas about grilling salmon differ from those of the other chefs. He likes to grill salmon with the skin off, because he says the skin sticks. He removes the skin by holding the knife at a 20° angle and moving it between the skin and the fish, which prevents the fish from tearing. Then he takes out the pin bones, seasons the fish well on both sides with salt and pepper, cleans and oils the grill, and rubs a little oil on the fish. He sets the fillet at 10 o'clock on the grill, doesn't touch it for a few minutes, then moves it to 2 o'-clock to achieve grill marks. Skin off or on, the important thing to remember when you grill fish is to leave it alone for the first few minutes on the grill so that it doesn't stick. Once it has cooked properly on the first side, it will be easy to flip. The glaze not only tastes great but helps the salmon retain moisture. Don't brush it on until shortly before the end of cooking or it will burn.

SERVES 6

Things to watch

` Don't disturb the salmon during the first 2 to 3 minutes on the grill.

` Don't grill the salmon for too long or it will be dry.

FOR THE GLAZE:

¼ cup orange juice concentrate

2 teaspoons caraway seeds, cracked

2 tablespoons butter

FOR THE SALMON:

6 salmon fillets with skin on, 6 to 8 ounces each

Salt and freshly ground black pepper to taste

Lemon wedges for serving

1. Make a very hot fire in your grill. Mix the caraway seeds with 1 tablespoon of the butter and chop. Combine the orange juice concentrate and caraway seeds in a saucepan and bring to a simmer over very low heat. Simmer 10 minutes, remove from the heat, and stir in the remaining butter.

2. Use tweezers or needle-nose pliers to remove the pin bones from the salmon fillets. Season with salt and pepper.

3. Place the salmon presentation side down at 10 o'clock on the hot grill and cook undisturbed for 2 or 3 minutes. Shift the fillets to 2 o'clock to create grill marks and grill another 2 minutes. Turn over and cook another 4 minutes, brushing with the glaze after a minute or two, until the fish pulls apart when pierced with a fork. Remove from the heat.

4. Brush the fillets with additional glaze and serve.

INTRODUCTION TO WINES

I learned a lot about wine when I lived in Paris, but most of that knowledge is limited to the wines of France. My familiarity with New World wines is spotty. I know little about Italian wines, and even less about those from Germany, Spain, and South Africa. So I'm always eager to take a class or participate in a tasting, and the two Boot Camp afternoons devoted to understanding wine are time well spent.

Our lecturers at Boot Camp help us to understand what we are looking for when we taste wine. Brian Smith, one of the wine professors at the CIA and a coauthor of their huge textbook *Exploring Wine*, kicks off his lectures with a question that is perfect for getting the ball rolling at any introductory wine seminar, no matter what the range of knowledge among the students: what makes a wine good? It boils down to three objective criteria: the grapes, the winemaking, and the source of the grapes, or the terroir, and its influence.

The Grapes

We spend most of the first day with Brian discussing different grape varieties that lend their names to the wines that are made from them. We taste eight different wines, four whites and four reds, each made from a different type of grape. The next day we also taste eight different wines, but this time we compare the influences of winemaking and terroir by tasting side by side two glasses of wine made from the same grape variety but from different places. Of the many wine classes I've been to, this is one of the most instructive.

Grapes have a variety of flavor profiles. Some are big, some are narrower. Brian tells us that three of the basic tastes—sweet, bitter, and sour (or acidic)—can be present in wine, and he guides us in our attempts to detect them as we taste.

"First try to detect one of these tastes, then define it. Move your head around." Our sensors for sweetness are in the front of the mouth, he explains; those for sour are on the sides and in the back of the roof of our mouth. We can also tell if a wine is high in alcohol if it leaves a slight tingling sensation (called a "burn") in our throat when we swallow it. Bitterness in wines comes from tannins, which are in the skins. Tannins are astringent—they draw the saliva from our mouth, resulting in a drying sensation. Tannins are instrumental in aging wine: as the wine ages, the tannins retreat. The reason tannic wines can be so pleasant with food, especially with meat, is because fats will denature the tannins, allowing the other fruity flavors to emerge. "But never drink tannic wines with cream sauces," Brian warns, "because the tannins will curdle the milk!"

In addition to detecting flavors in wine, we should ask ourselves if the wine is heavy or light, smooth or rough, complex or straightforward. All of these are objective criteria that help us decide whether or not we like the wine and what we might want to pair it with. In general, lightly flavored wines go with lightly flavored foods. Heavier, more tannic wines are better supported by richer

A flight of wines is often selected to complement the diverse courses of a meal.

meat dishes. Wines can enhance foods by virtue of their similarities—tastes, flavors, and textures—or they can highlight foods through contrast. For example, the sweet fruitiness of a Riesling works well with the smokiness of delicately smoked salmon or trout. But if there's too much flavor in the food, the delicacy of a Riesling will be lost. A rich, sweet wine might better accompany something savory and rich, such as foie gras or cheese, rather than dessert, whose sweetness might overpower the more nuanced sweetness in the wine. On the other hand, a sturdy, mouth-filling wine such as a Shiraz can stand up to the kind of aromatic Mediterranean food that is eaten in the southern climates where this grape thrives.

Having discussed some of these concepts, Brian pours each of us four glasses of white wine—a Riesling from Germany, a Sauvignon Blanc from South Africa, a California Chardonnay, and a California Viognier—and urges us to have open minds as we observe the objective criteria in each. He advises us to note the color differences, which often indicate something about the flavor.

Lightness of color indicates a light aroma and a delicate flavor; a green hue might foretell a grassy flavor. Young wines from colder climates often have that greenish hue. The deeper, yellower wines point to riper fruit, a warmer climate, and wood aging. A more viscous appearance reflects a richer wine.

Before we taste, we raise the glasses to our noses and breathe in. We swirl the glasses and breathe in again. Do we detect flowers or fruit? What kind of fruit do we detect? Citrus (lemons, orange peel, limes, grapefruit)? Green apples? Bananas? Tropical fruit? Or do we sense something more vegetal, like grass or hay? Is the nose on the wine aggressive (which indicates acidity) or restrained? Are we reminded of other smells, such as lanolin or gasoline, barnyards or cat piss? Strangely enough, there are some smells that can be unpleasant in life but can have a subtle place in wine.

The Riesling does have a fruity, sweet, character, but with enough acid to balance it beautifully. You would not call it a sweet wine; rather, it's an intensely fruity wine. People find hints of green apple, grapefruit, and lime. The

Sauvignon Blanc has a more aggressive aroma. It is less floral and more grassy, and seems bigger and more muscular than the Riesling. We detect more acid as well.

With its big, heavy, oaky, buttery flavors, the Chardonnay is smooth and rich, almost oily. It tastes heavy after the first two wines, typical of the in-your-face style that many California Chardonnays display. We wonder how this wine would pair with food. Bill Guilfoyle, the instructor I have in my other session at Boot Camp, condemns California Chardonnays as "disastrous" with foods, and I tend to agree. It is the heavy oaking that we are tasting on this wine, and it's overbearing.

The last white we taste, a Viognier from California, has been enjoying a lot of recent popularity. This is probably because it's so immediately accessible. Viognier is a fruity grape with low acid and a round, soft, tropical flavor. Brian contrasts it with the Riesling—if Riesling is a green banana, Viognier is a ripe one.

We then go on to taste the reds: a Pinot Noir from Oregon's Willamette Valley, a Sonoma County Merlot, a Napa Valley Cabernet Sauvignon, and a Mendocino County California Syrah. Brian explains, as we look at the limpid Pinot Noir, how this grape is the thinnest-skinned of the red grapes. The color of red wine is derived from the skins, which is also where the tannins reside, so it follows that Pinot Noirs have the lightest color and the least amount of tannin of any of the red wines. In contrast, Cabernet Sauvignon is the smallest red grape and has the highest ratio of skin to grape. Cabernets are dark, tannic wines.

We find many nuances in the Pinot Noir. It smells of earth and dry clay, smoke and fruit—decidedly red fruit. It is light and acidic, long in the mouth with hints of cinnamon. The Clos du Bois Merlot is pleasant, simple, and fruity. It is easy to drink, and that explains why Merlots are so popular in the United States. The Cabernet Sauvignon, from Stag's Leap in Napa Valley, is much less immediate. There are layers of leather (tannic acid is what is used to cure, or tan, leather) and tobacco playing against the berry-like red fruit. I taste figs as well, something close to the tree. There is promise in that bottle; however, to my taste it is not yet ready to drink. But the Syrah is; this is a grape—the same grape is known as Shiraz in Australia—that tastes ripe and luscious. We perceive lots of red fruit, but also spice, earth, and herbs.

Terroir

Terroir is a French word that refers to place, or the soil in which the grapes are grown. In wine parlance, terroir also implies how vines are grown—the viticulture—and the way in which the wine is vinified. The farming of grapes and the techniques used for making wine are place-specific.

AOC

Any discussion of terroir must begin with an understanding of the AOC. The letters stand for "Appellation d'Origine Controlée," which means, literally, "controlled naming of origin." The concept of appellation has been adopted by wine regions all around the world and generally refers to a defined, named geographic area considered to have distinct attributes derived from the soil and/or climate. A wine's appellation, if it has been awarded one, should give the drinker an indication of what that wine will be like.

At least that's the case in Europe. The French AOC system pinpoints the place the wine comes from, and in so doing defines the way in which the wine is made—what grapes may be used, how they must be grown, the yield, the alcohol content, and the vinification process.

But in the United States, there are two types of appellation. One is a preexisting geopolitical unit, such as a state or a county. The other is an agricultural unit based on common natural or historical attributes, such as Napa Valley. Generally, the larger the geographic area in the appellation, the less the appellation tells you about the wine. Napa Valley, for example, is a very large area, with great fluctuations in climate and sun exposure. Consequently there is talk now of subdividing these larger appellations into smaller, more cohesive ones.

In any wine-producing region, appellations can cover areas ranging from large to very small. Burgundian AOCs are like Russian dolls, with smaller appellations located inside larger ones. The smaller the appellation, generally, the more prestigious (and more expensive) the wine. The hierarchical Burgundian appellations go from region (Burgundy) to district (Côte de Beaune) to village (Puligny-Montrachet) to individual vineyard (Les Folatières). The vineyards are further ranked

into categories known as crus, which range from cru ordinaire through premier cru and up to grand cru at the highest end.

If a vineyard has no recognized cru status, its wine will have only village appellation status, and the appellation phrase beneath the name of the wine will read Puligny-Montrachet Controlée. If the wine from a particular vineyard is judged a cru ordinaire, the appellation on the label will name the village plus the name of the vineyard (for example, Appellation Puligny-Montrachet Les Folatières). If the wine from a vineyard is considered to have premier cru (or 1er cru) status, the appellation phrase will also denote that status (Appellation Puligny-Montrachet Les Folatières, 1er Cru Controlée). If a vineyard is judged to have Grand Cru status, the label appellation will only name the individual vineyard (Appellation Montrachet Controlée).

New World wines are not burdened by such rigorous and hierarchical labeling practices. Here labeling most often refers to the grape varieties. The appellation refers to the place the wine is from, but sometimes that tells you little about the wine, because the region—like Napa—may be so large. By contrast, we know that a bottle of Puligny-Montrachet will always be a white wine from that village, and it will be made with the Chardonnay grape.

To illustrate how terroir can help us to identify and appreciate wines, we do a comparative tasting of wines made with the same grapes but from different parts of the world (France and California). This is incredibly revealing: the wines from France are consistently more subtle and elegant than the wines from California. The French wines are all lighter, with lower alcohol content. But there are other, more nuanced differences that speak of the soil, the climate, and the vinification.

We taste a Sancerre (made from the Sauvignon Blanc grape) from the Loire Valley against a Sauvignon Blanc from the Napa Valley. The Sancerre is more fragrant with fruit than the Napa wine, which has more mineral aspects in the nose. The California wine jumps out at you more. It is more acidic, with more alcohol (this is described as a "higher burn," because the alcohol burns the back of your throat). Both wines are pleasant to drink.

The Chardonnays are completely unalike. The Burgundy, a Puligny-Montrachet, is light and citrusy, very floral in the nose, with nuances of ripe fruit and smoke. The California Chardonnay is big, buttery, and oaky—assertive, even aggressive. I enjoy sipping it, but I can imagine drinking it only as an aperitif, not as an accompaniment to food.

The French reds are also quite distinct from the California equivalents. The Pinot Noir from Burgundy, a Chambolle-Musigny Premier Cru, is like a field of fruit, long in the mouth, but light. You can notice the oak in it,

A CORKED BOTTLE

The term *corked* refers to a bottle of wine that has spoiled due to a reaction with a mold that has gotten into the cork. We have the opportunity, if you can call it that, to taste a corked wine when Brian Smith opens the first bottle of Clos du Bois for our comparative tasting. We taste our glasses before he does, and none of us has much to say. I don't think the wine has much finish—or is it that I wouldn't want to finish the wine? A corked wine has a moldy, musty smell; when you taste it, you think of a damp room filled with molding newspapers, certainly not fruit. It's not a wine you'd like to continue drinking through a meal. It's a wine that needs to be sent back, if you're in a restaurant, or poured out, if you're at home.

Bottles with twist-off tops or plastic corks will soon become the norm in the industry. We don't yet know if these bottles will age well, but we do know that wine that is not stoppered with cork will not be subject to this type of spoilage. And that will be good for the wine industry and for us.

but it isn't overpowering. The California Pinot Noir has more vegetal aspects—leaves and mushrooms rather than all red fruit. It is more severe than the French wine. The Bordeaux that we drink next to a Clos du Bois (65 percent Cabernet Sauvignon in the French wine, 54 percent in the California wine) is by far the most complex wine that we taste. It makes us think of leather and barnyards, of herbs and cigars and fruit. The California wine is mostly just big and fruity. It isn't as tannic as the French wine, and we wonder how well it will age.

We learn this afternoon just to what degree California producers make a different sort of wine than their French counterparts. Everything we taste has merit, and clearly the California style has great appeal, especially in the United States. In the end, it's a matter of taste.

DINNER AT AMERICAN BOUNTY RESTAURANT

Our wine instructor, Brian Smith, joins us for dinner at American Bounty Restaurant, another one of the CIA's elegant restaurants located in Roth Hall. He has carefully selected a menu and wines to go with it, only to find when we arrive that some of the wines haven't been ordered. We manage. The menu is an interesting one, and this time the service is on track, possibly because we are all having the same thing, so the students in the kitchen can get the timing right while putting their banquet-style cooking skills to good use.

American Bounty is so called because the dishes on the menu reflect the cultural diversity of this country and are made with local ingredients whenever possible. This is a good place to see how classically trained chefs can branch out, layering the knowledge they have gained in the teaching kitchens of the CIA with their creative impulses. Regional specialties are dressed up and modernized. Pan-fried Florida Rock Shrimp Cakes, for example, are served with a Hearts of Palm and Chayote Salad and a Red Pepper Sauce. In the New England Seafood Sampler a Fricassée of Maine Lobster is served with Garlic Orzo Custard. Bordering countries are not ignored here: the fall menu features a signature Canadian Yellow Split Pea Soup (albeit served with Smoked Potatoes and Chive Sticks), an Escabèche of Sea Scallops with Jalapeño, Lime, Pineapple, and Cactus Leaves, and Jamaican Jerk Duckling with Cassava Tots (a playful spin on tater tots), Pineapple-Jícama Slaw, and Braised Greens.

In keeping with the name and menu, all of the wines on the list come from the United States. Most of them, understandably, are from California, but Washington State, Oregon, and New York State (including the Finger Lakes, Hudson River, Millbrook, and North Fork regions of Long Island) are all well represented. If you want to sample these different wine-producing regions, you can order a flight of Chardonnays and taste two very different wines, one from Greystone Cellars (at the West Coast campus of the CIA) and the other from Dr. Konstantin Frank in the Finger Lakes region of New York. Or you can taste a flight of whites, which includes an Oregon Pinot Blanc, a Napa Valley Chenin Blanc, and a Friulian-inspired blend (Big House White) from Bonny Doon Vineyard in Santa Cruz, California. Go for a flight of reds and you'll get 2 ounces each of a Pinot Noir from Millbrook, New York, a Merlot from the California Central Coast, and a Mourvèdre from Sonoma Country.

Our first course is Pastrami-Cured Atlantic Salmon, which is really an American twist on Gravlax. Brian ordered both a Monteviña Pinot Grigio from Amador County, California, and an Iron Horse Rosé from Green Valley, California, to accompany this course. The Pinot Grigio is available, but we have to substitute an Iron Horse sparkling rosé from their Sonoma Valley vineyard for the Green Valley rosé. I always enjoy a dry sparkling wine with smoked or cured salmon, and this suits me just fine.

Brian has decided on a vegetarian entrée that will showcase both white and red wines. Interestingly, it is the same dish that I ordered at this restaurant nine months earlier, when I came in January with my first Boot Camp. I'm not sorry to have the Roasted Mushroom and Goat Cheese Strudel again, especially since this time around it's much better (it had been way too dry when I'd ordered it in January). The chef must have reworked the recipe, for now the mushrooms are nice and moist in their generous goat-cheese-infused sauce, beautifully packaged in a crisp, golden filo tube. The strudel is cut into two pieces on the diagonal, like Japanese nori rolls, one standing on end, the other lying down. Creamed spinach and braised pumpkin bring color to the plate, and lentils add a savory dimension that marries well with the strudel. Nothing seems out of place. I will remember this presentation when we have our lecture on plating a few days hence, because it is so well executed. The main item is certainly the focal point, and it is enhanced and set off by the side dishes.

Both of Brian's wine choices (both, thankfully, in stock) are wines I would choose myself to go with this dish. There is a Navarro Gewürztraminer from Anderson Valley, California, for the white-wine drinkers, and a Pinot Noir from Russian River Valley in Sonoma for those who want red. The Navarro Vineyards Gewürztraminer is a nice floral/spicy match for the entrée. I am always on the lookout for a red wine that will go well with vegetarian entrées, and Brian has given me a newfound appreciation of Pinot Noirs, which are light and delicate and go well with fish and vegetables. The David Bruce Pinot Noir is just what I wanted to try with this course, and I'm not disappointed.

Even our dessert has a comforting American feel to it. It is a Warm Dark Chocolate Pudding Cake, and it is served with a glass of Quady Elysium from Madera County, California. Don't confuse this with Madeira, the Portuguese dessert wine. The Quady winery does specialize in dessert wines made with muscat grape varieties, and in ports, but it is in Madera County, California. They named their black muscat dessert wine Elysium because, in their words, "Drinking this, you can almost feel you have fallen into a rose garden and been transported to heaven." And I must say I do. I transport myself to bed instead, thinking what an appropriate meal this has been after our first wine lecture, and about the wines I will serve with my own next dinner party.

Hilde Potter Room, American Bounty Restaurant

Day 4

MOIST HEAT COOKING METHODS

I am not a macho cook. High heat, speed, and kitchen gymnastics are not what I love about cooking. I like a slow simmer, and flavors that develop over time and keep evolving even after the fire is turned off. That's why, when it comes to cooking meat, I'm most attracted to stews and braises, those hearty, big-flavored country dishes that begin with tough, well-exercised cuts of meat and end up, miraculously, fork tender. It's a method of cooking that I don't find as mysterious as others, because it's easier for me to ascertain when the dish is done. I taste the sauce and stick a fork into the meat. If it's tender and the sauce surrounding it is delicious, it's good to go. And it will be even better if I wait a day to serve it.

DAY 4 TEAM PRODUCTION ASSIGNMENTS

Team 1

Ossobuco alla Milanese (page 188)

Saffron Risotto with Porcini Mushrooms and Basil (page 217)

Green Beans with Bacon and Shallots (page 204)

Sautéed Red and Yellow Peppers (page 219)

Team 2

Yankee Pot Roast (page 174)

Polenta (page 213)

Braised Fennel with Parmesan Cheese*

Oven-Roasted Vegetables (page 211)

Team 3

Poached Fillet of Sole with White Wine Sauce*

Potatoes with Saffron and Parsley (page 191)

Carrot Flan (page 195)

Sautéed Snow Peas with Sesame Seeds (page 220)

Team 4

Poached Chicken Breast with Tarragon Sauce (page 170)

Mashed Turnips and Potatoes (page 212)

Hot and Spicy Mixed Vegetables (page 208)

Haricots Verts (page 208)

Team 5

Braised Lamb Shanks (page 173)

Spinach Spaetzle with Sapsago Cheese (page 224)

Glazed Beets (page 199)

Deep-Fried Parsnips (page 198)

*Recipes and photographs on pages 88–90 and 94–96

COMBINATION METHODS

Braising and stewing are combination cooking methods that use both dry and moist heat. Meat is usually first seared, then simmered with mirepoix and aromatics in a closed vessel, either on top of the stove or in the oven. Simmering results in flavor extraction and tenderizing. Tough cuts of meat—the ones that come from the working parts of the animal, such as the shoulder and the shank—are rich in collagen, a protein found in connective tissue that holds the muscle bundles together. When you cook in a moist environment, the collagen gets converted into gelatin, which is soluble in water and leaches out. But if you simmer meat for too long, too much will leach out and the meat will dry out, become fibrous, and fall apart.

Between my first Boot Camp, in January, and the one I attend in September, the chefs have changed the menus somewhat and substituted a dish called Swiss Steak for the Yankee Pot Roast we made with Chef John. Some of the instructors feel that there isn't enough time to make a proper, tender pot roast, so they have gone for Swiss Steak, which is a lot like pot roast, but the brisket (or chuck or top roast) is cut into portion-size pieces before it's cooked. Chef Hinnerk is totally against this idea, and to prove that he can make the pot roast work within the allotted time, he demos it for us, and has it simmering by the time we get to work on our assignments. The chef who was instrumental in changing the menu is teaching in Skills Kitchen II and comes over from time to time to banter with Chef Hinnerk. He is skeptical, but in the end he will have to shake our chef's hand and concede.

Chef Hinnerk uses a pot that is wide enough for the meat, liquid, and other ingredients, but not too big. He blots the meat dry and seasons it well. Then he barely covers the bottom of the pot with oil and browns the meat on all sides, using tongs to lift it when he browns the ends. The heat is fairly high, though not so high as to burn the meat; you need to go for dark color when you sear.

He removes the meat from the pan and browns the mirepoix. "The caramelized vegetables contribute to the flavor of the dish," he tells us. "If you need to add some oil, do it." Then he turns the heat down a little, adds a tablespoon of tomato paste, and caramelizes it, using his nose to ascertain when it is done. Next he adds red wine and reduces it until the pan is almost dry. He adds the aromatics (since the liquid will be strained, there is no need to make a sachet). He returns the meat to the pot, barely covers it with stock (the amount you use depends on the size of the pot—the recipe does not know).

Before seasoning the liquid, he tastes it to ascertain how much he should add, then he brings it to a simmer and covers it. The pot roast can cook in the oven or on top of the stove.

Two and a half hours later a platter of sliced pot roast with gravy joins our stews, braises, and side dishes on the buffet in Skills Kitchen I. It is as tender as can be. And

BASIC PROCEDURE FOR BRAISING AND STEWING

1. Season or marinate the main item. Sometimes the main item is lightly floured.

2. Sear the main item on all sides in hot oil. The oil should just cover the bottom of the pan. Searing adds flavor and color. In some stews the main item is blanched rather than seared. This is the case, for example, in Phô Bo, the signature Vietnamese beef and noodle stew.

3. Remove the main item and set aside in a bowl.

4. Add mirepoix and caramelize. Add tomato paste and cook until rust-colored with a sweet aroma (pinçage).

5. Add the liquid, stir to deglaze the pan, and bring it to a simmer over direct heat. Do not allow the liquid to boil; boiling toughens the meat. Return the main item to the sauce; add aromatics. Cover and simmer gently at low heat, either on top of the stove or in the oven, until it is fork tender. ("Fork tender does not mean falling apart," says Chef Hinnerk, "which could indicate that the food has been overcooked.") Taste the liquid from time to time and adjust seasonings. Periodically test the main item for doneness.

6. Remove the main item and keep warm.

7. Strain the liquid and return it to the pot. Reduce, thicken, and adjust seasonings. Garnish as desired.

8. Slice or carve the main item (if necessary) and serve it with the finished sauce and appropriate garnish (if desired).

BASIC PROCEDURE FOR STEWS

Follow the above steps through Step 5. Then correct flavor and consistency of the sauce, thickening it if necessary.

---

frankly, I am happy that we did not make Swiss Steak, as the name evokes only one thing for me: a school cafeteria.

Ingredients for Braising

When it comes to meat, braising usually involves large cuts such as lamb shanks, or multi-portion cuts that are carved after cooking. Food that is braised is usually half-submerged in a well-flavored liquid, such as stock, wine, or a combination, and the resulting sauce is commonly strained and thickened. For stews, the meat is cut into bite-sized pieces and submerged in the liquid, which will not be strained at the end of cooking. But as far as the cooking techniques are concerned, they are identical in all other ways.

Braises and stews should be cooked in large, heavy, tightly lidded pots that are wider than they are tall, but not too large for the amount of food that is being prepared. The food can be browned in this pot or in a separate pan, which would be deglazed and the contents added to the braising pot. Foods that are suitable for braising and stewing include beef, veal, lamb, pork, poultry, game, organ meats, and vegetables. There are, to be sure, seafood stews, but the seafood is never stewed for a very long time. However, the vegetables and aromatics that make these dishes so delightful might have a good long simmer before the fish and/or shellfish is added.

Cuts suitable for braising: Pork cottage butt (upper left), lamb shanks (lower left), osso bucco (top center), short ribs (bottom center), duck legs (far right).

Vegetables can also be braised and stewed. But they tenderize in a different manner. What determines tenderness in vegetables is fiber, which, if it's water-soluble, will soften and eventually dissolve in water. Keeping your eye on the time and on your food, then, is important when you're braising and stewing vegetables.

At Boot Camp we make braised fennel, cooking it first on top of the stove and finishing it in the oven with a golden Parmesan topping; and we braise greens with bacon. These were both comforting dishes, as braises and stews tend to be.

Accompaniments

Braises and stews are commonly served with a starch, unless the stew itself is filled with potatoes (like in Irish Stew). Steamed or mashed potatoes, steamed rice, and noodles are the most common accompaniments, as they're wonderful for soaking up the flavorful sauce. But there are many other possibilities, including polenta (page 213), couscous, orzo, and grains such as bulgur, farro (also called spelt), or barley. Sometimes I just serve thick slices of toasted country bread. At Boot Camp I make a truly wonderful, colorful spaetzle that has spinach and sapsago cheese in it (page 224), to go with the braised lamb shanks I'm also making. Another team's menu calls for a delicious saffron and porcini risotto (page 217) to go with Ossobuco alla

Things to watch

- Do not allow the liquid to boil during cooking (it toughens the meat and causes it to shrink excessively).

- Do not use too much liquid (it weakens the flavor of the sauce). A standard ratio for braising is 1 pound of the main item, 1 ounce of mirepoix (at Boot Camp we usually use more), and 1 pint of liquid.

Milanese (a bit excessive, I think, as the risotto can stand alone as a starter or main dish, but it still tastes good).

One of the best things about braises and stews, even in a professional kitchen, is the fact that they actually get even better when you let them rest overnight before you serve them. You'll find that larger cuts, like a brisket of beef, are easier to slice when chilled. Any excess fat in the braise has a chance to rise to the surface, chill, and harden. That makes it easy to lift it away from the dishes for a calorie and fat savings. Most important, the flavors in the sauce mellow and deepen as the dish rests overnight. Reheat braises in the oven to keep the main ingredients from falling apart; be sure to cover the pan tightly before it goes into the oven. Stews are easy to reheat right on the stove, but remember to start out on a very low temperature.

1. Many vegetables lend themselves to this method of cooking, which is why there are signature vegetable braises and stews from all over the world. Think of the many different types of vegetable tagines that are served with couscous throughout North Africa, the marvelous braised artichokes à la barigoule and ratatouilles from Provence, and slow-cooked greens from the American South. We leave some of the fennel's core in place so that it will hold together throughout its cooking time.

2. Mirepoix and aromatics—sachet d'épices or bouquet garni—are always present for flavor, but in addition pork products (pancetta, bacon, salt pork, or ham), tomato paste, tomatoes, and other vegetables are often important components of a stew or braise. Other elements might include a marinade and the thickener. The stock can be thickened simply by means of flour that has been added to the fat and mirepoix or has been used to dust the meat before browning; other possibilities for thickening include a slurry added after being reduced, a roux, or a liaison.

3. You can turn a vegetable braise into a more substantial dish by preparing it as a gratin. As the chefs explain to us, gratin doesn't automatically indicate cheese (although it is a common topping), but rather that a dish is cooked in such a way that the sauce is perfectly reduced and the top (with cheese or without) baked into a perfect, golden-brown crust. To control the way the crust is forming, you can cover a braised dish with a lid or some aluminum foil as it cooks and then remove the cover during the final 10 or 15 minutes of cooking time, or quickly broil the dish to brown the top just before serving.

4. Braises benefit from a short resting period before you dish them up. When you take them from the oven, they are bubbly and very hot, but if you give them a 15-to-20-minute rest, they are easier to serve. In addition, this brief rest improves the flavor of the dish. Be sure to evaluate the sauce when the braised foods are fully tender. You may want to lift them from the braising liquid to a serving dish, then adjust the sauce by seasoning it, letting it thicken by reduction, or adding other ingredients to finish the sauce, such as cream or a liaison.

BRAISED FENNEL WITH PARMESAN CHEESE

I love the fact that we make so many pleasing vegetable dishes at Boot Camp. When we toured the CIA storage rooms earlier in our stay, it was the array of produce that impressed me the most. Fennel is a great candidate for braising, being a tough vegetable that stands up to long, slow cooking. Here it's braised first, then gratinéed with the Parmesan. When you cook the fennel, leave the core in so that it won't fall apart. Then cut it out before you finish the dish.

SERVES 6

> 3 good-sized fennel bulbs, trimmed and cut in half lengthwise
>
> ½ medium onion, sliced
>
> 1 stalk celery, diced
>
> Juice of 1 lemon
>
> 1 garlic clove, chopped
>
> 1 cup Brown Veal Stock (page 140)
>
> 1 teaspoon salt
>
> ¼ teaspoon freshly ground black pepper
>
> ¼ cup grated Parmesan
>
> 2 tablespoons butter or olive oil

What the recipe doesn't know

` Whether you have veal stock (probably not). If not, you can use chicken stock.

Things to watch

` Don't let the liquid boil away completely; if that appears to be a possibility, cover the pan so that the fennel doesn't dry out and burn.

1. Preheat the oven to 325°F. Bring a large pot of generously salted water to a boil and drop in the fennel. Boil until partially cooked, about 5 minutes. Drain.

2. Combine the fennel with the remaining ingredients except the Parmesan and the butter or olive oil in a casserole or Dutch oven. Bring to a simmer on top of the stove, cover, and place in the oven. Braise for 45 minutes, or until the fennel is thoroughly tender but still holds its shape, and the liquid has reduced; check from time to time to make sure it isn't boiling away, and add more if necessary. Remove from the oven and turn the oven up to 425°F.

3. Using tongs, remove the fennel from the pot and cut out the core, using a carving fork or a towel to steady the bulbs. Cut the pieces in half lengthwise and transfer to a baking dish or gratin dish, overlapping the slices. Pour on any liquid from the pan and sprinkle on the Parmesan. Dot with butter or drizzle with olive oil, and cover the pan.

4. Return the fennel to the oven and bake about 15 minutes, until the cheese melts. Uncover and continue to bake until the top is browned, 5 to 10 minutes more.

STEAMING

Food that is steamed is cooked by a vapor bath, which surrounds the food in a closed vessel. The item that is being cooked never touches the liquid and so loses little of its flavor and nutrients during the cooking process. Food that is steamed has a delicate flavor and texture and is often served with a sauce, which is made separately.

Items that take well to steaming include naturally tender cuts of meat, fish, or poultry, as well as shellfish, vegetables, and fruit. I use steaming most often for vegetables, and occasionally for fish. The liquid used should be water. Every once in a while when I steam, I'll add an aromatic to the water, such as bay leaf or lemon peel or herbs, though Chef Hinnerk disagrees: "A waste of time and ingredients," he says. "The food won't absorb any of the flavors." But, he adds, that doesn't mean that steamed food has to be bland.

Like poached foods, once the moist heat source is removed, steamed foods begin to dry out. So sometimes foods that are steamed are wrapped to help them retain moisture. Wrappings include lettuce leaves, seaweed, vine leaves, corn husks (think tamales), and leek strips.

POACHING

The Boot Camp lesson on these cooking methods is one of the most interesting to me. I've done my fair share of poaching, steaming, and cooking en papillote, but after this class I realize how little I understood about them. I didn't know, for instance, that there are two kinds of poaching—shallow and deep. Indeed, listening to the chefs, I concluded that I'd been poaching wrong for years!

Foods that are prepared using these methods are generally subtly flavored, with a simple, straightforward appeal. I love Chef Hinnerk's assessment of poaching: "It's a very honest method of cooking. It's all about you and the food. If you poach a piece of fish correctly, and the fish is fresh, it will be good. But if the fish wasn't good to begin with, no matter how well you poach it, it won't be good."

Success in poaching is all a matter of temperature. The water should be between 140°F and 185°F. "What does this look like?"

BASIC PROCEDURE FOR STEAMING

1. Bring the liquid to a boil.

2. Add the main item to the steamer on a rack in a single layer.

3. Cover the steamer.

4. Steam the food to the correct doneness.

5. Serve the food immediately with the appropriate sauce and garnish. If holding, hold with moist heat and keep covered.

Chef Hinnerk asks us rhetorically. "There are no *bubbles*." This is when I realize that I've been poaching all these years at a simmer, which is between 185°F and 205°F, when bubbles begin to break lazily on the surface, and too high. He admonishes us not to bring our poaching liquid to a boil first and then lower the heat. If the temperature goes too high, meat will toughen and become too dry (we knew this from our graphic demonstration of denaturing proteins); fish will dry out and fall apart. When you poach, the moisture stays in and the flavor stays in.

With the exception of fish, which is often poached whole (poached salmon being the most well known example), items that are poached are usually portion-sized tender cuts. Chicken, variety meats, fish and shellfish, fruits and vegetables, and eggs are all good candidates for this cooking method.

I associate poached foods with French cooking. That's probably because poached meats and fish are typically served with a sauce. Chef Hinnerk says that sauce is essential for poached items, because they're so plain. Indeed, they are the perfect vehicle for rich French sauces. The sauces go on top, both to moisten the food and to add some sheen to what would otherwise be a dull-looking surface.

Shallow and Deep Poaching

"Shallow poaching is the moist heat counterpart to sautéing," explains Chef Hinnerk. Items that are shallow-poached are cooked by a combination of liquid and steam. Additional fats or oils are not necessary, though butter can be used to lubricate the pan. The food is

---

BASIC PROCEDURE FOR SHALLOW POACHING

1. Butter a sautoir and place the aromatics (such as shallots or mirepoix) in an even layer.

2. Season the main item and add it to the pan.

3. Add enough liquid to cover the items by half. Add seasonings and any additional aromatics such as herbs or spices.

4. Bring to just below a simmer—165°F to 185°F is an ideal temperature range. Cover the pan with a circle of parchment paper (cartouche) or a lid. Finish cooking over direct heat or in the oven.

5. Remove the main item, moisten it with a little of the poaching liquid, and keep it warm.

6. Carefully strain the poaching liquid (cuisson), return to the pan, reduce if necessary, and prepare a sauce as desired.

7. Serve the main item with the sauce spooned over and an appropriate garnish.

partially submerged in a liquid containing an acidic ingredient such as wine, lemon juice, or vinegar, and covered to catch the steam. Shallots line the bottom of the pan; they're there for flavor and to elevate the item. You could also use a brunoise-size mirepoix, called a matignon, which is cooked first (you eat it with the sauce).

The size of the cooking vessel is important, to minimize the amount of liquid you'll need. The less we use, the more flavorful the sauce will be. A sautoir is ideal for shallow poaching. The liquid is brought to temperature on top of the stove, and the item is placed in it and covered. Generally a cartouche is used to cover the item. Chef Hinnerk likes to use a lid but admits that there's a greater risk of overcooking the food if you use that instead of a cartouche. The pan is then transferred to the oven (usually set at 350°F) to finish the cooking, which makes it easier to control the temperature.

When shallow-poached food is done, it is removed from the pan and must be kept moist. Once exposed to air, poached food dries out quickly. A small amount of the poaching liquid should be spooned over the top, then the food should be covered while you make the sauce.

In addition to the amount of liquid used, the main difference between shallow and deep poaching is that in shallow poaching the cooking liquid is used as a base for the sauce, and in deep poaching it is not. Deep-poached items are generally served with a sauce, but the sauce is derived separately and added just before serving. Larger items, such as whole fish or whole unboned chicken breasts, are usually deep-poached. They are completely submerged in the liquid and are cooked uncovered. Like shallow-poached foods, once meat or fish has been deep-poached it must be covered and kept moist, and served quickly.

BASIC PROCEDURE FOR DEEP POACHING

1. Bring the cooking liquid to a simmer (185°F).

2. Lower the item into the poaching liquid, using a rack if necessary. Be sure the main item is fully submerged.

3. Finish the food over direct heat or in an oven.

4. Remove the main item and serve at once, or moisten it, cover, and keep it warm while preparing a sauce. You can also allow the item to cool in the liquid, or you can hold it in hot liquid that is below 140°F.

5. Cut or slice the main item and serve it with the appropriate sauce and garnish.

Note: For both shallow-poached and deep-poached foods, to achieve a clear broth begin the food in cold liquid.

1. Delicate fish fillets such as sole are often rolled up before being poached, to prevent them from curling during the cooking. The rolls are called paupiettes, and they will cook more evenly and look more attractive than curled-up pieces of once-flat fish. One thing I learn to look for when poaching fish and chicken breasts is a white residue that accumulates on top. This is protein (I always wondered what that was), and it indicates that your fish or chicken is done.

2. Chef John changes my cooking life forever when he explains that fish cannot cook in liquid that has a temperature lower than 140°F. "So when you've got guests coming for dinner, and some of them are late, and you've already begun poaching your fish, turn off the heat when it's done and leave it in the warm liquid. It won't continue to cook and it will stay moist and warm."

$3.$ The poaching liquid left in the pan, called the cuisson, is reduced and used for the sauce. We make a rich white wine sauce for our sole fillets, built from the white wine cuisson and sweet whole butter that we cut into cubes and keep cool until ready to whisk into the sauce. Adding cream to a butter sauce helps it hold together better, something my chefs refer to as "stabilizing" the sauce. If you reduce the cream before you add it to the sauce, it gives the sauce a richer body with better cling. This type of rich sauce is a perfect foil for such subtly flavored foods as poached fish or chicken.

$4.$ Instead of pooling the sauce onto warmed plates, we spoon the sauce over the top of the fish. It gives the dish a beautiful glossy ivory color. We choose some accompanying dishes that are in the same family of flavors and textures and one that provides a splash of contrast.

POACHED FILLET OF SOLE WITH WHITE WINE SAUCE

The reason you roll up fish fillets into paupiettes when you poach them or bake them is to prevent them from curling. I always thought the rolled fillets of sole I got in restaurants were rolled up for presentation only (and a silly one at that). All the while I just lived with the fact that my sole fillets curled when I poached them, and always broke apart when I lifted them out of the pan. You can also fold them in half or twist them to prevent this from happening.

SERVES 6

> 6 sole fillets, about 5 to 6 ounces each, trimmed
>
> Salt and freshly ground pepper to taste
>
> 1 tablespoon butter, plus more for the pan
>
> 3 tablespoons minced shallots
>
> 1¼ cups dry white wine
>
> 2 cups Fish Stock (page 143)
>
> 1 cup plus 2 tablespoons heavy cream

1. Preheat the oven to 350°F. Butter a flameproof pan or ovenproof skillet large enough to hold the rolled fish fillets in one layer. Trim the fish fillets and season with salt and pepper. Gently roll them up, fold them, or twist the fillets once.

2. Heat a small saucepan over medium heat and add the butter. Add the shallots and cook until translucent, 3 to 5 minutes. Transfer to the baking dish and spread in an even layer.

3. Lay the sole fillets on top of the shallots. Add the wine and stock and bring to a simmer over direct heat.

4. Cover the sole with buttered parchment paper (a cartouche) and place in the oven for 5 to 8 minutes, until the flesh turns opaque. Watch very carefully. Remove from the heat and gently transfer the sole to a warm serving platter. Cover and keep warm.

5. Bring the liquid in the pan to a boil and reduce by half. Add the cream and continue to reduce until the sauce coats the front and back of your spoon. Taste and adjust seasonings. Pour over the fish and serve.

Things to watch

` Don't overcook the fish or it will fall apart.

` Don't allow the liquid to evaporate from the pan when you reduce it after cooking the fish.

` This is a last-minute dish: don't cook it ahead.

SIMMERING AND BOILING

Simmering takes place at temperatures between 185°F and 205°F. It's the most frequently used temperature range for cooking in liquid, be it a stock or soup, stew, or braise. Foods of all kinds will tenderize when cooked in this temperature range. It is most often used to cook sturdy vegetables, legumes, tough cuts of meat, and pasta (yes, I learned, pasta is simmered, not boiled). Shellfish is often simmered but never boiled; if you boil shrimp or lobster or crab, it becomes tough and rubbery.

When liquid is simmering, you do see bubbles. But they're small, lazy bubbles. They rise slowly to the surface every few seconds and break with hardly a sputter. Boiling liquid, on the other hand, which has reached a temperature of 205°F or above, is rolling. The bubbles rise and break continuously at the surface.

Few foods are cooked by boiling. They can be partially cooked this way, as in parboiling or blanching. Vegetables are blanched—cooked for less than a minute in boiling water—to remove skin, set color, remove impurities, or cook ever so slightly before stir-frying. Meat is sometimes blanched as well before being stir-fried or simmered. The term is routinely misused in recipe directions, which instruct the cook to blanch a vegetable before finishing it in a sauté pan, when what they really mean is to parboil it. When a food (usually a vegetable) is parboiled, it's boiled rapidly for a few minutes to minimize cooking time and retain color and texture. Then it's usually shocked in an ice-water bath and drained. Parboiling is never for very long, because after 7 minutes of boiling, cellulose breaks down and foods will be overcooked.

DEVELOPING A MENU

By now our final exam plans are well under way. Every time there is a coffee break, teams huddle together to talk about their menus or confer with the chef. They scurry to the library from the afternoon lecture to research recipes, and one Boot Camper spends hours in the kitchen making brown sauce.

S.C.H.I.F.T.

The instructors at the CIA have codified menu development with an acronym, S.C.H.I.F.T., that outlines the things you are supposed to keep in mind when putting together a menu.

Shape. Avoid contrived food shapes. This can be accomplished by using a combination of sliced, molded, loose, and whole food items.

Color. Use a combination of earth tones and naturally vibrant colors. Usually, compatible flavors naturally provide an exciting combination of color.

Height. Use the natural shape of food to provide varied but not extreme height. This will enhance the flow on the plate.

Items. The choice of items will be based on practicality, portion size, number of items on the plate, and degree of difficulty.

Flavor. This is the single most important factor. Through the use of fresh, compatible flavors the presentation will be enhanced naturally.

Texture. By varying cooking methods and the cutting of vegetables, a variety of textures will be achieved.

Our course materials include Menu Development Worksheets. All of the things we are to think about are listed, with a few lines underneath for our notes. None of us on the team actually fills in the worksheets, but when we settle on our menu, it is clear that we've covered the bases. Anybody who loves to cook and to entertain on any scale naturally incorporates these menu considerations into his or her choices.

Flavor combinations

Number of components on the plate (a variety of complementary items)

Portion size (appropriate for the course)

Proper cooking technique (basics executed well)

Colors (vibrant versus earth tones)

Height of food (varied but not drastically different)

Texture variations

Plate layout (traditional versus nontraditional)

Practicality (should not require too much handling; should be able to be done consistently)

Plating, balance, and composition (sliced, whole, loose, molded, and special cuts)

Trends (use common sense)

When I plan a dinner, sometimes I begin with one ingredient I want to use. It can be an inspiration from the farmers' market—maybe beautiful baby artichokes or fava beans have come in—or perhaps there's some great wild salmon available at my fish market, or the Dungeness crabs have begun to arrive. Sometimes I plan a menu around a dish I want to try (or need to test). Wherever my thought process begins, I fill out the menu by balancing flavors and colors, thinking about what will be time-consuming and what will be ready more quickly. If one item on the menu is complex, I will choose a simple accompaniment. I consider how easy it will be to serve the food; I never want to have more than one item on the menu that requires last-minute preparation unless I have people helping me. I must admit that before Boot Camp I didn't really think much about the height of the food, but when I plated it, there was always some variation.

My idea for the scallops we've been assigned for our appetizer is to marinate them in a ginger and soy marinade, then sauté them so they have a thin glaze and serve them on a mesclun salad with a ginger vinaigrette. Christine, however, is strongly against the marinade. She has a great deal of respect for the pure flavor of the fresh scallops and wants to just lightly brown them in butter. I have no objection; in fact, I think she is right. The clean, fresh flavor of the scallops against the ginger vinaigrette on the greens will provide a nice balance of compatible flavors. And flavor, we know, is the single most important factor when it comes to menu development. We need some bright color on the plate, and decide to use very thinly sliced—julienned, really—red bell peppers for that. As for the starch, we'll stick to the Asian theme and slice wontons into strips, then deep-fry them for a crispy garnish.

We have been assigned beef tenderloin as our main dish protein, and I'm happy about this, as I rarely plan a menu around steak. Christine is contemplating butterflying the meat and stuffing it, but Chef John thinks that would be a bit busy for such a tender and delicious cut of steak. Just before I left for Boot Camp I saw Wolfgang Puck make beautiful pan-cooked steaks encrusted with black, white, green, and red peppercorns, and so we decide to cut our tenderloin into thick steaks and do the same (see pages 115 and 189). We'll serve a mushroom ragoût on the side, which can also serve as a sauce for the meat. This is looking very French, so we decide on a traditional potato gratin as our starch, and simple haricots verts as our vegetable. The bright green will be welcome against the earth tones of the steak, mushrooms, and potatoes, and the simplicity will also be appreciated.

I research recipes in the library. I want to use my new knowledge of Sauce Espagnole and take advantage of the veal stock we've made, which I've never had access to at home and will probably never make again. I read recipes in classical French books like Ann Willan's *La Varenne Technique* and more contemporary cookbooks such as Patricia Wells's *Bistro Cooking*, and write out recipes for a Morel and Wild Mushroom Ragoût (page 227) and a traditional Gratin Dauphinois (page 228). I use my own recipe for an Asian Vinaigrette for the starter salad. All that we need to do now is make up our lists for our supplemental food orders and give them to the chef. Oh, and pull off the cooking.

TURNING SKILLS INTO RECIPES, FROM BASIC TO "STEPPED UP"

Even though Chef Hinnerk insists that the purpose of Boot Camp is to make us fluent in kitchen skills so that we won't need recipes to cook, we always have recipes to work from during production. But the chef never hesitates to make changes in these recipes if he feels there is a better way to do something, or if he perceives an inaccuracy. For example, my Boot Camp Spinach Spaetzle with Sapsago Cheese recipe (page 224) tells us to blanch the spinach that is going into the spaetzle batter. But Chef Hinnerk recommends that we just throw the spinach into the blender with the eggs (and to use six of them instead of the four called for), and the spaetzle made this way is much brighter and more vivid-tasting than the spaetzle we prepared following the recipe in the last Boot Camp. The Glazed Beets recipe says to cook the beets with all of the ingredients, then remove the lid and reduce to a glaze. But Chef Hinnerk knows that the liquid will dry up before the beets are done if we cook them this way, and he insists that we cook them first.

The Boot Camp dishes are simple ones, classic preparations chosen so that we can develop our kitchen skills. Chefs build on these skills to create more complex dishes—"stepped-up" dishes, they call them at the CIA—that look interesting on the plate and are memorable on the palate. For example, the chef at Ristorante Caterina de' Medici came up with his popular raw tuna appetizer (page 104) by "stepping up" a plate of tuna carpaccio. First of all, he pounded the tuna slices paper-thin. Then he decided on a sauce for embellishing the tuna. This being an Italian restaurant, he selected an olive-oil-based Salsa Crudo with pungent ingredients such as capers and olives, garlic, chile, and lemon juice. For texture and color, he built a very small salad of frisée, arugula, fennel fronds, and julienne of radishes dressed with the Salsa Crudo and placed it in the middle of the tuna. One more element—tiny deep-fried croutons—adds texture and a bit of starch, but nothing too busy, to the composition. Once the recipe was fully worked out, he entered it into the computer in a format that is useful for chefs, so that all of the students who come through the kitchen will be able to turn out this appetizer with a certain level of consistency. At the end of our intensive week in the kitchen, we will be expected to create these kind of stepped-up dishes for our final exam.

Building a dish around an assigned protein is an interesting exercise for me. Writing recipes is what I do for a living, but I've never approached my work in this way, because I'm not a chef. My menu thoughts usually begin with the type of dish I want to make, not with a specific meat or fish. This is probably due in part to my vegetarian cooking origins, and also to my interest in Mediterranean and Mexican cuisines, where meat does not fall

*Recipe Name:*_____

YIELD: 6 PORTIONS

Ingredients: **Amounts:**

Method

_____

_____

_____

_____

_____

_____

_____

_____

_____

_____

_____

_____

so neatly into the center of the plate. Oh, I'm sometimes inspired to create a dinner party around an ingredient that may be fish or meat—say it's Dungeness crab season or the coho salmon are running. But if I cook meat, usually it's because I want to make a stew or eat a roast chicken, and not because I've suddenly been given some stew meat or a chicken to work with.

Nonetheless, the process of building a recipe is the same no matter where you start. First you must decide what your focal point is. What sort of dish do you want to make? Do you want to make a roast with your tenderloin and serve it with a sauce? Or do you want to wrap it in pastry and make Beef Wellington? Perhaps you'd like to cut it into steaks to grill or sauté and serve with an interesting sauce. What kind of sauce do you envision? Then you research ways to do this—there is always more than one—until you come up with a recipe. It's always a good idea to write the recipe down, and included in our Boot Camp materials are recipe templates. They are from the standard program that restaurants use, with the recipe name at the top, then the yield, followed by two columns, one for ingredients and one for amounts. This takes up half the page; the rest is for the method.

Having decided on your focal point, you need to envision the rest of the plate. What would be interesting and delicious? What's in season? What colors and textures will make the plate come alive without making things too busy, both on the plate and for you in the kitchen? The chef who developed the Crudo di Tonno had to fulfill the same criteria that we have been given: he had to create an appetizer using a protein, a sauce, a vegetable, and a starch. The little salad fulfills the vegetable requirement, and the croutons are a brilliant way to work in a little bit of starch.

Our team has decided on cutting our tenderloin into steaks, coating the steaks with cracked peppercorns, and sautéing them. Rather than make a pan sauce, we'll make a rich slurry-thickened wild mushroom ragoût, which, as I've noted, will serve as both sauce and side dish. The steak is straightforward, but the ragoût requires some research. I've made many a mushroom ragoût, but this time I wanted to use veal stock, something I'd never use at home, yet a classic ingredient in a French mushroom ragoût. Having read through a number of recipes in French cookbooks, I came up with the dish we've decided to prepare, which is little more than a stepped-up version of sautéed mushrooms.

DINNER AT RISTORANTE CATERINA DE' MEDICI

The ochre Mediterranean-style villa that houses the Colavita Center for Italian Food and Wine, and within it Ristorante Caterina de' Medici, is the newest addition to the CIA campus. It looks a little out of place among the other red brick New England buildings, yet it's a welcome sight on a freezing gray winter day. During January Boot Camp, the formal herb gardens that have been landscaped in the villa's backyard are a dramatic setting for the students' large ice sculptures. In the warm Indian summer of my September Boot Camp the gardens are flourishing, and I love crossing them each time I go from the Continuing Education Center to the Conrad Hilton Library, stopping always to admire and smell the herbs.

Everybody loves Ristorante Caterina de' Medici with its contemporary Italian cuisine. When I speak with friends who have been to the CIA restaurants, this one always gets the highest marks. I particularly like the set menu designed for my Boot Camp group. The meal begins with the appetizer whose

Pollio Pizza Station and Victoria Packaging Coop. Antipasto Bar, Ristorante Caterina de'Medici

creation I describe above: Crudo di Tonno alla Battuta, a plate of thinly sliced raw tuna embellished with a very Mediterranean sauce of olive oil, capers, garlic, green picholine olives, lemon juice, parsley, and very finely diced red onions and celery heart. There is something a little bit picante in this sauce, and when we see the recipe—we rave about the dish so much that they decide to give it to us—I see that the heat comes from finely diced jalapeño chiles. This is classic Italian with a New World twist. In the middle of the plate, on top of the paper-thin tuna slices, is a very small salad of frisée and arugula, fennel fronds, and julienned radishes, and around the fish are scattered the tiniest of croutons.

Our second course is lamb chops ("Scotta Dita" al Rosmarino con Caponata), three of them, rubbed with rosemary and grilled rare, then set over a pungent caponata and garnished with roasted cipollini onions. It is interesting to note the difference between these lamb chops and the Roast Rack of Lamb with Rosemary Jus that was on the menu at Restaurant Escoffier. The meat, in both cases, is juicy and rare, the outside rubbed with rosemary before being grilled (at the Italian restaurant) or roasted (at Escoffier). But the Caterina de' Medici lamb chops are Mediterranean through and through. Meat is more likely to be grilled than roasted in the Mediterranean for the simple reason that people in these countries traditionally did not have ovens. They would cook meat over coals or in a pan on top of the stove. Since grilled meat is not going to render a jus that can be recuperated, the meat will be garnished with something else, typi-

cally something with big flavors, such as this menu's caponata, a sort of sweet-and-sour ratatouille.

It doesn't immediately occur to me to wonder why pasta isn't part of this Italian dinner. But Italian cuisine is not just about pasta and pizza, and soon I come to see that the courses were chosen as much to be a vehicle for pairing Italian wines with food as to showcase the restaurant's cuisine.

I have a fairly good grasp of wine when it comes to French and New World wines, but I've always regretted my lack of knowledge about the rich world of Italian wines. My meals at Caterina de' Medici give me the opportunity to fill in some of the gaps. Bill Guilfoyle, the wine lecturer at my first Boot Camp, makes wine selections that go wonderfully with our set menu. Two white wines, a Vernaccia di San Gimignano from Teruzzi and Puthod in Tuscany, and a Gavi di Gavi from Bava in Piemonte, are poured with the tuna carpaccio. We are served a Valpolicella "Classico Superiore" from Masi in the Veneto and an Aglianico del Vulture from Tenuta le Querce in Basilicata with the meat.

The Vernaccia di San Gimignano, a distinctive dry white wine made from the Vernaccia grapes grown around the Tuscan town of San Gimignano, is a light, crisp wine that doesn't fight with the pungent flavors in the Salsa Cruda. The Gavi, a Piemontese wine made from the Cortese grape, is a bit more complex, fruity and aromatic. Gavis were originally produced to serve the fish restaurants along the Ligurian coast to the south of the Piedmont, and indeed, this is a very suitable wine for our fish course.

Like the two whites served with the appetizer, the two reds we have with the meat course crescendo in complexity. Valpolicella is a vast red-wine-producing area in the Veneto, and its wines vary tremendously in their quality. Unfortunately, the bulk of today's Valpolicellas are mass-produced, thin, acidic wines. But at their best, when they're labeled "Classico Superiore," they can be fruity, medium-bodied wines that are very drinkable, and this is the case with ours.

I keep seeing the other red wine, an Aglianico del Vulture from Basilicata, on restaurant menus, and we keep ordering it, mostly out of nostalgia for Basilicata, where my husband and I spent a few lovely days soon after we'd met. Each time we love it for its fruitiness and complexity but lack of severity. It turns out that the Aglianico del Vulture is one of the most important wines coming out of southern Italy. Florence-based wine writer Daniel Thomases says that the best bottles of Aglianico del Vulture are beginning to "offer worthy competition to a fine (and pricier) Sangiovese of Tuscany or Nebbiolo of Piedmont."[1]

Bill also chooses a lovely dessert wine to accompany our Seasonal Fruit Upside-Down Cake (in January this is based on dried fruit). It is a light, sparkling Moscato d'Asti from the Piemonte. This is a wonderful dessert wine, very fragrant, only slightly fizzy, and not too sweet. It's made from, and tastes of, the delicious white muscat grape, one of my very favorite fruits.

When I come back to Boot Camp the following autumn we order our dinner à la carte and choose wines from the extensive list, which is exclusively Italian, with the interesting inclusion of "New World Italian" wines—American wines made from Italian grapes. The menu at Caterina de' Medici is very extensive, with hot and cold antipasti that include salads and soups, cured meats, small cooked dishes such as Wood-Oven-Roasted Shrimp with Rosemary and White Beans, and the ineffable raw tuna I've eaten before. There's a wide selection of primi piatti (pasta, gnocchi, risotto), and at least ten entrée (secondi) choices. This time I do eat pasta, pappardelle served with a classic Ragú Bolognese. I have the great good fortune to be sitting at the table with the wine importer son of one of my fellow Boot Campers, and we taste six different Italian wines, each one of them new to me, throughout the course of our dinner. Ours is a lively table.

[1] Jancis Robinson, ed., *The Oxford Companion to Wine*, 2nd ed. (Oxford University Press, 1999), p. 7.

Day 5

OUR FINAL EXAM

I oversleep on the last day of Boot Camp. It's 6:40 when I get out of bed, but somehow I manage to dress, pack my car, and drive the short distance to the CIA by 7 a.m. I burst into the classroom just as our chef instructor is beginning his lecture on plating. And I'm glad I haven't missed it, because it's one of the liveliest sessions of the week.

INTO THE KITCHEN, FOR THE LAST TIME

We're learning about plate and platter presentation techniques because today is the big day of our final exam, when each team will produce its own menu. Presentation is an important element in this exercise. Because I almost always serve my meals family style, plating has never been a huge concern. Boot Camp, though, teaches me to pay more attention to this, and when I go home my husband will notice, congratulating me on my newfound plating skills.

Our chef instructor takes us through a series of slides of individual plates and larger platters, and we discuss which ones are good or bad and why. The first slide, labeled "The Times Are A-Changing," is a picture of an old-style presentation of a roast turkey, glazed and covered with frills and garnishes made from leaves and chives and tomato roses. It used to be that platters were so decorative that chefs "prayed to the Lord that nobody would eat from them," as Chef Hinnerk puts it during the September Boot Camp. We're all glad those times are over. We learn that the finished plate should be in

your mind before you begin to cook. And as I think about it, many of my menus are inspired by just a vision of food on a plate. I have these thoughts while walking through a market, swimming laps, or just musing.

The items on your plate or platter should be recognizable. They should, above all, be edible. Chef Hinnerk, in particular, hates "nonfunctional garnishes," or NFGs, as he calls them. He stresses that it is not imperative to garnish: "If you want to serve lemon wedges with your fish, pass them on the side." And then he tells the story of the terrible tomato wedges, the inevitable garnish that his mother used at her restaurant in Germany, the "love" that she insisted go out on every plate, no matter what the season. When Chef Hinnerk and his wife and daughter moved in with his parents so that he could run the restaurant after his mother became ill, he refused to put the tomato wedges on. "Where is the love?" his father and the wait staff asked him whenever he sent out a plate. "Eventually I acquiesced. I would have had to leave otherwise."

According to the CIA, a nonfunctional garnish is any item, edible or inedible, that does not contribute to the taste or texture of a dish. A functional garnish is one that adds

color, texture, taste, and interest—all four—to the plate or platter. It harmonizes with the main item and doesn't distract from the focus. If you ask yourself what purpose your garnish serves and the only answer that you come up with is that it adds color to the plate, chances are you've got a nonfunctional garnish.

My Boot Camp group judges plates of food for shape, color, balance, food selection, unity, and flow. One that has a variety of shapes set in straight and curved lines looks very much alive, whereas another looks unappetizing because the food is dark and gelatinous, everything is round, and you can't figure out what it is. In some photos, the colors are good but the layout is not. A plate of two green cabbage rolls side by side on a tomato sauce has nice color, but it could be improved if the rolls were cut on the diagonal and stacked. Sometimes a garnish, like pointy toasts sticking way up on a plate, takes over the plate and distracts from what should be the focal point. Though height is important, here it is greater than the width of the plate—the toasts look downright threatening. A plate on which a hunk of meat is placed next to a pile of noodles, with vegetables on the side, looks flat, and the noodles look dry: "This looks like a typical plate that you would find in a restaurant on the highway," our chef instructor comments.

Unity, when it comes to plating, means that the layout of the food should work as a cohesive unit. The components should be brought together on a plate to emphasize that the entrée is a single offering of foods that work well together. If foods are distributed willy-nilly on the plate, there won't be one single focal point and the plate won't express the idea that the foods are working together to make a delicious meal. Items on the plate or platter should not distract from the focal point.

Flow is another presentation term. It refers to a sense of movement on the platter, which can be achieved if there is a strong focal point. If the layout is asymmetric, there is usually a stronger sense of flow. Flow will

EXAMPLES OF NONFUNCTIONAL GARNISHES

A wedge or slice of orange placed on a plate of eggs
A wedge or crown of lemon on a dish that has a sauce served with it
Lettuce leaves that are used as underliners for hot food on hot plates
The traditional sprig of parsley or watercress (though there are times when watercress or parsley is appropriate—for example, watercress can be used on a plate that contains a simple grilled or roasted item)
Orange, lemon, or lime "baskets"
Tomato roses and apple birds
Paper or foil frills

be interrupted if items that are sliced are not placed in the order in which they were sliced (sequencing) and facing the same direction.

Choosing the right plate is also important. A colorful plate doesn't always contribute positively to the presentation. It should enhance the food rather than fight with it. Sometimes a plain plate on a fancy liner is the solution. Sometimes a functional dish, such as a tagine, is very nice for presentation, even if you haven't used it for the cooking. And—very important—the rim of the plate is for the guest and the waiter only. Don't lay food on the rim!

The same checklist used for menu development, S.C.H.I.F.T., can also be applied to presentation.

Shape. The shapes on the plate should be complementary; they should not all be the same. On the other hand, they should flow. A huge pointed chip can be meaningless as a garnish.

Color. Most importantly, your plate should not be drab; all of the food should not be brown. There should be more than one color on the plate, at least one of them bright.

Height. The plate should not look like somebody sat on it. The look of the plate is enhanced if the main item is elevated. This can be done easily by draping it over a side dish or, if it is shaped already, like a stuffed leaf or filo pastry, standing it up.

Items. The different foods on the plate should not be all the same type or color. There should be a variety, but the plate should not be too busy either. The food should look alive. There should be a sense to the composition—a sauce or puree that enhances a main dish, with a side dish that complements it. There should also be flow and sequencing (arranging items in the order in which they were cut from a large piece). There should be a sense of movement. If the food is too symmetrical, it looks dead; asymmetric layouts provide for a strong sense of flow. Lines should be strong. The layout should work as a cohesive unit, with areas of reduced focus and an emphasis on food items that are inter-related.

Flavor. Flavors should be contrasting. If one dish is spicy, another should be bland. If one is sweet, another should be sour or savory. Everything on the plate should not have the same flavor profile (such as garlic). Some contrasting flavors/attributes:

> Spicy/cool
>
> Sour, tart/sweet
>
> Warm, hot/cold, frozen
>
> Crisp/soft, tender
>
> Rich, fatty/lean

Texture. Similarly, textures should also be balanced through contrast: crunchy and soft, for example. By varying cooking methods and the cutting of vegetables, a variety of textures can be achieved.

OUR FINAL EXAM MENU

Sautéed Filet Mignon with Mixed Cracked Peppercorns (page 189)

Morel and Wild Mushroom Ragoût (page 227)

Gratin Dauphinoise (page 228)

Haricots Verts (page 208)

PRODUCTION

There are no more lectures after the coffee break on this, the last day. We don't have time. We have to get to the kitchen and start cooking. Every team knows what they have to do; they will find their ingredients assembled for them at their stations. The race is on.

Janice, Christine, and I worked out that Christine will be responsible for the appetizer, from start to finish, and I just hope I'll have a moment to watch her sauté those plump scallops. I'll start on the ragoût and the potato gratin right away, as these items need time. Janice, who has relaxed considerably over the course of the week will be our sous chef, and there's plenty for her to do. She sets about preparing the steaks, while Christine cleans the scallops, makes the salad and the dressing, and cuts wontons into ¼-inch-wide strips.

I get to work peeling and slicing potatoes for the Gratin Dauphinoise. Once the slices have been cooked until just tender, I layer half of them in my baking dish, season them, and top them with a layer of crème fraîche and then a layer of good Gruyère cheese, followed by more layers of potatoes, crème fraîche, and cheese.

The mushroom ragoût, also one of my assignments, is going to be luxurious: a thick sauté of wild and cultivated mushrooms, including reconstituted dried morels, in a sauce of reduced red wine, Madeira, and reduced veal stock and mushroom broth, lightly thickened with a slurry and enriched with butter at the end of cooking.

Christine goes to deep-fry the wonton strips. Janice, meanwhile, cuts very thin strips of red pepper to add a little color to the salad, and trims the haricots verts, which will be cooked in boiling salted water and tossed with a little butter at the last minute.

"Team 3, you'd better start cooking your steaks!" Chef John bellows, and I start to heat

In the second Boot Camp I attend, in September, I don't prepare a menu myself, but rove from team to team. This allows me to watch Chef Hinnerk coaching people along—he is very much hands-on with his teams. He shows one team how to oven-smoke their quail by setting them on a rack above wood chips in a roasting pan. The little quail are stuffed with dried cherries soaked in port, and Chef Hinnerk helps the team make a fabulous sauce with dried cherries and green peppercorns, spiced with the liquid that the peppercorns were bottled in. The quail is to be served as an appetizer over sautéed shredded cabbage. The team follows that with an herb-crusted roast loin of pork, sliced thin and accompanied by a medley of vegetables, including broccoli with cheese sauce, roasted red potatoes, and more cabbage, this time braised.

Team 3 is using their tenderloin to make Beef Wellington. Sam worked for hours yesterday on a Sauce Espagnole, reducing and doctoring the veal stock until it was rich and full of body. Today he adds four types of mushrooms to the sauce, deglazes the pan with Madeira, reduces that, and adds it to the Sauce Espagnole. Now the team is making mushroom duxelles, cooking down finely chopped mushrooms until they are reduced to a paste, which they will rub over the top and bottom of their seared tenderloin. Next they'll wrap it in puff pastry, which they'll brush and seal with egg wash. Finally they'll roast it until the meat is cooked medium rare, 120°F. The pastry will turn out a beautiful shiny mahogany, the meat will slice like butter, and won't that sauce be perfect? Equally rich, and quite original, is Team 3's Savoy cabbage side dish. They separate the light and dark leaves and blanch them separately. The light-colored leaves are blended with cream for the sauce, which is tossed with the shredded blanched dark leaves. Glazed carrots add some brightness. As if all of this isn't enough, Team 3 also has an ambitious appetizer: sole-filled dumplings with braised bok choy. They spoon the filling onto wonton skins, which they seal and fry. Their sauce is made with Asian ponzu, honey, rice wine vinegar, soy sauce, ginger, green onions, red pepper flakes, and orange juice.

the sauté pans. Once the pans are good and hot I turn the heat down ever so slightly and place a few steaks on—show side down, of course. They sizzle for about 4 minutes, and then I turn them. Four minutes more, and I do the touch test to see if they are cooked rare. They are. I remove them from the pan and keep them warm in the oven. All around us is a buzz of activity, with our chef instructor running here and there to help people out and calling out the time.

The clock is ticking. It's noon, and we need to finish up. Our Gratin Dauphinois is golden and beautiful, and our bright green beans glisten. The mushroom ragoût smells heavenly and the steak is done. Now it's time to compose our demo plates, with one portion of each dish we've prepared, and arrange the remaining portions artfully in a hotel pan.

1. The tenderloin is a gorgeous strip of meat. We cut it into six thick steaks, then season the steaks and encrust them with cracked peppercorns. Once they're prepped, they can be refrigerated until it is time to cook them at the last minute.

2. The Gratin Dauphinois is clearly the most time-consuming of our dishes. First the potatoes have to be peeled and sliced, then parboiled in a mixture of milk and water. Then the gratin is assembled and baked. It needs an hour in the oven, but if it's done before it's needed, it won't be harmed by sitting.

3. When the gratin goes into the oven, I get to work on the mushroom ragoût. I've already soaked the dried morels, which need a half hour to render a tasty soaking liquid that I'll add to my veal stock. Janice helps me chop shallots, garlic, and tarragon. We cut the cultivated mushrooms into thick slices and trim the stems of the wild morels and chanterelles.

4. Christine begins to brown the scallops. She heats a sauté pan, adds a little butter, and then, when the butter is good and hot, cooks the scallops on one side for just about a minute, until browned. Then she flips them over and cooks them on the other side. By the time the surface is lightly browned, the scallops are done—they're opaque.

5. We douse our salad with our ginger-lime vinaigrette (lime juice, balsamic vinegar, ginger juice, soy sauce, dark sesame oil, and peanut oil). Then we use a pair of tongs to toss the greens in the dressing until the entire salad is evenly coated and glistening. It makes a better salad than simply pouring the dressing on top.

6. Lightly browned scallops are dotted around the rim of the plate with a mound of freshly dressed greens in the center. For our hotel pan presentation for the chef, Christine makes a dramatic-looking plate with the scallops going down the middle, the salad on either side, and neat clumps of wonton crisps here and there.

SHOW TIME

I am challenged by plating the steak. In my experience, the steak would come to you in a single piece, and I drew it on our plate diagram that way. But I can't get any height or focal point on the plate with a rustic serving of potato gratin and a big round steak. So I decide to slice the steak and drape the slices over the mushroom ragoût, which is also to serve as the sauce for the meat. I place all the items together in the center of the plate, with some of the ragoût exposed, the green beans on the other side of the steak slices, and the potato gratin wedged in between the beans and the ragoût. For the hotel pan, we cut the remaining five steaks in half and run the beans down the middle, with the potatoes on the other side; the ragoût is served separately.

We are making these decisions quickly. The chefs are calling for our plates to be displayed on a buffet in Lecture Hall 1, our classroom, which has been transformed into a banquet room for our graduation lunch. A series of chafing dishes has been set up on another table, awaiting our hotel pans. Tables are set, and there is beer, wine, mineral water, and a big congratulatory cake.

One by one, appetizer and entrée plates come in to grace the display table. Each team makes a presentation, and the chef gives his critiques. A dish might need some color or some focus, but it's clear that we have all passed the final exam. We have all put our newly honed skills to good use.

With the pressure of my team's presentation behind me, I can take the time to appreciate what the other teams have done. Some have taken a simple approach to their final exam ingredients. Others have chosen more complicated menus. One team has made deep-fried "nests" of shredded potato for their appetizer of quail, which they marinated in a soy sauce, rice vinegar, and sesame oil mixture before roasting, and glazed with something similar. This clearly involves a huge amount of work, but with a fairly simple herb-crusted rack of lamb as their entrée, they could afford the time.

Another team has used their shrimp to make a tempura appetizer in a rice flour batter, which they serve with two colorful purees, a bright green avocado puree seasoned with garlic, cilantro, and lime, and a mahogany chipotle puree with a base of tomatoes and onions. Chef John comments that this is a successful example of fusion cuisine, though he suggested using an avocado salsa instead of a puree for more textural variation. This team also developed a rich main dish for their chicken breasts. They've sautéed them and deglazed the pan with wine, mushroom juice, and Madeira, then whisked in lots of butter for the sauce. The chicken is served on top of a big potato pancake that has a surprise filling of Boursin cheese—"Potatoes Anna with a twist," says Chef John. The sides, wilted spinach and oven-roasted vegetables, create a nice balance to the main items.

One team has produced an amazing salmon entrée: a majestic fillet marinated in a citrus-flavored mixture and poached in a couple of quarts of olive oil at 140°F. That temperature didn't really cook the fish—it still looks raw. But the proteins have been denatured, so we can cut through the salmon with a fork, and it absolutely melts in our mouths. On their demo plate, a thick slice of the fillet sits perched on a row of glazed mandarin slices above a pool of green puree made from pea shoots. It is decorated with one glistening, promising dab of beluga caviar. This is a truly amazing Thomas Keller recipe from the French Laundry. They've chosen to accompany the salmon with rice pilaf, grilled yellow squash, and glazed carrots, producing a plate with lots of color.

If the salmon is the high-end dish in this group, the most innovative is the turkey breast sandwich done by another team. When they were assigned the turkey breast, I wondered what they would do with it. Personally, I've never been inspired to buy a turkey breast; give me the whole bird or nothing at all. Everyone agrees, however, that turkey breast is good for one thing—sandwiches. And this team has taken that idea and run with it. They roasted the turkey breast, then grilled it lightly for a charred flavor. The bread is focaccia, spread with a delicious nut-cranberry-mayonnaise dressing. This unique turkey club has prosciutto instead of bacon (though the prosciutto was deep-fried, which I thought was a mistake) and mesclun instead of lettuce. It's a truly delicious sandwich and a humorous, satisfying, contemporary American plate.

GRADUATION

We sample each team's handiwork, and as we're polishing off this large meal our chef stands up to congratulate us and hand out our certificates of accomplishment. This is the closest thing to a diploma I've had since high school. It says:

The Culinary Institute of America hereby certifies

Martha Shulman

has successfully completed

Boot Camp I

and is awarded 3 Continuing Education Units

It is signed by the vice president of continuing education and the chef instructor. I'm proud of this diploma. It wouldn't get me a job in a restaurant kitchen, but the knowledge I acquired to earn it helps me in my own.

POSTSCRIPT

The other day, when I was helping out in a first-grade cooking class at my son's school, I was thinking about how much I'd learned at Boot Camp. We were making latkes for Hanukkah, and I was doing the frying. I felt very comfortable around the hot oil. I knew when it was hot enough to add the latkes to it, being careful not to crowd the pan, and helped some of the other volunteers as my potato pancakes sizzled away at just the right pace. We cooked to color, turning the latkes only once, when they were golden on the first side. When they were done we drained the latkes on a rack, and as soon as they were cool enough to eat, the kids gobbled them up. They were perfect, much better than the latkes I'd made the year before, in the days before Boot Camp.

MISE EN PLACE AND KNIFE SKILLS

When I think of chefs, I think of precise, fast chopping under pressure. When I first imagine what Culinary Boot Camp might be like, I envision military-style knife drills. Knife skills seem to me to fit the notion of "basic training," and I would love it if the entire first day of Boot Camp was devoted to working with a knife. But we aren't being trained to be chefs, and what we need to know about chopping and cutting can be covered in our first afternoon lecture.

We learn about the different types of knives and their care and sharpening. We also learn how to select the right tool for the job and different ways of holding a knife, depending upon the task or the ingredient at hand. We learn the names of and the techniques for producing various cuts. Throughout our week at Boot Camp we continue learning how to cut a variety of vegetables and fruits, from avocados to zucchini. I was hoping we'd be taught how to butterfly and debone a chicken, but there isn't time for everything, and we won't need this chef's skill to execute our recipes. Boning a chicken (or a duck) is a skill that all chefs must learn in cooking school; they'll do it often in restaurant kitchens. In truth, I've never needed to know how to do this, and can't imagine that I ever will, but I'm nevertheless a little disappointed that I don't acquire the skill in Boot Camp.

However, all of our knife skills have been well honed by the end of the week, over the course of which we do a lot of cutting and chopping. With our brand-new chef's knives, paring knives, and swivel peelers we spend hours peeling and chopping onions, carrots, and celery; we cut zucchini into bâtonnets and turn it into little footballs. We peel and slice and julienne, and we make concassé and chiffonade, oblique cuts and rondelles. We mince and grate, shred and dice. By the end of Boot Camp all of us are better with a knife than we've ever been before.

MISE EN PLACE

The purpose of all of this chopping and cutting is to prepare ingredients for cooking. This is called mise en place. Mise en place, Chef John emphasizes, is a crucial first step in any culinary undertaking. I can attest, having cooked in all manner of kitchens, both tiny and large, that cooking will always go more smoothly if you are properly set up to begin with. The term, which means literally "put in place," refers not only to the cut-up and measured ingredients that will be going into your dish but also to the equipment that will be required to execute the dish and the way your work area, or station, is organized. Because the CIA trains professional chefs, the standards for keeping the work area clean are very high. When you follow them at home, you'll find that your kitchen stays clean no matter how complex a dish you're cooking.

Your Work Area

Whether you are working in a tiny apartment kitchen or a spacious one with up-to-the-minute design and equipment, the way you organize your work area and the way you move about in it will affect the flow of your cooking and the quality of your food.

Maintaining an organized work area increases your efficiency and maintains a clean work environment.

Work surfaces. The height of your work surface should be neither too high nor too low, so that you are not stooping nor reaching up to cut. Cutting boards should be large. They will not move around on your work surface if you place damp paper or cloth towels between them and the surface. The boards can be either wooden or plastic. In commercial kitchens plastic cutting boards are required, as they are easier to sanitize.

Cleanliness. It's vital that you keep your work area clean and safe from cross-contamination. Cross-contamination occurs when pathogens from one kind of food—say, chicken or eggs—get into another type of food. Professional kitchens have to be very careful about this. If your work area is not right next to the kitchen sink, then included in your equipment should be a container of sanitizing solution (made by diluting a chemical sanitizer such as chlorine in water), wiping cloths, side towels, and gloves, so that you can clean off your work surface and knives after cutting each type of food. If you are next to the sink, rinse the board and knives with a sanitizing solution each time you finish a task. As towels become dirty, replace them with clean ones. All perishable foods should be kept cold until ready to prepare. If you are using a scale, have it handy, and cover the surface with plastic wrap or parchment. Change the paper with each new type of food to avoid cross-contamination.

Organizing your ingredients. Each prepped ingredient should go into a separate container. If all herbs and/or spices are going to be added at the same time to a dish, they can be measured into the same container. The ingredients should be placed on your work surface in the order in which they will be used during the cooking of the dish. That way your work will flow in one direction. Sometimes it helps to place the containers on a sheet tray, freeing up room on your work surface. Also have a container for trimmings that you might use in stocks, as well as one for trimmings destined for the compost pile, and a separate one for the trash.

Organizing utensils, pots and pans, and serving dishes. Get out the utensils and pots and pans you'll need, and put them where you'll need them. Measures and cutting tools should be at your work station, pots and pans and cooking implements on the stove. If ice water baths are called for, get them ready now. Put colanders in the sink, and have necessary strainers set over bowls at the ready.

OUR KNIFE KITS

We work mainly with two types of knife: an 8-inch chef's knife and a paring knife, which can range from 2 to 4 inches. A utility knife is a smaller version of a chef's knife and is also used for light cutting, slicing, and peeling chores. It's useful for cutting tomatoes. Our knife kit also contains:

- A long serrated knife, for slicing bread (also useful for citrus and tomatoes)

- A swivel-bladed peeler, for peeling carrots, potatoes, and cucumbers

- A bench scraper, for scraping off the work surface, and also for use in pastry
- A melon baller (also called a Parisian scoop), useful not only for making melon balls but also for scooping out cherry tomatoes and seeds from zucchini and cucumbers
- Measuring spoons
- A whisk
- A wooden spoon
- A heatproof rubber spatula
- A flat metal spatula
- Tongs

- A thermometer
- A sharpening stone made with two layers of coarseness, for sharpening knives
- A wine opener (also called a wine key)
- A boning knife, kept very sharp, for removing bones from large cuts of meat
- A slicing knife, for cutting softer items such as cakes and large roast
- A meat fork, used to hold meats in place while they're being sliced
- A sharpening steel, used alongside a sharpening stone, to refresh the edge put onto a blade

Professional knife kits house a variety of knives and tools, like the ones pictured here.

BASIC CUTS

Chef John begins by showing us the basic cuts that we will master as we work our way through the Boot Camp curriculum. He shows us how to curve the fingers of our guiding hand, the hand that is not holding the knife. The guiding hand is responsible for controlling the food that is being cut. The classic position for the guiding hand is with the fingertips slightly tucked under and holding the object, with the thumb behind them, so that the knife blade rests against the knuckles and the fingers cannot be cut. For some tasks, such as tournés and flutes, the guiding hand holds the food above the cutting surface and turns the food against the knife blade. When parallel cuts or angled parallel cuts are made—for example, when butterflying meat or slicing a bagel—the guiding hand rests on top of the food.

Use your guiding hand to control the food as you cut.

Rough Cuts and Precision Cuts

We have already learned that there are two basic styles of cutting fruits and vegetables: rough cuts and precision cuts. Chopping and mincing are rough cuts—the food is cut into small pieces in the case of chopping, and very small pieces in the case of mincing, but the pieces don't necessarily have to all be the same dimension. Precision and portioning cuts, on the other hand, such as dice, julienne, rondelles, and bâtonnets, are perfectly uniform. Precision cuts ensure that the foods will cook evenly and retain their appearance as they cook. When vegetables are used for flavoring but are strained out at the end, or when the dish is a rustic one, such as a stew

or a braise, precision cuts are not necessary. We watch and listen as the chefs cut, slice, dice, julienne, and more.

To dice foods, Chef John demonstrates, you peel and trim the item, then cut it into even slices, using your first slice as your guide. Stack the slices (not too high or they will slip and you won't get even dice) and cut even parallel cuts. Now gather the sticks together and, using your guiding hand to hold them in place, make crosswise parallel cuts through the sticks. All of the cuts should be the same thickness to produce even, neat dice.

To julienne and make bâtonnets, the chef first trims the item so that the sides are straight (this is called squaring off). Then he slices the vegetable lengthwise, using parallel

From left to right: fine brunoise, brunoise, small dice, medium dice, and large dice.

From left to right: fine julienne, julienne, and bâtonnet.

cuts. Using his first cut as a guide, he cuts the remaining slices the same size. The chef then stacks the slices, aligning the edges, and makes parallel cuts the same thickness through the stack (⅛ inch for julienne, ¼ inch for bâtonnets). The sticks should be 1 to 2 inches long.

The chefs show us all the precision cuts. They cut carrots into rondelles, slicing the long cylindrical vegetables crosswise. Rondelles can be varied by cutting on the diagonal to produce ovals, by cutting the vegetable in half lengthwise first to produce half-moons, or by scoring the surface with channels to produce flowers. They cut herbs into delicate shreds called chiffonade, and demonstrate oblique cuts (aka roll cuts) on parsnips. They bring out a heavy mandoline

and have fun cutting potatoes into allumettes (matchsticks), gaufrettes (waffle cuts), ripple cuts, and ribbons.

Chef Hinnerk demonstrates how to cut potatoes into football-shaped tournés. The tourné is a purely decorative cut and is usually used for garnishes, though I did spend the better part of a morning session in the kitchen cutting them. It's a tedious business. First peel the vegetable, if desired. Cut the vegetable into manageable sizes—quarters or sixths for large round vegetables such as beets or turnips; 2-inch lengths for zucchini, carrots, and potatoes. Then cut the vegetables with a paring knife, holding them in your guiding hand, so that they taper toward the end and have 4 to 7 even, flat surfaces.

Top row, from left to right: rondelle, tourné. Bottom row, from left to right: lozenge, fermiere, paysanne.

HOW TO CUT...

Onions

The CIA teaches its students how to peel the onions whole and leave them for use the next day (by trimming off the stem end, then peeling off the skin and the underlying layer if it contains brown spots). However, most of us peel our onions and use them right away. Whether you peel the onion whole and cut it later, or peel them and use them immediately, this is how you chop an onion:

Cut the onion in half lengthwise, through the root end. Peel away the skin from each half. Lay the onion half cut side down and make a series of evenly spaced, parallel lengthwise cuts with the tip of your chef's knife, leaving the root end intact. The closer together your cuts, the smaller your dice will be. Turn your knife parallel to your cutting surface and make two or three parallel cuts from the stem end to the root end, leaving the root intact. Now cut the onion crosswise through the existing cuts, from the stem to the root end.

Alternatively, you can make a series of lengthwise cuts through the onion, angling your knife with each cut to follow the natural curve of the onion and make cuts that are perpendicular to the onion's layers, a technique chefs refer to as radial cuts. Just as in the previous method, the more closely spaced your cuts, the smaller the finished cut will be. Give the onion a quarter turn, and cut crosswise through the radial cuts to dice or mince. This method eliminates the need to make horizontal cuts in the previous method, and I prefer it; if you leave the root end intact, the onion will hold together.

To slice rounds, peel the entire onion before cutting. Slice across the onion into rounds using a chef's knife, a mandoline, or an electric slicer.

Shallots

Shallots must be peeled, like onions, then separated into cloves like garlic, then minced. Trim and peel as you would an onion. Separate the cloves, then make a series of perpendicular and horizontal cuts, using the tip of your chef's knife or paring knife. If it makes it easier for you to steady the shallot cloves, cut them in half from stem to root end first so that you can lay them down on the cut side.

Garlic

As much garlic as I've chopped in my life, I never mastered the skill as I do at the CIA, following the chefs' tips. The CIA would be the first to point out that large quantities of garlic can be prepared in a food processor or a mini-chopper. However, smaller amounts are always best chopped by hand. To loosen the cloves, wrap an entire head of garlic in a kitchen towel and press down on its top to break it into individual cloves. To loosen the skin from each clove, crush the clove between the flat side of the knife blade and the cutting board. Lift off the skin and remove the stem end and any brown spots. If the garlic clove has sprouted, cut in half lengthwise and remove the green shoot.

Lay the skinned clove(s) of garlic on your work surface, and again crush them using the flat side of your chef's knife: hit the blade firmly with the heel of your hand or your fist. Then chop fine, using a rocking motion.

To finely mash the garlic, first sprinkle with salt, which acts as an abrasive. Angle the knife so that it is nearly flat against the cutting surface and mash the garlic to a paste against the cutting surface.

Carrots and Parsnips

This never would have occurred to me if I hadn't gone to Boot Camp. You know how carrots and parsnips can be very wide at one end and quite tapered at the other? The way to get even pieces is to cut the thick, wide parts in half lengthwise before you slice them. Even cuts are important, and although the shapes won't be exactly the same, the size will, and uniform size matters.

Celery

To get neatly cut stalks while keeping the heart of the celery intact, slice off the bottom of the celery, then pull off the stalks. Because celery is such an osmotic vegetable, it can be a bacteria carrier, easily subject to cross-contamination. Keep the celery that you aren't using well away from other foods, preferably upright in a small amount of water in the refrigerator.

Slice celery on an angle. To dice, cut the stalks into lengthwise strips, then cut across the strips.

Leeks

Leeks are almost always sandy, so they must be cleaned thoroughly before slicing or chopping. Rinse the leeks, then trim away the heavy dark green leafy portion by cutting it at an angle with a chef's knife. By cutting at an angle, you will avoid cutting away the light green part in the center. Cut away the root end, then cut the leek in half lengthwise (or into thirds or quarters). Run the cut leeks under cold water, fanning the layers to make sure the sand is washed away. Slice, julienne, or chop as desired.

Ginger

Chef John shows us how to peel ginger with a spoon. He holds the spoon so that the bowl of the spoon is inverted and uses the edge of the bowl to scrape away the peel. I think this is the neatest thing I've seen all day, but when I try it at home, it isn't as neat. My spoon feels more awkward than a paring knife, and it takes me longer to peel it this way, so I go back to the paring knife or the swivel-bladed peeler for my ginger. Try it both ways. Once you've peeled your ginger, slice it crosswise into quarter-sized pieces. Then either chop, mince, dice, or process.

Tomatoes

Tomatoes are peeled for most of the preparations we use them for at Boot Camp. Peeled, seeded, finely chopped tomatoes are called concassé, which is what our recipes call for. To peel tomatoes, bring a pot of water to a rolling boil while you core the tomatoes with the tip of your paring knife. If you wish, score the blossom end to make peeling easier (I never do this, and neither do many chefs). Drop a few tomatoes at a time into the boiling water and wait 10 seconds if the tomatoes are very ripe, 30 if they're less ripe, then transfer immediately to a bowl of ice water. Peel away the skin, using the paring knife to help if you wish (catch the skin between your thumb and the flat side of the knife). If the skin comes away in a thin, translucent layer, the tomato is ripe and properly blanched. If it sticks in spots, the tomato is not quite ripe. Use a knife to cut away the skin where it sticks.

To seed and chop, dice, or cube, cut round tomatoes in half across the equator, plum tomatoes lengthwise. Gently squeeze out the seeds. If necessary, use your fingertip to scoop out seeds that adhere. Make parallel and horizontal cuts of the desired width, then chop or cut into cubes or dice. If a recipe calls for tomato concassé, chop very fine.

For truly precise tomato julienne or dice, halve or quarter the skinned tomato lengthwise, and then cut the tomato seeds away from the outer layer of flesh. This is sometimes known as filleting the tomato. Finally, cut the tomato fillets into julienne or other shapes.

Avocados

Holding the avocado gently in your guiding hand, cut it in half lengthwise, down to the pit, and turn the avocado all the way around on the knife with the knife resting on the pit. Remove the knife and gently twist the two halves apart. Gently remove the pit with a spoon, or dig the heel of your knife into the pit with a short chopping motion and twist it free. To get the pit off the knife bade, use the edge of your cutting board or the lip of a container to help release the pit. The easiest way to peel a ripe avocado is to gently scoop it out from the peel with a spoon. You can slice or dice the avocado before you scoop it out, by scoring down to the skin with the tip of a paring knife or utility knife. Then scoop out the precut slices or dice with a kitchen spoon. If the avocado is too hard for this, peel it by catching the skin between the ball of your thumb and the flat side of a utility knife or paring knife, and pull the skin free from the avocado. Slice or dice as desired.

Peppers

Roast peppers by turning them over a gas flame until they blacken. If you don't have a gas stove, you can cut the peppers in half, place them cut side down on a baking sheet, and broil them. Once charred, place them in a plastic or paper bag so the pepper's own steam can loosen the skin. Once cooled, you can slip off the skin and pull out the seeds and ribs.

Bell peppers and chiles can be cut in two ways. For the first method, cut through the pepper from stem to blossom end. If desired, cut again into quarters. Using the tip of your knife, cut away the stem, seeds, and membranes. Then slice or dice.

In the second method, cut across the stem and blossom ends to remove the "shoulders" of the pepper and the pointed tail. Cut in half lengthwise, then, holding the pepper with your guiding hand so that it is stable, hold the knife blade parallel to the work surface and cut away the seeds and membranes. Slice, julienne, or dice as directed.

To skin a pepper that has not been roasted, cut into quarters following the directions for the chef's method, then, holding the pepper with your guiding hand so that it is stable, hold the knife blade parallel to the work surface and run it between the skin and the flesh.

Zucchini

Chef John points out that the mature seeds on the inside of the zucchini are mostly water, and when he juliennes or makes bâtonnets, he cuts the zucchini down each side of the middle, discards the middle with the seeds, then cuts his bâtonnets. If your zucchini are young and fresh, the seeds won't have matured so much as to be watery or tough. Since the first thing you do when julienning or making bâtonnets or tournés is to cut the squash into 2-inch lengths, you'll be able to have a look at the seeds and ascertain what you want to do with them.

Cut the zucchini into 2-inch lengths, stand upright, and made parallel cuts to the desired width. Stack the slices and make parallel cuts to the desired thickness. You may discard the center core if you wish. If cutting on the mandoline, pass each section of zucchini over the fine opening of the cutting blades. Give the zucchini a quarter turn when the seeds are exposed and continue cutting from each face until only the seeds remain.

Apples

When cutting up apples, have ready a bowl of water acidulated with the juice of half a lemon, and drop the apple wedges into the water as you cut so that they won't discolor upon exposure to air. I finally master coring apples after I watch Chef John demonstrate. If you need eight slices or more, you can slice and cut away the core as you go along by doing as follows.

Peel the apple if necessary, cutting away the stem and blossom ends with the tip of your paring knife first. Halve the apple from top to bottom and then cut into quarters. Cut the quarters in half from top to bottom. Lay each eighth of an apple on your work surface and, angling your knife, cut away the core in one slice. You may now continue to halve your slices until you have up to 32 thin slices.

If you need quarters or sixths, then core the apple sections in two cuts, working from the stem end and angling your cut to the midpoint of the core. Make a second cut from the opposite direction.

For chopped or diced apples, cut across the wedges.

Another way to cut an apple into neat, thin slices, by hand or using the mandoline, is to cut straight down the side of the core on all sides, then slice. If using the mandoline, you will slice the apple on the mandoline until you get to the core, then turn it over and remove slices from the opposite side. Finally, slice the narrow sides.

Pears and round, soft squash can be cut in the same way.

Citrus Fruit

Chef John shows us one trick that I'm convinced must be taught only to professional culinary students. You know how, when you squeeze a wedge of lemon onto food, the juice doesn't always go where you want it to? Well, if you cut away the white membrane on the edge of your wedge of lemon, that won't happen.

Zest, the colored portion of the citrus fruit, can be removed using a paring knife, a zester, a swivel peeler, a grater, or a microplane. To get rid of any residual bitterness, blanch the zest one to three times in boiling water. For sweetened zest, add sugar to the blanching water.

To cut sections or segments of flesh (called citrus suprêmes) away from the skin and connective membranes of the fruit, trim both ends of the fruit so that it sits flat on your work surface. Using a chef's knife, utility knife, or a paring knife, cut the skin and pith completely away from the fruit, following the natural curve of the fruit from top to bottom. Hold the fruit in your hand (over a bowl to catch juice) and slice next to the connective membrane on one side of each citrus segment, then twist the knife to turn the direction of your cut and scoop out the section.

Pineapples

I learn a thing or two about pineapples at the knife skills lecture, including two different ways to peel them. I always wondered why eating pineapple, which I cannot resist, irritated my mouth; I thought it was punishment for my gluttony. It turns out that this is because of the presence of an enzyme called bromelain, which is also a meat tenderizer. If you blanch pineapple for 15 seconds, you won't change the taste or texture, but you will neutralize the bromelain.

Another thing I learn is why almost all of the pineapples in supermarkets today are so sweet, whereas not too long ago you really had to pick and choose, smelling them and pulling out a leaf to ascertain whether or not they are ripe. Now there's a new hybrid called Supersweets, and that's what they're growing in Hawaii. They've taken the guesswork out of selecting pineapples.

The CIA teaches two methods for peeling a pineapple. For method 1, cut the ends off. Stand the pineapple upright and cut the skin away by cutting down the sides, following the curve of the pineapple. Chef John says, "It should be the same shape peeled as it was before it was peeled." Make sure that the cuts were deep enough to cut away the eyes, but not so deep that you cut away too much flesh.

For method 2, which is especially useful if you are going to make rings, cut away a slice from the pineapple's base, then trim away the peel as above, but trim it closer to the outside so that the eyes are left in. The eyes go in a spiral pattern around the pineapple. Use the tip of a paring knife or utility knife to cut the eyes out by cutting a V-shaped groove around and around the pineapple.

To dice or cube a pineapple, slice the pineapple down the sides of the core, as you would an apple. Discard the core and then cut as desired.

To make wedges, cut the peeled pineapple into lengthwise quarters. Cut away the core, then slice crosswise.

To make rings, slice the peeled pineapple crosswise and use a small round cookie cutter or corer to cut away the core.

Mangos

Chef John offers us a useful tip for cutting mangos: "Cut the mango flesh from the seed as you would cut off a chicken breast from the bone, cutting out, down, and in." In other words, cut down the broad side of the mango, slightly off center, from the stem end to the tip end. The knife should scrape against the pit. Repeat on the other side, cutting as close to the pit as possible. Cut the flesh from the sides of the pit, following the curve of the pit.

Lay each half, skin side down, on your cutting surface and score with the tip of your knife in a crosshatch pattern, down to but not through the skin. Turn the mango half inside out and slice the cubes away from the skin.

If you want to peel the mango before cutting, slice off a small piece of the end, stand the mango upright, and peel down the sides using a paring knife, between the skin and the flesh, as you would a pineapple.

Kiwis

This demo changes my kiwi-cutting life, such as it is, forever. To skin a kiwi, you don't cut the skin away. You cut off the ends, then slip a spoon inside between the skin and the flesh, scrape it around the inside of the skin, and pop out the kiwi.

Poultry

In our knife skills demo we are shown how to truss a chicken for roasting.

I never bothered to truss my chickens or turkeys before, but I find out from Chef Hinnerk that if you don't truss the chicken, it loses 25 percent more moisture as it roasts. Trussing makes the bird compact and allows it to cook more evenly. So when I get back from Boot Camp, I begin to truss my chickens before roasting. It only takes a couple of minutes.

There are many ways to truss a chicken or a turkey. Chef John uses a method that is pretty much identical to the one presented in the CIA's standard text on knife skills, *The Professional Chef's Knife Kit*. Chef Hinnerk uses a different method that gives the same results, plus a sort of handle that's handy for lifting the bird.

Whichever method you choose, to prepare a chicken for trussing first cut away excess fat and remove the wing tips at the second joint. Pull out the tips, and using the tip of your boning knife, make a cut that circles around the second joint of the wing bone. Bend the wing bone at the second joint to snap it, then continue to cut through the joint until the first two joints are removed. Season the bird generously inside and out with salt and pepper. If desired, place aromatics such as garlic cloves and herbs in the bird's cavity.

For Chef John's trussing method, take a long piece of kitchen twine and pass the middle of it underneath and around the ends of the drumsticks. Cross the ends of the string to make an X (this looks a little like you're playing cat's cradle). Pull the ends of the string down toward the tail, then back along the body, pulling the strings tightly over the joint that connects the thigh and drumstick. Continue to pull the string along the body toward the bird's back, catching the wing underneath the string. Pull one end of the string securely underneath the backbone at the neck opening and tie the two ends of the string with a secure knot.

I like Chef Hinnerk's method because the string doesn't jam up as much skin. But I do have to learn to tie a slipknot to do it. Using a slipknot, lasso one wing and pull the long end of the string tight. Wrap the other wing and pull the two together, then pull the long end of the string around to the legs and secure them by wrapping them together, crossing the string over one and under the other and back. Bring the string back around to the wing end and secure by using a double knot to tie the long end of the string to the short end hanging off the wing.

ADDITIONAL BOOT
CAMP RECIPES

Stocks and Sauces

BROWN VEAL STOCK

You begin this standard brown stock by roasting the bones, then simmering them with browned aromatics for 6 to 8 hours. What you get is a complex, full-bodied liquid that is traditionally used as a foundation for classic brown sauces such as demiglace and jus lié (see page 184). In addition to a large stockpot, you will need a large, heavy roasting pan for the bones. This makes a lot of stock, but if you're going to take the time to make this, you might as well make 4 quarts and keep it on hand in the freezer.

MAKES 4 QUARTS

8 pounds veal bones

Vegetable oil as needed

9 quarts water

1 large onion, finely chopped

1 medium carrot, finely chopped

1½ stalks celery, finely chopped

½ 6-ounce can tomato paste

1 sachet d'épices containing a bay leaf, a few sprigs each parsley and thyme (or ½ teaspoon dried thyme), ½ teaspoon cracked black peppercorns, all tied into a piece of cheesecloth (or just add these ingredients to the pot and forget about the cheesecloth)

½ teaspoon salt

1. Preheat the oven to 425°F. Meanwhile, rinse the bones well and pat dry.

2. Coat a large roasting pan with a thin film of vegetable oil and heat it in the oven for 5 minutes. Add the bones in an even layer and return to the oven. Roast for 15 minutes, then reduce the heat to 325°F. Roast the bones, stirring and turning from time to time (use tongs to move them around), until they are a deep brown color, 30 to 45 minutes.

3. Transfer the bones to a large stockpot and add cold water to cover. Add a cup or two of water to the roasting pan and stir and scrape

What the recipe doesn't know

· How heavy your roasting pan is and how big your veal bones are. This will impact the amount of time it takes for them to brown.

· The shape of your stockpot. You may need more water to cover the bones.

the bottom of the pan to deglaze. Add the deglazed contents of the pan to the stockpot. Slowly bring to a simmer over low heat, taking care not to allow the liquid to boil. Skim the surface as necessary.

4. Meanwhile, heat a heavy sauté pan or Dutch oven over medium-high heat and add a thin film of oil. Add the carrots and cook, stirring, until browned, about 10 minutes. Add the onions and celery and continue to sauté until the onions and celery have browned, about 10 more minutes, then reduce the heat slightly and stir in the tomato paste. Cook, stirring and taking care not to allow the tomato paste to burn, until the tomato paste takes on a rusty brown color and gives off a sweet aroma, about 1 to 2 minutes. Transfer to a bowl and set aside. This will be added to the stock during the last hour of cooking. Add a ladle of hot water to the pan and stir and scrape the bottom with a wooden spoon to deglaze. Add the deglazed liquid to the simmering stock.

5. Simmer the stock, making sure that it never boils—lazy bubbles should occasionally come to the surface—for 5 to 7 hours. Add the caramelized mirepoix and tomato paste, the sachet d'épices, and the salt. Continue to simmer for 1 hour, skimming and tasting from time to time, or until the stock has developed a rich flavor and a full body.

6. Remove from the heat and strain through a cheesecloth-lined strainer. Chill in an ice bath and refrigerate, freeze, or use. Skim off any fat that accumulates on the surface of the stock and discard.

TOMATO PINCÉ

In restaurant jargon, tomato sauce and tomato paste are called "tomato product," and lightly browned tomato product, in this case tomato paste, is called tomato pincé. It produces a deep, rich color and flavor in the stocks and sauces to which it is added. To pincé, you must lightly brown the tomato paste or sauce, being careful not to burn it (the high sugar content of the tomato paste or sauce is what allows it to brown so nicely, but it can also cause it to burn). The tomato product should smell noticeably sweet once it is properly browned; if it is still reddish orange and smells very tomato-like or acidic, it is undercooked and will create an orange rather than brown color in the stock or sauce to which it is added.

CHICKEN STOCK

Students at the CIA make this chicken stock every day. It's a classic stock made with several pounds of chicken bones, which give up their flavor over a long 4-hour simmer. Simmering is not boiling: you should see lazy, occasional bubbles breaking at the surface, no more movement than that. The recipe from the CIA calls for tying the bay leaf, parsley and thyme stems, and peppercorns into a cheesecloth (this is called a sachet d'épices), but I've never seen the need to do this, as you strain the stock at the end. To my delight, Chef Hinnerk felt the same way. The aromatics are added only during the last hour, because after an hour they have released all of their good flavors, and overcooking will release sulfuric compounds in vegetables—not desirable flavors.

MAKES 4 QUARTS

What the recipe doesn't know

The shape and size of your pot. You may need more or less water to cover the chicken bones, depending on the shape and size of your pot.

8 pounds chicken bones
6 quarts cold water
1 large onion, finely chopped
1 medium carrot, finely chopped
1½ stalks celery, finely chopped
1 bay leaf
A few sprigs each parsley and thyme
6 peppercorns
½ teaspoon salt

1. Rinse the chicken bones and combine with the water in a large stockpot. Bring to a boil over low heat. As the mixture comes to a boil, skim the foam and scum that come to the surface. Continue to skim regularly until the water has reached a boil.

2. Turn the heat to low and simmer slowly for 3 to 4 hours, until the stock smells very fragrant. Add the onions, carrots, celery, bay leaf, parsley and thyme stems, peppercorns, and salt. Simmer for another hour.

3. Strain the stock through a fine wire mesh sieve or a large strainer lined with cheesecloth into a bowl or another pot. Chill in an ice bath and skim off any fat that accumulates on the surface of the stock and discard. Refrigerate, freeze, or use.

Variation: **BROWN CHICKEN STOCK**
Before combining the bones with the water, brown them in a heavy pan in a 375°F oven for 25 to 35 minutes, along with an onion, a carrot, and a stalk of celery, all coarsely chopped. Add the browned vegetables during the last hour of cooking.

FISH STOCK

Since fish stock is best used the day it's made, this recipe is only for 2 quarts. When making fish stock, use bones and heads from white-fleshed fish, and avoid salmon, mackerel, and other strong-tasting, fatty fish. Mahi is not good for fish stock because it's an acidic fish. Chef Hinnerk likes to soak the bones in salt water for an hour before making his fish stock. If you do this, your fish stock will be clearer and won't have an overly fishy flavor. Most fish stores and supermarket fish departments fillet their fish before displaying them, so you'll want to call ahead to order the bones and heads.

MAKES 2 QUARTS

4 to 6 pounds fish bones and heads
3 quarts cold water
½ large onion, finely chopped
½ medium carrot, finely chopped
1 stalk celery, finely chopped
¾ cup mushroom trimmings (optional)
¼ teaspoon salt, or to taste (optional)

1. Combine all of the ingredients in a large pot and bring slowly to a simmer. Skim off any scum and foam that rise to the surface. Simmer, without boiling, for 30 to 60 minutes.

2. Remove from the heat and strain. Chill in an ice bath and refrigerate until ready to use.

Variation: FISH FUMET

4 to 6 pounds fish bones
2½ quarts cold water
2 cups dry white wine, such as sauvignon blanc
⅓ cup finely chopped onion
⅓ cup finely chopped leek, white part only
⅓ cup finely chopped parsnips
½ cup finely chopped celery

Follow the instructions for fish stock using the above ingredients.

What the recipe doesn't know

` Whether or not you can obtain fish bones. If you can't, use a whole white-fleshed fish.

` The size of your fish carcasses, and the size and shape of your pot. As our chef said, the amount of water you use "is not a federal law." Put the bones in first, then cover them with water.

VEGETABLE STOCK

At Boot Camp I learned all kinds of things I never knew about a stock I've been making for over 30 years: for example, that tomatoes and mushrooms are essential to a flavorful vegetable stock, because they both possess a highly flavorful compound called glutamic acid. Also, vegetables will begin to release sulfuric compounds if you cook them too long, which is why you only simmer this stock for 30 minutes. If you are a vegetarian or are cooking for vegetarians, this is the stock to use in place of chicken stock.

MAKES 4 QUARTS

- ½ pound onions, sliced
- 1 pound leeks, white and light green part only, cleaned and diced
- ½ pound celery root, diced
- ½ pound carrots, diced
- ½ pound turnips, diced
- ½ pound parsnips, diced
- 1 pound tomatoes, chopped
- 8 garlic cloves, crushed
- ½ pound Napa cabbage, diced
- 1 pound mushroom stems or whole mushrooms
- 1 tablespoon plus 1 teaspoon fennel seeds
- 1 tablespoon plus 1 teaspoon dried thyme
- 1 tablespoon plus 1 teaspoon dried oregano
- 4 bay leaves

Place all of the ingredients in a large stockpot and cover with 5 quarts of water, or enough to cover the vegetables. Bring to a boil, reduce the heat, and simmer gently for 20 to 30 minutes. Taste and adjust salt.

CHICKEN VELOUTÉ

The chefs demonstrated this velouté to illustrate soup production, as velouté is the base for most cream soups. The word velouté comes from the French word for velvet, and indeed, chicken velouté is a classic, velvety white sauce. It's made by thickening chicken stock with a pale roux, a mixture of flour and butter that has been cooked until the floury taste is gone but the mixture is not browned (that's what the book says, but Chef Hinnerk cooked the roux just until it was ever so slightly toasty and nutty-smelling). It is the basis of most creamed vegetable soups. There is, as with so many classic recipes, more than one way to make a velouté. If you already have a roux made, it can be stirred into the stock. Otherwise the stock is usually added to the roux. You can use chicken stock alone, or make a more aromatic velouté by simmering mushroom trimmings and bay leaf in the sauce. Chef Hinnerk likes to use a pure fat for the roux, either clarified butter or oil; we used regular unsalted butter.

MAKES 1 QUART

- 1 quart Chicken Stock (page 142)
- 2 ounces (½ stick) butter, preferably clarified (page 26)
- 3 ounces (scant ⅔ cup) all-purpose flour
- ¾ cup mushroom trimmings (or chopped mushrooms), optional
- 1 bay leaf, optional
- 1 to 2 teaspoons salt (to taste)
- ½ teaspoon ground white pepper

1. Warm the chicken stock in a saucepan; do not let it get too hot.

2. Melt the butter over medium heat in a heavy saucepan, and when it begins to bubble, stir in the flour. Stir until the mixture is smooth and continue to cook, stirring, until the mixture is smooth and has the consistency of wet sand at low tide. Cook just until the flour begins to smell toasty and nutty, but no further. The roux needs to cook so that the flour will break down, which is what makes the sauce so smooth.

3. Whisk most of the stock into the roux, leaving a little behind for thinning out later, and incorporate vigorously. Bring to a simmer, stirring frequently to make sure the mixture doesn't scorch on the bottom of the pan. As the mixture slowly comes to a boil it will begin to thicken; it is also at this point that there is the greatest risk of scorching, so be vigilant. Add the mushroom trimmings and bay leaf, and simmer 30 to 60 minutes, skimming the impurities as they rise to the surface of the sauce.

4. Strain the sauce through a strainer lined with a double thickness of cheesecloth. Taste and adjust seasonings. Keep warm.

Things to watch

- Don't brown the roux too much.

- Add cold or warm stock to the roux, but not hot stock. The roux needs the time to disperse into the stock before it comes to a boil.

- If you already have roux on hand, add it to the stock, but make sure to warm the stock first.

- Hold back a little stock, which you may need later for thinning.

- Stir frequently and watch carefully so your mixture doesn't scorch, especially when it is just coming to the boiling point.

- Taste the velouté just after it thickens: you will be able to discern a raw cereal taste at the back of your palate. By the end of cooking, that flavor should no longer be there.

PEANUT SAUCE

This spicy Southeast Asian sauce is a classic accompaniment to beef, chicken, or shrimp satay. It also makes a great all-purpose dip, and it's good with dumplings.

MAKES 2 CUPS

- 1 tablespoon peanut oil
- 1 tablespoon minced garlic
- 1 cup smooth peanut butter
- 6 slices chile pepper, such as serrano, jalapeño, or Thai chiles, minced
- 1 tablespoon sugar
- ½ teaspoon cayenne pepper
- ¼ cup fresh lime juice
- ¼ cup soy sauce
- ¾ cup water or stock (chicken or vegetable)
- 1 tablespoon minced lemongrass

1. Heat the oil over medium-low heat in a medium saucepan and add the garlic. Cook, stirring, until fragrant and translucent, about 1 minute. Add the chile peppers and cook for another minute, until they soften slightly. Add salt to taste.

2. Add the remaining ingredients and bring to a simmer, stirring. Thin with water or stock if the sauce is too thick. Simmer a few minutes and remove from the heat. Serve warm or cold.

MUSTARD TARTAR SAUCE

This sauce is served with the Crab and Cod Cakes on page 160. It goes well with most fish, especially shellfish. Some chefs like to keep the egg, cornichons, and dill separate, serving them as a garnish, and put the mayonnaise-mustard mixture into a squeeze bottle to sauce their crab cakes. I like everything mixed together. Creole mustard (one brand is made by Zatarain's) is sold in the condiments section of most supermarkets.

SERVES 6

- ¼ cup diced red onions
- ¼ cup mayonnaise
- 2 tablespoons Dijon mustard
- 1 tablespoon Creole mustard
- ¾ teaspoon sugar
- 2½ teaspoons cider vinegar
- 1 hard-cooked egg, finely chopped
- ¼ cup finely chopped cornichons
- 2 tablespoons minced fresh dill
- Salt to taste

1. Bring a small pot of water to a boil and add the chopped onion. Blanch for 5 seconds, then transfer to a bowl of ice water, drain, and dry on paper towels.

2. Combine the mayonnaise, mustards, sugar, and vinegar in a small or medium bowl. Add the remaining ingredients and mix together well. Taste and adjust salt. Cover and refrigerate until ready to serve.

POMMERY MUSTARD BEURRE BLANC

Beurre blanc is a thick, rich sauce that is made by combining shallots and an acid, usually wine and/or vinegar, with a lot of butter, which is whisked in and emulsifies in the acid. It's a simple sauce, but a lot can go wrong. In some recipes the beurre blanc is strained after the butter is swirled in. Chef Hinnerk strained the flavorful reduction, then returned it to the pan and added a bit of cream to stabilize it, then added the butter, swirling the pan vigorously and constantly. If the sauce does fall apart, he told us, you can rectify it by adding a splash of water. This pungent beurre blanc, with lots of mustard added at the end, is perfect with grilled meats, especially lighter ones such as the pork chops on page 187.

MAKES 1 CUP, ENOUGH FOR 6 SERVINGS

6 tablespoons dry white wine, such as Sauvignon Blanc

2 tablespoons cider vinegar

Juice of ½ lemon (optional)

3 peppercorns, crushed in a mortar and pestle or a spice mill

1 small shallot, minced

3 sprigs fresh thyme

1 bay leaf

2 tablespoons heavy cream

6 ounces (1½ sticks) butter, cut into pieces

1 tablespoon Pommery mustard

Salt and freshly ground pepper to taste

1. Combine the wine, vinegar, lemon juice, crushed peppercorns, shallots, thyme, and bay leaf in a small saucepan and bring to a boil. Reduce until the pan is almost dry (if it dries out, add a splash of water). Strain the reduction and return to the pan over medium-high heat.

2. Add the heavy cream and reduce until it coats the front and back of a spoon (nappé).

3. Piece by piece, whisk in the butter and continue to whisk and/or swirl the pan until the mixture is thick and emulsified. If you see that the sauce is about to break, add a little water and whisk vigorously. Whisk in the Pommery mustard.

4. Remove from the heat, transfer to a bowl, and season with salt and pepper. Keep the sauce warm by placing the bowl above a pot of hot water. (See photo on page 186.)

TOMATO AND ROASTED RED PEPPER COULIS

This beautiful, savory sauce goes well with grilled meat, poultry, and fish.

MAKES 2 CUPS

> 1 tablespoon olive oil
>
> ½ small onion, chopped
>
> 1 garlic clove, minced
>
> 2 tablespoons tomato paste
>
> ⅓ cup red wine
>
> ¾ pound tomato concassé, fresh or canned (page 148)
>
> 1 large red bell pepper, roasted (page 134)
>
> 1 cup Chicken Stock (page 142)
>
> 1 bouquet garni, consisting of a bay leaf, a few sprigs of parsley, and a few sprigs of thyme
>
> ½ teaspoon salt (or to taste)
>
> ¼ teaspoon freshly ground pepper (or to taste)

1. Heat the oil over medium heat in a sauté pan or wide saucepan and add the onion. Cook, stirring, until translucent, about 3 to 5 minutes. Add the garlic and cook for another minute or two, until fragrant.

2. Add the tomato paste and cook over medium heat until the color deepens and it smells fragrant, about 3 minutes. Add the wine and stir and scrape the bottom of the pan to deglaze.

3. Add the tomatoes, roasted pepper, the chicken stock, and bouquet garni, bring to a simmer, and simmer 45 minutes over medium-low heat, or until the tomatoes have cooked down and the sauce is thick enough to coat the front and back of your spoon. Stir often.

What the recipe doesn't know

> The size and shape of your pan. If it's wider than it is tall, the sauce will cook down more quickly. Keep your eye on the sauce and stir frequently.

4. Remove and discard the bouquet garni. Puree the sauce in batches in a blender, being careful not to allow the hot sauce to splash. Return to the pot and adjust the consistency by either continuing to reduce or adding more hot stock to thin. Season to taste with salt and pepper.

TOMATO CONCASSÉ

Tomato concassé is simply peeled, seeded, chopped tomatoes. When a recipe calls for a quantity of tomato concassé, there's usually no reason not to use canned, especially when tomatoes aren't in season.

Fresh tomatoes

1. Bring a pot of water to a boil while you core the tomatoes. Use the tip of your knife to score the blossom end of the tomatoes, making sure not to cut too deep. Prepare an ice bath for shocking the tomatoes.

2. When the water comes to a rolling boil add the tomatoes and blanch them until their skins begin to peel back from the core, 10 to 30 seconds, depending on their ripeness (blanch less ripe tomatoes longer). Transfer with a spider to a bowl of ice water. Peel off the skins and return to the ice water, or proceed to seeding, making sure that your board is clean.

3. Cut the tomatoes in half (across the widest part, or belly, for slicing tomatoes and from top to bottom for plum tomatoes). Squeeze gently to press out the seeds and use the tip of your knife or a small spoon to scoop out any seeds that remain. Chop the tomato into pieces that are approximately the same size.

TOMATO COULIS

Any coulis is a sauce thickened by its main ingredient. The recipe calls for peeled, seeded, chopped tomatoes, but by all means used canned tomatoes if you wish, and absolutely use them when fresh local tomatoes are not in season. This simple tomato sauce is great with pasta and makes a delicious accompaniment to deep-fried fish such as the flounder on page 182.

MAKES 1 QUART

- 3 cups Chicken Stock (page 142)
- 2 tablespoons olive oil
- ½ medium onion, minced
- 2 cloves garlic, minced
- 5 tablespoons tomato paste
- 2 pounds fresh or canned tomatoes, peeled, seeded, and finely chopped
- 1 bouquet garni made with a bay leaf and 3 sprigs each thyme and parsley

- ½ teaspoon salt, or to taste
- ¼ teaspoon freshly ground pepper, or to taste
- Pinch of sugar (optional)

1. Bring the stock to a simmer in a saucepan.

2. Heat a wide, heavy sauté pan or saucepan over medium heat and add the oil. When it is hot, add the onions. Sweat the onions until translucent, 5 minutes, and add the garlic. Cook until fragrant and translucent, another 30 seconds.

3. Add the tomato paste. Sauté, stirring, for another 2 to 3 minutes, until the tomato paste takes on a rusty color and has a sweet aroma.

4. Add the tomatoes, stock, bouquet garni, salt, pepper, and sugar and bring to a simmer. Simmer for ½ hour, until fragrant and thick. Remove and discard the bouquet garni. Taste and adjust seasonings.

5. Purée the tomato sauce in a food processor fitted with the steel blade or a blender and return to the pot. If it seems too thick, thin with a little more chicken stock. If it seems too thin, continue to simmer until it reaches the desired consistency. Taste and adjust seasonings. (See photo on page 183.)

Things to watch

- Don't burn the garlic.

- Don't burn the tomato paste.

Appetizers and Soups

BEEF SATAY

Chef John yelled, "Demo!" and we stopped what we were doing to watch him cut the narrow strips of flank steak, with his knife held at an angle, that we would thread on skewers. It only took a couple of minutes, and I thought as I watched, "This is what I came here to see."

MAKES 20, SERVING 6 TO 8

- 3 pounds flank steak or beef top round
- 1 cup peanut oil
- 3 shoots of lemongrass, shredded
- 6 garlic cloves, minced
- ½ teaspoon crushed red chili pepper
- 2½ tablespoons curry powder
- 1½ tablespoons honey
- 1½ tablespoons fish sauce

1. Soak 20 wooden skewers in water for 30 minutes while you prepare your ingredients. Meanwhile, working with the knife at a slight angle, trim the flank steak and cut across the grain into thin strips, about ½ inch wide. Thread the meat onto the skewers.

2. Combine the peanut oil, lemon grass, garlic cloves, crushed chili pepper, curry powder, honey, and fish sauce in a bowl. Transfer to a long baking dish, and set the skewered meat in it. Turn the skewers over several times to coat evenly. Cover the dish and marinate for 1 to 3 hours.

3. Prepare a hot grill. Set the skewers on the grill and grill the meat until done, about 2 minutes per side. Serve with the peanut sauce (page 146).

BRUSCHETTA WITH OVEN-ROASTED TOMATOES AND FONTINA CHEESE

When you roast tomatoes for a very long time at low heat, they caramelize slowly and melt down into something utterly luscious. Of course it helps if you start with delicious, in-season tomatoes, but even the nondescript imported Romas we used in January tasted pretty good with help from the balsamic vinegar and olive oil, and especially the rich fontina cheese.

MAKES 12, SERVING 6

- 12 to 24 plum tomatoes, cut in half lengthwise
- 1 teaspoon crumbled dried marjoram
- 2 tablespoons balsamic vinegar
- 3 tablespoons extra-virgin olive oil, plus additional for brushing the bread
- 1 teaspoon salt, or to taste
- ½ teaspoon freshly ground pepper, or to taste
- 24 ¾-inch-thick slices French bread, cut on the diagonal
- 24 thin slices fontina cheese (about 6 ounces cheese; use a cheese slicer for cutting)

1. Preheat the oven to 300°F. Place a rack over a sheet tray. Scoop out the seeds of the tomatoes and place each half on a rack, cut side down. Roast until the tomatoes have shriveled and dried partially, about 1½ hours. Keep the oven on.

What the recipe doesn't know

The size of your tomatoes. They will shrink down tremendously in the oven, so have enough to cover the slices of bread.

2. Toss the roasted tomatoes with the marjoram, balsamic vinegar, olive oil, salt, and pepper.

3. Brush the bread slices with olive oil and toast or grill on both sides.

4. Place the fontina on the grilled bread and top with 2 to 3 tomato halves (depending on their size; there should be one layer). Place on a baking sheet and heat through in the oven until the cheese has melted. Serve hot.

GOAT CHEESE IN PHYLLO WITH ROASTED PEPPER SALAD

This is a lovely variation of a classic French salad. Instead of herb- or breadcrumb-crusted rounds of goat cheese, the goat cheese is wrapped in phyllo and baked until the phyllo is browned. Then it's sliced and served with a colorful salad of greens and roasted red and yellow peppers.

SERVES 6

2 cups Chicken Stock (page 142)

20 pearl onions

One 12-ounce log goat cheese

⅓ cup chopped fresh herbs, such as parsley, chives, chervil, and tarragon

6 sheets of phyllo dough

¼ cup (½ stick) butter, melted

1 egg, beaten with 1 tablespoon water for egg wash

2 tablespoons red wine vinegar

1 tablespoon balsamic vinegar

1 teaspoon salt, or to taste

½ teaspoon freshly ground pepper, or to taste

½ cup extra-virgin olive oil

2 large red bell peppers, roasted (page 134)

2 large yellow bell peppers, roasted (page 134)

2 large green bell peppers, roasted (page 134)

3 cups baby salad greens

1. Bring the chicken stock to a boil in a saucepan and drop in the pearl onions. Reduce the heat to medium and simmer until the onions are very tender, 30 to 45 minutes. Drain and set aside.

2. Preheat the oven to 400°F. Line a baking sheet with parchment. Roll the cheese log in the chopped herbs.

3. Layer the phyllo sheets on a piece of parchment paper, brushing each sheet lightly with melted butter. Work quickly so that the phyllo doesn't dry out or it will crack when you roll it.

4. Place the goat cheese log along the long edge of the stacked phyllo. Tuck the ends of the dough over the ends of the log. Using the parchment paper as a guide, roll up the dough tightly, completely enclosing the goat cheese. Brush the roll with melted butter and egg wash, and score into portions, cutting one-third the depth of the strudel. Place on the parchment-lined baking sheet and bake for 20 minutes, until golden brown.

5. To make a vinaigrette, combine the red wine vinegar, balsamic vinegar, ½ teaspoon salt, and ¼ teaspoon pepper. Whisk in the olive oil.

6. Toss together the roasted peppers, simmered onions, and half the vinaigrette. Season with salt and pepper to taste. In a separate bowl, toss the salad greens with the remaining vinaigrette and season with salt and pepper.

7. For each portion, arrange the dressed salad greens on one side of a plate and a small mound of the pepper salad on the other. Slice the phyllo log and serve on the pepper salad.

CHICKEN AND FENNEL BANDILLEROS WITH TOMATO AND ROASTED PEPPER COULIS

These grilled chicken and fennel skewers, served with a tomato and roasted pepper coulis, make a pretty appetizer.

SERVES 6

- 1 medium bulb fennel, cored, layers separated and cut into ¾-inch cubes
- 1 pound boneless, skinless chicken breasts or thighs, cut in ¾-inch cubes
- Juice of 1 lemon, rind reserved
- 1 tablespoon minced garlic
- ¼ cup extra-virgin olive oil
- 1 teaspoon crumbled dried Greek oregano
- 1 teaspoon salt
- 1 teaspoon freshly ground black pepper
- 1 recipe Tomato and Roasted Red Pepper Coulis (page 148)

1. Place the fennel in a large, lidded pan and add enough water to cover the fennel halfway. Bring to a boil, reduce the heat, cover, and pan-steam until the fennel is tender and the water has evaporated, about 10 minutes. If the water evaporates before the fennel is tender, add more to the pan. Drain and allow to cool.

2. Combine the fennel and chicken in a bowl and toss with the lemon juice, garlic, olive oil, oregano, salt, and pepper. Cover and refrigerate for one hour or longer, stirring every once in a while. You can also marinate the mixture in a zip-close bag.

3. Soak wooden skewers in a combination of lemon rind and water for 15 to 30 minutes. Prepare a medium-hot fire in a grill or preheat a grill on high. Thread 5 pieces of fennel and 3 cubes of chicken, alternating the chicken and fennel, onto each skewer.

4. Grill on medium-high heat until cooked through, about 3 to 4 minutes on each side. Serve hot with Tomato and Roasted Pepper Coulis.

COCONUT SHRIMP WITH SWEET AND SOUR SAUCE

You could serve these dramatic deep-fried, coconut-crusted shrimp as an appetizer, presented on a platter with the sauce in a bowl, or you could pass them as hors d'oeuvres. Make sure to remove the tails so that guests don't bite into shells hidden beneath the golden coconut coating.

SERVES 6

FOR THE BEER BATTER:

2 cups flour

1½ teaspoons baking powder

1 teaspoon salt

½ teaspoon freshly ground black pepper

1/8 teaspoon sweet paprika

1 cup beer

FOR THE SWEET AND SOUR SAUCE:

1 tablespoon vegetable oil

1 tablespoon minced fresh ginger

1 tablespoon minced garlic

¼ cup minced scallion

¾ cup sugar

¾ cup rice wine vinegar

½ cup reduced sodium soy sauce

¼ cup dry sherry

2 cups Chicken Stock (page 142) plus more as needed

2 tablespoons dark sesame oil

1 tablespoon cornstarch

¼ cup water

FOR THE SHRIMP:

1 pound large shrimp (21–25 count), shelled, tails removed

½ cup flour for dredging

1 cup grated unsweetened coconut

Vegetable or peanut oil for deep frying

1. Sift together the flour, baking powder, salt, pepper, and paprika into a medium bowl. Gradually stir in the beer and mix until well blended. Allow to rest at least 30 minutes.

2. Make the sweet and sour sauce: Heat the oil over medium heat in a saucepan and add the ginger, garlic, and scallion. Cook until fragrant, stirring frequently, about 5 minutes. Add the sugar, rice vinegar, soy sauce, sherry, chicken stock, and sesame oil. Bring to a boil.

3. Stir together the cornstarch and water to make a slurry. Add the slurry to the sauce and bring back to a boil. When the sauce thickens, remove from the heat. If necessary, thin with chicken stock. Set aside.

4. Clean and devein the shrimp. Dry on paper towels.

5. Dredge the shrimp in flour and remove excess. Place the shrimp in the beer batter. Put the coconut in a bowl.

6. Heat 1 inch of oil to 350°F in a wide, heavy saucepan or deep fryer. Remove the shrimp from the batter one at a time. Let the excess batter drip off into the bowl, then dredge the shrimp in the coconut. Slowly lower the shrimp into the oil and fry until golden brown, about 2–3 minutes. Remove from the oil, drain briefly on racks, and serve with the sauce.

MOZZARELLA ROULADE

Watching Chef John demo this was a revelation. "Ah, so that's how mozzarella is made," I thought, as I watched John submerge a colander full of cheese curd into a pot of salted hot water and work it with a spoon until it became a stringy mass. Then he gently kneaded it into a smooth ball, which he carefully pressed into a rectangle. This he stuffed with prosciutto and basil and rolled up. It was a sight to see, and it tasted good too. Many cheese companies sell cheese curds; you can find them on the Internet and in some supermarkets.

MAKES 16 PORTIONS

⅓ cup salt

2 quarts water

1 pound cheese curd, cut in 1-inch cubes

½ teaspoon freshly ground black pepper

20 basil leaves

10 paper-thin slices prosciutto

Basil leaves, cut into shreds, for garnish

Extra-virgin olive oil, for garnish

Aceto balsamico tradizionale di Modena, for garnish

1. Combine the water and salt in a large saucepan or Dutch oven, and bring to 170°F.

2. Place the cheese curds in a colander and submerge in the hot water. Press and work the cheese with the back of a spoon until it becomes one mass and takes on some stringiness.

3. Remove the cheese from the water and knead lightly with the spoon while it is still in the colander, until the mass becomes smooth. Don't overwork, as that will toughen the mozzarella; you need to have it pliant enough to press out into a rectangle.

4. Lay a sheet of plastic wrap on your work surface, place the mozzarella on top, and spread it by hand into a ⅛-inch-thick rectangle.

5. Sprinkle the pepper evenly over the warm cheese, and then cover with the basil leaves and a thin layer of sliced prosciutto.

6. Using the plastic wrap to help guide the cheese, roll up like a jelly roll into a tight roulade. Wrap with plastic wrap and secure the ends tightly with string. Use your hands to shape the roulade into a nice round cylinder, then wrap again with aluminum foil so that it holds its shape. Refrigerate for a minimum of one hour.

7. To serve, cut in 1-inch slices and place on a plate. Add droplets of olive oil and aceto balsamic in a random pattern around the roulade. Garnish with basil.

Note: You can make this in two batches, forming two roulades, if you find it difficult to work with 1 pound of curds. Aceto balsamico tradizionale di Modena is an expensive commodity, sold in tiny bottles. It has a rich, mellow flavor that is without compare.

PORK AND CORN DUMPLINGS WITH CILANTRO CREAM SAUCE

This is a fusion recipe if there ever was one—Chinese dim sum filled with pork and sweet corn and served with a creamy, French-style sauce whose defining ingredients are cilantro, chiles, and ginger. This is pure CIA, a training ground for American chefs who will want to appeal to eclectic American palates and will rely on their classical, mostly French training to achieve this.

SERVES 6

FOR THE DUMPLINGS:

1½ cups fresh or frozen corn kernels

3 green onions, white and light green parts, minced

3 garlic cloves, finely minced

1 pound ground pork

1 egg

1½ tablespoons oyster sauce

1 tablespoon dry sherry

1 tablespoon dark sesame oil

1½ teaspoons Asian chili sauce

36 round wonton skins

1 teaspoon cornstarch, plus additional as needed for the parchment

2 tablespoons water

FOR THE SAUCE:

1½ cups chopped fresh cilantro

1½ tablespoons chopped fresh ginger

2 garlic cloves

1 to 3 serrano chiles, or to taste, stemmed

1½ teaspoons cornstarch

1¼ cups Chicken Stock (page 142)

1 cup heavy cream

½ teaspoon salt, or to taste

FOR COOKING THE DUMPLINGS:

3 tablespoons peanut oil per batch

¾ cup water

1. Make the dumplings. Combine 1 cup of the corn, the green onions, garlic, ground pork, egg, oyster sauce, sherry, sesame oil, and chili sauce and mix together thoroughly.

2. Place 2 teaspoons of the filling in the center of each wonton skin. Dissolve the cornstarch in the water and moisten the edges of the wrapper with your finger. Fold over the wonton and pinch together, then bring the outside corners toward each other and crimp together like a tortellini, with the sealed side on top and the folded side on the bottom. Press down lightly so the bottom of the dumpling is flat. Line a sheet tray with parchment and dust with cornstarch. Place the wontons on the parchment and refrigerate.

3. Make the sauce. Place the cilantro, ginger, garlic, serranos, cornstarch, and chicken stock in a blender and process until completely liquefied. Transfer to a saucepan, stir in the cream and salt, and blend well. Bring to a boil, stirring frequently, and boil until thick enough to coat the back of a spoon (nappé). Remove from the heat and set aside while you cook the dumplings.

4. Cook the dumplings. Heat the oil over high heat in a large sauté pan until almost smoking. Add the dumplings—as many as will fit without crowding the pan—and fry until the bottoms turn golden brown, about 2 minutes.

Add ¾ cup water, cover the pan, reduce the heat to medium, and cook the dumplings until firm to the touch, about 2 minutes. Transfer to a serving dish and keep warm while you repeatwith the remaining dumplings.

5. Serve the dumplings with the sauce, garnishing with the remaining corn.

CRAB AND COD CAKES

I'd never really thought about combining crab and cod in a crab cake, but it's a great idea, and sure does keep the cost of the dish under control. Just make sure that you remove all of the bones once the cod is cooked. They're easy to feel and pull out.

SERVES 6

Butter as needed for the pan

Water as needed

½ pound fresh cod

½ cup mayonnaise, or as needed

1 scallion, thinly sliced

1½ teaspoons Dijon mustard

½ teaspoon Old Bay seasoning, or to taste

Pinch of cayenne

½ teaspoon Worcestershire sauce

¼ teaspoon Tabasco

4 ounces bacon (about 2 strips), cut in fine dice

2 stalks celery, minced

½ pound crabmeat, picked over for shells

2 tablespoons beaten egg

Salt to taste

½ cup crumbled Ritz crackers

½ to 1 cup all-purpose flour, as needed for dredging

2 eggs beaten with ½ cup milk, for breading

Vegetable oil as needed for pan-frying

1 to 2 cups panko, as needed for breading

1. Preheat the oven to 325°F. Generously butter a baking dish large enough to accommodate the fish in one layer. Season the cod, place in the buttered baking dish, add ¼ cup water, and place in the oven. Cook until opaque and firm, about 10 minutes. Remove from the heat and allow to cool.

2. Meanwhile, mix together the mayonnaise, scallions, mustard, Old Bay seasoning, cayenne, Worcestershire, and Tabasco. Set aside in the refrigerator.

3. When the cod is cool enough to handle, remove any bones and, using your fingers, flake into 1/2-inch pieces. Set aside.

4. Heat a sauté pan over medium heat and add the bacon. Cook until almost completely crisp, and pour off most of the fat from the pan. Add the celery and continue to cook until the celery is tender, about 5 minutes. Transfer to a strainer and allow to drain.

5. Combine the mayonnaise mixture, cod, bacon mixture, crab meat, egg, salt, and crumbled crackers in a bowl. Mix well. If the mixture is too moist, add more cracker crumbs. If it is too dry, add more mayonnaise. Taste and adjust seasoning. Shape 2-ounce rounds and place on a sheet tray.

What the recipe doesn't know

` The size of your pan. This will impact the amount of oil you'll need for frying the crab cakes.

` How moist or dry your crab and cod mixture will be when you combine the ingredients. You may need to add more crumbled crackers or more mayonnaise.

6. Heat the oil over medium-high heat in a large sauté pan. Meanwhile, dredge the crab cakes in the flour, dip in the egg-milk mixture, and coat with the panko. When the oil is hot, pan-fry until golden, flipping the crab cakes halfway through. Do not crowd the pan (cook in batches if necessary). Drain briefly on a rack, and serve with Mustard Tartar Sauce (page 146), garnished with Warm Coleslaw (page 226) and Corn Bread (page 196).

STEAMED MUSSELS WITH CHORIZO, PEPPERS, AND TOMATOES

Although we made this marvelous, spicy mussel dish as an appetizer, I would gladly serve it as a main dish.

SERVES 6 AS AN APPETIZER (4 AS A MAIN DISH)

60 mussels

¾ pound chorizo

¼ cup olive oil

¼ cup minced garlic

¼ cup minced shallots

1 red bell pepper, cut in medium dice

1 yellow bell pepper, cut in medium dice

1 quart Chicken Stock (page 142)

4 plum tomatoes, cut in medium dice

¼ cup chopped Italian parsley

¼ cup chopped cilantro

¼ cup (½ stick) butter

1 teaspoons salt, or to taste

½ teaspoon freshly ground pepper, or to taste

1. Scrub the mussels, debeard, and discard any that are cracked or opened. Rinse several times and set aside.

2. Fill a saucepan with water and heat to just below a simmer (180°F). Add the chorizo and poach for 6 minutes. Shock in ice water and drain. Cut the sausages in half lengthwise, and then cut into ⅛-inch-thick half-moon-shaped slices. Set aside.

3. Heat a large, heavy, lidded frying pan or a Dutch oven over medium heat and add the oil, garlic, shallots, peppers, and sausages. Cook gently without browning, until the vegetables are tender, about 8 minutes.

4. Add the mussels and the stock and bring to a boil. Cover tightly and steam until they open wide, stirring once if necessary, about 5 minutes. Remove the lid and discard any unopened mussels.

5. With a slotted spoon, distribute the mussels, vegetables, and chorizo evenly among soup bowls. Sprinkle with the tomatoes and herbs, and top with a dollop of butter.

6. Taste and adjust the seasonings in the broth, and pour over the mussels. Serve hot, with crusty country bread.

CHICKEN BROTH

The difference between a stock and a broth, I learned at the CIA, is that a broth is made with meat and bones, and a stock with bones only. A broth will not simmer as long as a stock, because you only simmer the broth until the meat is done. If you have an older hen, this will take a couple of hours; if you're using a younger chicken, 1 hour will suffice. It's important to remove excess fat from your chicken before you begin the broth. This is the broth to make for chicken noodle soup or the Amish-Style Chicken and Corn Soup on page 163.

MAKES 4 QUARTS

- 1 stewing hen, about 5 pounds, rinsed and disjointed
- 6 quarts cold water
- Salt to taste
- 1 medium onion, chopped
- 1 medium carrot, chopped
- 1½ stalks celery, chopped
- ½ pound tomatoes, chopped (optional but recommended)
- 1 bay leaf
- A few sprigs each parsley and thyme
- 6 peppercorns
- Freshly ground pepper to taste

1. Remove any excess fat from the stewing hen. Place in a stockpot and cover with cold water. Add salt to taste. Bring slowly to a simmer, stirring from time to time and removing

What the recipe doesn't know

` If you were able to get a hen. If not, use a chicken, and only simmer for an hour, or until done.

the scum that rises to the top. Simmer gently, uncovered, for 2 hours (1 hour for a younger chicken).

2. Add the onions, carrots, celery, and tomatoes. Continue to simmer for 30 minutes, skimming regularly and tasting from time to time. Adjust seasoning as necessary.

3. Add the bay leaf, parsley and thyme sprigs, and peppercorns, and simmer for another 30 minutes.

4. Using tongs, carefully remove the poultry from the broth and set aside in a bowl. Cover the bowl so the meat doesn't dry out. Carefully strain the stock through a chinois or strainer lined with a coffee filter or cheesecloth. Degrease the broth by skimming away any fat that remains with a serving spoon, or chill the broth and lift off fat later.

5. Taste, adjust seasoning, and serve with the garnishes of your choice.

AMISH-STYLE CHICKEN AND CORN SOUP

This is basically a chicken-noodle soup, with spaetzle (page 223) standing in for noodles. The CIA categorizes this soup as an ethnic soup, a group that would also include gumbo and the Santa Fe Chili Soup on page 168. The saffron and the spaetzle garnish distinguish this from other farmhouse chicken and vegetable soups. The chef's demonstration of making the spaetzle with the special tool called a spaetzler was one of the high points of that day in the kitchen for me, as I'd never made spaetzle and didn't even know that a special tool for it existed (I bought one at the CIA store that very day). If you happen to have some leftover chicken and some chicken stock in your refrigerator or freezer, this is a great way to use it up.

SERVES 6 TO 8

FOR THE SOUP BASE:

1 stewing hen, quartered

1 bay leaf

A few sprigs each parsley and thyme (or ½ teaspoon dried thyme)

½ teaspoon cracked black peppercorns

2½ quarts Chicken Stock (page 142) or water

½ cup finely chopped onion

¼ cup finely chopped carrot

¼ cup finely chopped celery

2 teaspoons saffron threads, crushed

1 teaspoon salt, or to taste

½ teaspoon freshly ground pepper, or to taste

3 cups corn kernels

3 cups diced celery

FOR THE GARNISH:

3 cups diced chicken meat (reserved from the stewing hen)

½ cup chopped fresh parsley

1 recipe cooked Spaetzle (page 223), or 6 ounces soup pasta, cooked

1. Combine the hen, sachet d'épices, and stock in a large, heavy soup pot or Dutch oven and bring to a boil. Reduce the heat, cover partially, and simmer gently for 1½ hours (45 minutes for a chicken), skimming as necessary.

2. Add the chopped onions, carrots, the 2 tablespoons finely chopped celery, and the saffron, and simmer for an additional ½ hour.

(continued)

3. Remove the chicken and let stand in a bowl until it is cool enough to handle. Remove the meat from the bones, dice, and set aside.

4. Degrease and strain the broth. If you aren't serving the soup right away, chill and before reheating, lift the layer of fat from the surface and discard. Reheat and season to taste with salt and pepper.

5. Before serving, bring the soup to a simmer, add the diced celery and corn, and simmer 10 minutes, or until the vegetables are tender. Add the garnishes to the soup, or distribute them between 6 bowls, spoon on the soup, and serve.

Note: You can make the spaetzle while the soup is simmering, drain it, and spread it on a half-sheet or finish it in a sauté pan with butter, and hold until you're ready to serve the soup.

What the recipe doesn't know

Ingredients you may have on hand. Don't feel that you have to garnish this with corn and celery. If you have squash, broccoli, or carrots on hand but not the corn or celery, use them. It's a chicken noodle soup with vegetables, after all. No spaetzle or you don't want to make it? Use noodles. Cook the vegetables separately and add them at the last minute, or simmer them in the soup just until tender and serve.

Whether you can find a hen. If not, use a younger chicken, make chicken broth (page 162), and use the chicken meat for the soup.

CHICKEN CONSOMMÉ

Years ago, a caterer friend showed me how to clarify a consommé. It seemed complicated then, and it must have intimidated me, as I never again attempted to do it. But when I observed the process at Boot Camp it struck me as magical and beautiful to watch, rather than complicated or intimidating. The process is called "building a raft," and students at the CIA must master it during their first three weeks of cooking. That we also did this was almost as miraculous as the raft itself.

MAKES 2 QUARTS, SERVING 10

5 egg whites
1¼ pounds ground chicken thigh
1 large tomato, chopped
1 teaspoon kosher salt, or to taste
¾ cup finely chopped onion
⅓ cup finely chopped leek, white part only
⅔ cup finely chopped celery
6 parsley stems, chopped
1 bay leaf
A few sprigs of thyme
½ garlic clove
1 allspice berry
6 peppercorns
2½ quarts cold Chicken Stock (page 142)
For garnish, cooked fresh or thawed frozen peas and Tomato Concassé (page 148) to taste, or other cooked finely diced vegetables of your choice, such as carrots and turnips

1. In a medium or large mixing bowl, combine the egg whites and ground chicken and beat together vigorously. Add the tomato and a gener-

ous amount of salt, and continue to beat vigorously (the agitation plus the salt and the acid in the tomato will denature the protein, which is essential). Add the onions, leeks, celery, parsley stems, bay leaf, thyme sprigs, garlic, allspice berry, and peppercorns. Continue to stir vigorously for another minute or two. Stir into the soup, and then bring the mixture to a boil over high heat, stirring frequently so the meat doesn't sink to the bottom of the pot and burn.

2. Once the stock comes to a boil, do not stir anymore, or the ingredients will be redispersed through the stock. Move the pot slightly off-center on the burner, so that the stock only boils on one side; allow it to boil over the raft mixture, pushing it to one side. Turn the heat to low and taste your stock. Add salt as needed ("Taste the stock now and add salt," noted Chef Hinnerk, "so that your soup will be well seasoned. If you do it later, it will just taste salty.")

3. Simmer the raft in the stock for 45 minutes to 1½ hours, until the soup is perfectly clear and a vivid, intense flavor has been achieved.

4. Strain the soup. This is tricky, because you don't want to break the raft, ruining the results of all your hard work. There are two ways to do this: you can turn off the heat and wait ten

BUILDING A RAFT AND CLARIFYING A CONSOMMÉ

The principle behind the raft is that raw, denatured proteins attract cooked proteins. Egg whites, ground meat, and white mirepoix—the "raft mixture"—are mixed in a bowl, added to the stock, and brought to a boil. The ingredients you use in your raft will impact the flavor of the consommé. For the chicken consommé our chefs used ground chicken—the thigh, which has more flavor but also more color (which you may not want). You stir the mixture as the stock comes to a boil, and as you stir, the proteins in the broth fix onto the raft mixture. When the stock comes to a boil the raft floats to the surface. Then you reduce the heat and simmer the mixture for 10 minutes, at which point the liquid is miraculously clear; all of the proteins in the broth have coagulated onto the raft. You let the raft simmer for about an hour so that the flavors of the consommé intensify, and then you let it sit. You can remove the raft at this point, let it settle to the bottom itself (it will after about 10 minutes), or push it down. Then you strain the soup, which you have to do carefully so that the particles don't go back into the consommé.

minutes for the raft to sink, and then carefully ladle the consommé through a fine-mesh sieve or strainer lined with cheesecloth or a coffee filter, being very careful not to agitate the raft. Or you can carefully push the raft down to the bottom of the pot with the bowl of a ladle and ladle out the consommé. Use paper towels to blot the fat from the surface of the consommé, then carefully strain, pouring the soup around the edges of the strainer so that you don't dump it on top of itself and release the solids back into the soup.

5. Return your beautifully clear consommé to the soup pot and reheat. Taste and adjust salt. Serve at once, garnishing each bowl with bright green peas and tomato concassé.

CREAM OF MUSHROOM SOUP

This is a classic cream soup or velouté, and a formula you can use with other vegetables such as carrots, broccoli, spinach, or cauliflower. The French term for the method is singer (singe)— you sweat the mushrooms in butter, and then add flour, and a velouté is created around the mushrooms. At the Culinary Institute they use a blender to puree the soup. I asked the chef if an immersion blender or a food processor would work, and he insisted that you could only get the proper degree of velvety smoothness with a blender.

SERVES 6 TO 8

6 tablespoons (¾ stick) butter

½ large onion, finely diced

2 stalks celery, finely diced

2 pounds mushrooms, cleaned and sliced

¾ cup all-purpose flour

2½ quarts Chicken Stock (page 142)

1 sachet d'épices containing a bay leaf, a few sprigs each parsley and thyme (or ½ teaspoon dried thyme), and ½ teaspoon cracked black peppercorns, all tied into a piece of cheesecloth

1 teaspoon salt, or to taste

½ teaspoon freshly ground pepper, or to taste

1 cup heavy cream

FOR THE GARNISH:

2 tablespoons butter

3 ounces mushrooms, sliced

1 teaspoon salt, or to taste

½ teaspoon freshly ground pepper, or to taste

1. Heat the butter over medium heat in a large, heavy soup pot or Dutch oven and add the onions, celery, and mushrooms. Cook until tender but not browned, stirring often, about 5 minutes. Add the flour and stir together for a few minutes.

2. Stir the roux and vegetables constantly while you add the stock. Add the sachet d'épices, salt, and pepper, and bring slowly to a boil, taking care to stir often so the bottom doesn't scorch. Reduce the heat to low, cover, and simmer until the vegetables are very tender and fragrant, 20 to 30 minutes. Remove the sachet.

3. Make the garnish while the soup is simmering. Heat a large, heavy sauté pan over high heat and add the butter. Turn the heat down slightly and add the mushrooms. Brown the mushrooms, about 5 to 8 minutes, season with salt and pepper, and set aside.

4. Puree the soup in batches in a blender until very smooth. Return to the soup pot and stir in the cream. Bring back to a simmer; taste and adjust seasonings.

5. Serve the soup with the garnish stirred in, or with a spoonful of the sautéed mushrooms placed in the middle of each bowl.

SANTA FE CHILI SOUP

This soupy chili can be hot or mild, depending on your taste. All you need to do is add more chili, cayenne, or Tabasco to get a hotter version than the one we did at Boot Camp.

SERVES 6 TO 8

2 tablespoons canola or vegetable oil

1 large onion, diced small

1 pound boneless beef bottom round roast, cut in ¼-inch cubes

1 tablespoon ground cumin

1½ teaspoons chili powder

2 garlic cloves, mashed to a paste with a pinch of salt in a mortar and pestle

½ cup all-purpose flour

¼ cup tomato puree

1½ quarts Brown Veal Stock (page 140)

2 teaspoons salt, or to taste

2 plum tomatoes, peeled, seeded, and finely chopped

½ teaspoon cayenne, or to taste

½ teaspoon crushed red pepper, or to taste

½ teaspoon Tabasco sauce, or to taste

1. Heat the pot over medium-high heat in a large, heavy soup pot or Dutch oven, add the oil, and when it is hot, add the onions. Sauté until translucent, about 5 minutes.

2. Add the beef, cumin, and chili powder, and brown the meat lightly on all sides, about 10 minutes. Turn the heat down to medium.

3. Add the garlic and sauté for about 30 seconds, until fragrant. Stir in the flour and mix well with the juices and fats in the pan to form a roux. Cook the roux for 3 minutes, stirring, for a few minutes, until it smells fragrant, and stir in the tomato puree and brown stock. Bring to a simmer, add about a teaspoon of salt, cover and simmer until the meat is tender, about 1 to 1½ hours. Add the chopped tomatoes and simmer 10 minutes longer. Skim off the fat from the top.

4. Add cayenne, crushed red pepper, Tabasco, and salt to taste. Serve, or refrigerate overnight and serve the following day, skimming off more fat first.

What the recipe doesn't know

Whether you have brown stock. You can make this with canned beef broth or even water if you wish.

SHRIMP BISQUE

When I went to my first Culinary Boot Camp we made lobster bisque, and I was happy to be part of the team that made it. However, I will probably never make it again. If I'm going to buy a lobster, I'll eat the lobster. By the time I went to Boot Camp the second time the instructors had changed the curriculum and we made shrimp bisque. It's a lot easier to make, and I would make this one at home.

MAKES 2 QUARTS

1 pound medium shrimp

6 tablespoons (¾ stick) butter

1 medium onion, minced

1 garlic clove, minced

1½ teaspoons paprika

2¼ teaspoons tomato paste

¼ cup brandy

¾ cup all-purpose flour

2 quarts Fish Stock (page 143), plus more as needed

1 teaspoon salt, or to taste

1½ cups cream

2 tablespoons dry sherry, or to taste

Old Bay seasoning, or to taste

Tabasco sauce, or to taste

Worcestershire sauce, or to taste

1. Peel and devein half the shrimp, and set aside in a covered bowl in the refrigerator. Leave the shells on the remaining half pound of shrimp and chop coarsely.

2. Heat a heavy soup pot or Dutch oven over medium-high heat and add the butter. When it foams, add the onion and chopped shrimp in their shells, and sauté until the shrimp is pink and the onion is tender, about 5 minutes. Stir in the garlic and cook until fragrant, stirring, about 30 seconds. Turn the heat down slightly, add the paprika and tomato paste, and cook until the tomato paste begins to brown and smell sweet and fragrant, 2 to 3 minutes.

3. Add the brandy to the pot and stir with a wooden spoon to deglaze. Stir in the flour and cook, stirring constantly, until you have a blond roux. Add the fish stock, stirring vigorously to incorporate the roux. Add salt to taste. Bring to a simmer, stirring often and taking care that the mixture doesn't sink and scorch on the bottom of the pot. Simmer, stirring frequently, for 45 minutes.

4. Transfer the soup, in batches, to a blender and blend, shells and all, until smooth. Strain the mixture, pressing all of the fragrant liquid through, and return to the pot. If the mixture is too thick, thin with more stock.

5. Heat the heavy cream and stir into the soup.

6. Dice the peeled, deveined shrimp that you set aside, and sauté in butter until opaque. Stir into the soup, along with the sherry, Old Bay seasoning, Tabasco sauce, Worcestershire sauce, and additional salt to taste. Taste, adjust seasonings, and serve.

Entrées

POACHED CHICKEN BREAST WITH TARRAGON SAUCE

A poached chicken breast can be a pretty plain item until it's sauced with this rich, velvety tarragon sauce, which is nothing more than a velouté enriched with cream and seasoned with fresh tarragon. You can poach the chicken ahead and hold it in the poaching liquid (be sure to cover it so it doesn't dry out). If you're making the sauce right away, make sure to cover the chicken with plastic wrap.

SERVES 6

4 tablespoons (½ stick) butter

2 shallots, minced

6 boneless, skinless chicken breasts

½ cup Chicken Stock (page 142)

¾ cup dry white wine, such as Sauvignon Blanc

A few peppercorns (optional)

2 cups Chicken Velouté (page 144)

2 teaspoons chopped fresh tarragon

⅓ cup heavy cream

Salt and freshly ground black pepper to taste

1. Preheat the oven to 350°F. Butter a shallow ovenproof pan generously and sprinkle with the shallots. Add the chicken breasts, the stock, and the wine and bring to a gentle simmer on top of the stove. Add a few peppercorns to the broth if you wish. Cover with parchment paper and place in the oven.

2. Poach in the oven until the chicken breasts are cooked through, about 15 minutes. Remove from the oven and transfer the chicken breasts to a platter or pan. Cover tightly with plastic wrap and keep warm.

3. Strain the poaching liquid into a saucepan and reduce to about ¼ cup. Add the velouté and tarragon and bring to a simmer. Add the cream, season with salt and pepper, heat through, and serve over the chicken breasts.

Served with Haricots Verts (page 208) and Mashed Potatoes and Turnips (page 212)

Served with Potato Puree (page 215) and Tournéed Zucchini and Carrots (page 222)

BRAISED LAMB SHANKS

This was the only lamb dish we made, a perfect way to put our lessons about braising and stewing to work. Chef John showed us how to "block" a lamb shank. That's what they do in restaurants to make the shank nice and even at both ends. They cut the long, bare bone down and cut away the rounded end. In Chef Hinnerk's class, the shanks came to us unblocked, and he had to send them back a couple of times to the fabrication room so they could saw off the elbows and the ends with a band saw. We browned these bones and threw them into the simmering braise, to add flavor to the sauce. Braised lamb shanks should be fork tender and the sauce rich, thick, and flavorful.

SERVES 6

6 lamb shanks, well trimmed
Salt and freshly ground black pepper to taste
Vegetable oil as needed
1 medium onion, finely chopped
1 medium carrot, finely chopped
1 stalk celery, finely chopped
2 garlic cloves, minced
2 tablespoons tomato paste
1¼ cups dry white wine
⅓ cup all-purpose flour (optional: see sidebar)
1 quart Brown Veal Stock (page 140), plus more as needed, heated
3 to 4 sprigs parsley
½ teaspoon dried thyme
½ teaspoon cracked black peppercorns
If thickening with a slurry: 1 tablespoon cornstarch dissolved in 2 tablespoons water

THICKENING THE SAUCE: ROUX OR SLURRY

You have two choices here for thickening the sauce. You can make a roux, as directed, or if you don't want to do that, you can thicken the sauce at the end with a cornstarch slurry, which is what they usually do in restaurants. A roux will give you a more velvety texture, but a slurry is simpler, and the intensely flavored slurry-thickened sauce that Chef Hinnerk instructed me to make was fine to my taste.

1. Season the lamb generously with salt and pepper. Heat a large Dutch oven or casserole over medium-high heat, add enough oil to film the bottom, and when it shimmers, sear the lamb shanks to a deep brown on all sides, in batches if necessary to avoid crowding the pan. Remove from the oil and transfer to a pan or bowl. Set aside.

2. Pour off all but a thin film of the fat from the pot. Add the onions, carrots, and celery and cook, stirring, until caramelized. Turn the heat down to medium low, add the garlic, stir together for about half a minute, and stir in the tomato paste. Stir until the tomato paste turns a darker color and gives off a sweet aroma, about 1 minute. Add the white wine and stir and scrape the bottom of the pan with a wooden spoon to deglaze. Cook until the wine reduces by about half.

3. Add the flour (if using) to the mixture and cook, stirring, for several minutes, until you have achieved a blond roux. Add the brown stock and bring to a boil, stirring vigorously. Reduce slightly, then return the lamb shanks to the pot, along with the parsley, thyme, pepper

(continued)

corns, and salt to taste. Turn the heat to low, cover the pan, and braise the lamb until it is fork tender, about 1 1/2 hours (you can also transfer the pot to a 275°F oven and braise it there).

4. When the meat is tender, remove the lamb shanks from the sauce, cover with plastic so they won't dry out, and keep warm. Strain the sauce, degrease it, and return to the pot. Adjust consistency, reducing it if it is too watery or adding a little stock if it is too thick. If you have not used a roux, bring the sauce to a simmer, stir the slurry, and add it to the sauce. Stir until the sauce thickens and remove from the heat. Taste and add salt and pepper if desired. Return the lamb shanks to the sauce, stir together, and serve.

Note: If you are having your lamb shanks blocked by your butcher, ask him to give you

What the recipe doesn't know

` The size of your pot. This will impact the amount of oil you will need to brown your lamb shanks, as well as the amount of stock you'll need to barely cover them. You will probably have to brown the shanks in batches so that you don't crowd the pan.

` The type of stock you have on hand. If you don't have access to brown veal stock, use canned or boxed beef stock.

the trimmings. Roast them in a 425°F oven until brown, and add them to the pot. They will intensify the flavor of the sauce. When the shanks are done, remove the trimmings from the broth and discard.

YANKEE POT ROAST

This classic pot roast can be cooked on top of the stove or in the oven in a mixture of reduced red wine and brown veal stock. The resulting gravy is dark and rich. Make it a day ahead for even better results, and reheat the meat in the gravy.

SERVES 6

2½ pounds beef chuck, top butt, or brisket

Salt and freshly ground pepper to taste

Vegetable oil as needed

1 medium onion, chopped

½ medium or 1 small carrot, chopped

½ stalk celery, chopped

4 tablespoons tomato paste

1 cup red wine

1 quart Brown Veal Stock (page 140), plus more as needed

3 or 4 parsley sprigs

½ teaspoon dried thyme

½ teaspoon cracked black peppercorns

½ cup Brown Roux (page 24) or 1 tablespoon cornstarch dissolved in 2 tablespoons water

1. Trim the beef, blot it dry, and season generously with salt and pepper. Heat a large Dutch oven or heavy lidded pan over medium-high heat and add a thin film of oil. Sear the beef on

' The size of your meat. The pan should be slightly larger but
not too much larger.

' The size of your pot. This will determine the amount of
stock you will need. It should barely cover the meat.

' The degree to which your stock is seasoned. This will determine how much additional salt you'll need.

You can also cook the roast in a 350° oven.
Turn it over from time to time so that it is
evenly moistened by the stock.

4. Remove the beef from the stock and keep
warm. Strain the stock into a saucepan, bring
to a boil, and reduce by about half. Taste and
adjust seasonings. Add the roux or slurry and
simmer another 20 minutes, until you have a
smooth, thick gravy.

5. Slice the beef across the grain and serve
with the sauce.

all sides to a dark brown, using tongs to turn the
meat and hold it up so you can sear the ends.
Transfer to a pan and cover to keep warm.

2 Turn down the heat slightly and add the
onions, carrots, and celery. Cook, stirring, until
golden brown, about 6 to 8 minutes. Add the
tomato paste and cook until it turns a deeper
color and gives off a sweet aroma, about 1 to 2
minutes.

3. Add the red wine and stir and scrape the
bottom of the pan with a wooden spoon to
deglaze. Boil the wine until there is just a small
amount left in the pot, and stir in the bay leaf,
parsley and thyme, and peppercorns. Return
the beef to the pan, along with any juices it
may have released. Add enough stock to barely
cover the meat, and bring to a gentle simmer.
Taste the stock and add salt as needed, keeping
in mind that you will be reducing it later. Cover
the pan, turn the heat to low, and braise the
beef until it is fork tender, about 2 to 3 hours.

Variation: **SWISS STEAK**

Some of the Boot Camp instructors felt strongly
that there wasn't enough time to make a proper
pot roast in the 3-hour window we had in the
kitchen (although, especially during my second
Boot Camp, this window was usually stretched
by about a half hour). So they introduced the
Swiss Steak recipe, which is like a portion-sized
pot roast. Chef Hinnerk wouldn't hear of this
and demonstrated the pot roast, which turned
out fine. But if you do want to make Swiss Steak
instead (I confess I had not even heard the name
of that dish since boarding school), instead of using a single large piece of beef, use six 4-ounce
portions of beef chuck, top butt, or brisket. Proceed with the above recipe, adjusting the cooking time for the smaller cuts of meat. Cook the
dish on top of the stove.

RAINBOW BEEF

This is a typical Chinese stir-fry, with sweet and pungent flavors and lots of colors. We made it on the day Chef John covered stir frying, pan frying, and deep frying. We were all working away on our assignments when the chef yelled, "Demo!" and we stopped to watch him cutting up the flank steak. This was a revelation to me. He cut the strips not only across the grain but on the diagonal, angling the knife to get very thin, tender slices that would stir-fry to medium-rare in just minutes. Make sure you cut your pepper julienne very thin, so that they cook quickly.

SERVES 4 AS A MAIN DISH, 6 IF PART OF A LARGER CHINESE MEAL

1 pound flank steak

1 egg

2 tablespoons cornstarch

¼ cup oyster sauce

1 tablespoon hot bean paste

2 tablespoons light soy sauce

½ teaspoon freshly ground black pepper

½ teaspoon sugar

1 tablespoon sesame oil

¼ cup vegetable or peanut oil

1½ teaspoons minced ginger

1½ teaspoons minced garlic

1 tablespoon chopped scallion

1 green pepper, seeds and membranes removed, cut in julienne

1 red pepper, seeds and membranes removed, cut in julienne

1 yellow pepper, seeds and membranes removed, cut in julienne

1. Slice the steak across the grain, with the knife slanted at a 45-degree angle, into thin 1-by-3-inch strips. Beat the egg in a medium bowl, whisk in the cornstarch, and mix with the beef.

2. Mix together the oyster sauce, hot bean paste, soy sauce, pepper, sugar, and sesame oil and set aside.

3. Heat a wok or large sauté pan over medium-high heat and add the oil. As soon as it coats the surface of the pan and feels hot when you hold your hand above it, add the ginger, garlic, and scallions. Sauté for a few seconds, only until aromatic, and add the beef. Stir-fry for about 2 to 3 minutes, until medium-rare. Add the peppers and stir-fry for a couple of minutes, just until they begin to soften. Stir in the sauce mixture and stir-fry until heated through, about 1 minute. Serve with rice.

Note I have substituted miso paste and a couple of pinches of cayenne when I couldn't find hot bean paste. I have also made the dish with hoisin sauce instead of black bean sauce. It was excellent both ways.

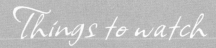

Things to watch

` Don't burn the garlic and ginger.

Served with Steamed Rice (page 222)

Served with Broccoli Rabe with Garlic and Oil (page 194)

PAN-FRIED BREAST OF CHICKEN WITH PROSCIUTTO AND MOZZARELLA

Prosciutto and mozzarella make a classic stuffing for chicken breasts. All you need to do to make the pocket is cut a horizontal slit in the middle. Once stuffed, the chicken breasts are lightly breaded and pan-fried.

SERVES 6

FOR THE CHICKEN BREASTS:

6 boneless, skinless chicken breasts

6 slices prosciutto

6 slices mozzarella

¼ teaspoon chopped fresh basil

¼ teaspoon chopped fresh marjoram

¼ teaspoon chopped fresh thyme

¼ teaspoon chopped fresh parsley

5 cloves garlic, minced

½ teaspoon salt, or to taste

¼ teaspoon freshly ground black pepper, or to taste

Vegetable oil or olive oil as needed (about ⅓ to ½ cup)

FOR THE BREADING MIXTURE:

2 eggs

¼ cup milk

½ cup flour, as needed

1 cup fresh or dry bread crumbs, as needed

FOR THE SAUCE:

2 tablespoons minced shallots

2 tablespoons olive oil

½ cup dry white wine, such as Sauvignon Blanc

1 cup Chicken Stock (page 142)

Pinch each chopped fresh basil, marjoram, thyme, and parsley

¼ cup (½ stick) butter

½ teaspoon cornstarch dissolved in 1 teaspoon water, if necessary

1. Place a chicken breast on a cutting board. Hold your knife parallel to the board and cut a horizontal slit in the middle of each breast, making sure that you don't cut through the other edges of the chicken breast. Repeat with the remaining chicken breasts. Wrap each piece of mozzarella in a slice of prosciutto, and stuff into pockets in the chicken breasts.

2. Mix the herbs and garlic together in a large bowl and toss the chicken breasts in the mixture. Season with salt and pepper.

3. Coat the chicken breasts with the breading mixture using the standard breading procedure described on page 44. Set aside in a single layer on a sheet pan in the refrigerator if not cooking right away.

4. Make the sauce. Heat the oil in a wide, heavy saucepan over medium-high heat and add the shallots. Sauté until translucent, 3 to 5 minutes, and add the white wine. Stir and scrape the bottom of the pan with a wooden spoon to deglaze and bring to a boil. Boil until the wine has reduced by half, about 5 minutes, and add the stock, herbs, and butter. Bring to a boil and reduce until the sauce is thick. If you wish, thicken further by stirring in the dissolved cornstarch, and remove from the heat. Season to taste with salt and pepper.

(continued)

5. Cook the chicken breasts. Preheat the oven to 350°F. Heat a large, heavy sauté pan over medium-high heat and add the oil. When it ripples, add the chicken breasts. Do not crowd the pan; cook in batches if necessary. When the chicken breasts are dark golden brown on the first side, after about 3 to 5 minutes, turn and cook on the other side until nicely browned. Transfer the pan to the oven for about 10 minutes to finish.

6. Drain the chicken breasts briefly on paper towels. Spoon some sauce onto each plate, top with a chicken breast, and serve.

Things to watch

` Make sure the oil is hot enough, but don't allow it to get too hot.

` Don't crowd the pan.

` Cook to color.

PAN-FRIED BUTTERMILK CHICKEN WITH COUNTRY-STYLE GRAVY

This pan-fried chicken is very much like traditional southern deep-fried chicken, but not as much fat is used. The chicken is marinated in a mustardy buttermilk mixture, which gives it a terrific flavor. Make sure the oil is hot enough when you cook the chicken, but also be sure that it isn't so hot that the flour burns, or your gravy will be bitter.

SERVES 6

> 2 cups buttermilk
> ¼ cup Dijon mustard
> 2 tablespoons minced fresh tarragon
> ¾ teaspoon Bell's poultry spice
> 3 fryer chickens, about 4 pounds each, butchered into 8 to 10 pieces each
> ½ teaspoon salt, or to taste
> ¼ teaspoon freshly ground black pepper, or to taste
> 3 cups all-purpose flour for dredging, plus ½ cup for the gravy
> ¾ teaspoon cayenne pepper
> 1 to 2 tablespoons Old Bay seasoning mix, to taste
> Vegetable oil as needed for pan frying
> 3 cups milk

1. Whisk together the buttermilk, mustard, tarragon, and poultry spice in a large bowl. Season the chicken pieces with salt and pepper,

toss well in the buttermilk mixture to coat, cover, and refrigerate for 4 hours or overnight. You can also transfer the chicken and marinade to resealable plastic bags and place them in bowls in the refrigerator.

2. Combine 3 cups flour with the cayenne and Old Bay seasoning. Mix well. Begin heating ½ inch of oil in a large, straight-sided frying pan over medium heat. Preheat the oven to 350°F and arrange racks over 2 sheet pans.

3. Dredge the chicken pieces in the flour and let sit several minutes on sheets of parchment. Dredge the chicken in the flour again. Discard any remaining flour. When the oil in the pan reaches 350°F, add the chicken in a single layer, being careful not to crowd the pan. Pan-fry until the first side is golden brown and crisp, 5 to 6 minutes. Turn over and pan-fry on the other side until golden brown and crisp, 5 to 6 minutes. Drain briefly on absorbent paper, then transfer to the racks and finish in the oven for 10 minutes, or until breast portions have an internal temperature of 170°F and thigh and leg portions have an internal temperature of 180°F. Keep warm while you make the gravy.

4. Strain the fat from the pan. Scrape away and discard any burnt bits of flour that may be adhering to the pan, and return ¼ cup of the strained fat to the pan. Add ½ cup flour and cook, stirring over medium heat, until you have a golden roux, about 5 to 6 minutes. Add the milk to the roux and whisk together well. Bring to a simmer and cook, stirring often and skim-ming as necessary, for 15 to 20 minutes, until there is no longer a floury taste. Season to taste with salt and pepper, transfer to a gravy boat, and serve with the chicken.

Things to watch

` Make sure your oil is hot enough when you add the chicken.

` Discard any bits of burnt flour before making the gravy.

` Cook the chicken until it is a golden brown color; control the temperature of the oil so that the outside of the chicken doesn't burn before the inside is cooked.

DEEP-FRIED FLOUNDER WITH TOMATO COULIS

This was one of my favorite Boot Camp dishes. If it's done properly, so that the batter is crisp and light, it's like a very classy fish and chips. The coulis is a perfect accompaniment.

SERVES 6

FOR THE BEER BATTER:
1 cup all-purpose flour
1½ teaspoons baking powder
1 tablespoon sugar
1 tablespoon salt
¼ teaspoon ground white pepper
1 cup light beer

FOR THE FISH AND GARNISH:
6 flounder fillets, about 5 ounces each
Salt and freshly ground black pepper to taste
1 quart vegetable or peanut oil
All-purpose flour as needed
2 cups Tomato Coulis (page 149)
6 lemon wedges for garnish
Deep-fried parsley sprigs (see sidebar)

1. Make the batter at least 30 minutes before cooking the fish. Sift together the flour, baking powder, sugar, salt, and pepper. Whisk in the beer and stir until smooth. Allow the batter to rest at room temperature for 30 minutes.

Things to watch

` Make sure the oil is at 350°F and that you bring it back up to this temperature between batches.

` Don't crowd the pan.

` The fillets should go directly from the batter to the oil.

` Your tomato coulis should be all ready to go before you begin.

2. Pat the fish fillets dry with paper towels and season with salt and pepper.

3. Begin heating the oil in a deep fryer, a wok or a wide saucepan. When the oil reaches 350°F. it is ready for the fish.

4. Dredge the fillets in flour and shake off the excess. One by one, dip the fillets into the batter and, using tongs, turn over to coat evenly. Using the tongs, transfer from the batter to the hot oil. Do not crowd the pan. The fillets will sink to the bottom, then "swim" to the top of the fryer. Deep-fry until golden brown, flipping the fillets once for even browning. Drain briefly on absorbent paper and serve with Tomato Coulis, with lemon wedges and fried parsley on the side.

DEEP-FRIED PARSLEY SPRIGS

Deep-fried parsley sprigs are a classic garnish and are especially pleasing with fish. The parsley should be fried in fresh oil, very close to serving time. Make sure to dry the sprigs well. Heat about 1 inch of vegetable oil in a frying pan over medium heat to about 350°F. Dip a piece of parsley into the hot oil; it should sizzle. Add the parsley to the oil and fry for 30 to 45 seconds. Remove from the oil using a slotted spoon or spider and drain on paper towels. The sprigs should be a brilliant, almost translucent green, and brittle.

ROAST SIRLOIN OF BEEF WITH JUS LIÉ

When you roast a big piece of sirloin like this, the drippings can be easily turned into a simple sauce.

SERVES 6

Things to watch

` Use a meat thermometer to be sure that you don't overcook the meat.

` Give the meat time to rest before carving.

- 1 3-pound boneless beef sirloin, tied at 1-inch intervals
- ½ teaspoon salt, or to taste
- ¼ teaspoon freshly ground black pepper, or to taste
- Vegetable oil as needed
- ⅓ cup diced onion
- ¼ cup diced carrot
- ¼ cup diced celery
- 2 tablespoons tomato paste
- 2½ cups Brown Veal Stock (page 140)
- 1 teaspoon cornstarch dissolved in 1 tablespoon water

1. Season the meat generously with salt and pepper. Place a rack in a roasting pan and preheat the oven to 350°F.

2. Heat a film of oil over medium-high heat in a large sauté pan and brown the meat on all sides. Transfer to the roasting pan. Add the onions, carrots, and celery to the roasting pan. Insert a thermometer into the meat and place in the oven.

3. Roast until medium-rare (125°F internal temperature), about 1 hour. Remove from the heat, cover loosely with foil, and let stand for 20 minutes while you make the jus.

4. Pour off the excess fat from the pan and add the tomato paste. Place over medium heat on top of the stove and cook the vegetables and tomato sauce, stirring, until caramelized, 3 to 5 minutes. Add the stock and stir and scrape with a wooden spoon to deglaze the bottom of the pan.

5. Stir the cornstarch and water and add to the sauce. Bring to a boil. As soon as the sauce thickens, remove from the heat and strain. Season to taste with salt and pepper.

6. Slice the meat and serve with the jus.

PORK RIBS WITH ASIAN-STYLE BARBECUE SAUCE

Baby back ribs should be grilled slowly over indirect heat. In this recipe they are initially seared over high heat, then moved to low heat and left to cook until done. The fire should occupy only part of the grill bed, and the ribs should be placed on the part of the grill that is not above direct heat. They can also be baked in the oven once they're seared on the grill. This sauce is very sweet; feel free to tone it down a bit if it's too sweet for you.

SERVES 6

FOR THE SAUCE:

2¼ cups hoisin sauce

1 cup plus 2 tablespoons plum sauce

¾ cup oyster sauce

½ cup honey

4½ tablespoons soy sauce

4½ tablespoons dry sherry

2 tablespoons plus ¾ teaspoon Asian chili sauce

4½ teaspoons curry powder (optional)

1⅛ teaspoons five-spice powder (optional)

2 tablespoons plus ¾ teaspoon grated lemon zest

2 tablespoons plus ¾ teaspoon grated orange zest

8 garlic cloves, finely minced

¼ cup finely minced ginger

6 tablespoons toasted sesame seeds

1 heaped cup minced green onions

1 heaped cup chopped fresh cilantro

FOR THE RIBS:

4 slabs pork baby back ribs, each with 8 ribs

1. Combine all of the ingredients for the sauce.

2. Place the rack on your work surface, meaty side down, and with the help of a small, sharp knife, begin to peel away the membrane. Once you've freed about an inch of membrane, grip it firmly and pull the entire membrane away from the rack.

3. Make a hot fire in your grill or preheat the oven to 350°F and set a rack over a baking sheet or pan. Brush the ribs with the sauce and place over the heat to sear them. Turn and sear on the other side. Then push the coals to one side of the grill, or turn off one part of the gas grill, and place the ribs on the part that is not heated. Place a foil pan underneath to catch drips. Cover. Or transfer the ribs to the rack in the baking sheet and cover the pan with foil. Grill or roast for approximately 45 minutes, basting with the barbecue sauce every 10 minutes. The ribs are done when they shrink down on the bone about 1 inch and are easily pierced with a fork.

Served with Boiled or Steamed Potatoes with Parsley (page 191) and Glazed Carrots (page 200)

GRILLED PORK CHOPS WITH POMMERY MUSTARD BEURRE BLANC

I never really thought a pork chop could be fancy until I tasted these. It helps, of course, to begin with top-quality meat; and you must be very careful not to overcook it. It's the mustardy beurre blanc that turns these chops into dinner party material.

SERVES 6

6 pork chops

½ teaspoon salt, or to taste

¼ teaspoon freshly ground black pepper, or to taste

1 teaspoon minced garlic

1 tablespoon Worcestershire sauce

1 tablespoon vegetable oil

1 recipe Pommery Mustard Beurre Blanc (page 147)

1. Season the pork chops generously with salt and pepper. Mix together the garlic, Worcestershire sauce, and vegetable oil and brush the chops with the mixture on both sides.

2. Prepare a medium-hot grill. Preheat the oven to 350°F. Place the chops presentation side down on the grill and grill for 3 to 4 minutes, turning at a 45° angle halfway through to achieve grill marks. Turn the chops over and grill 3 to 4 minutes more. Finish if necessary in the oven, until the internal temperature is 155°F.

3. Serve with Pommery Mustard Beurre Blanc.

Things to watch

`Don't grill the pork chops for too long.

OSSOBUCO ALLA MILANESE

Ossobucco, braised veal shanks, is a classic long-simmering braise. Ideally we should have had an extra hour before lunch for the braising and stewing class, for the meat needs 2 to 2½ hours to become meltingly tender. But we did get to test our skills, and the broth tasted good, though our time was up after the meat had simmered for only 1½ hours.

SERVES 6

Six 2-inch-thick slices veal shank, with the bone in

½ teaspoon salt, or to taste

¼ teaspoon freshly ground black pepper, or to taste

Flour as needed for dredging

Olive oil as needed

⅔ cup diced onion

½ cup diced carrot

½ cup diced celery

1 teaspoon (1 clove) minced garlic

2 tablespoons tomato paste

1 cup dry white wine, such as Sauvignon Blanc

1 Roma tomato, peeled, seeded, and finely chopped

1 quart Brown Veal Stock (page 140), plus more as needed

FOR THE GREMOLATA:

1 garlic clove, minced

2 teaspoons lemon zest

2 tablespoons chopped flat-leaf parsley

2 anchovy fillets, chopped

1. Preheat the oven to 350°F. Season the veal shanks with salt and pepper. Dredge them in flour and shake off the excess.

2. Heat a large, wide, heavy casserole or Dutch oven over medium-high heat and add enough olive oil to film the bottom of the pot. When the oil is hot, add the veal shanks, in batches if necessary, and sear to a deep brown on all sides, about 5 minutes per side. Remove the meat from the pot and transfer to a large pan or bowl. Cover to keep warm.

3. Pour off the fat from the pot, leaving enough to generously film the bottom, and add the onions. Turn the heat to medium and cook, stirring from time to time until golden brown, about 7 to 8 minutes. Add the carrots and celery and cook, stirring, until nicely browned, about 5 minutes. Add the garlic and cook for a minute or two more, until fragrant. Add the tomato paste, lower the heat slightly, and cook

Things to watch

Make sure to simmer the meat long enough, until it is fork tender.

The liquid should not boil, but should be kept at a slow simmer.

until it turns a darker color and gives off a sweet aroma, about 1 minute. Add the white wine and stir and scrape the bottom of the pan with a wooden spoon to deglaze. Bring to a boil and reduce the liquid by half.

4. Stir in the tomato and stock, bring to a boil, stirring, and boil until the mixture has reduced by half, about 10 to 15 minutes.

5. Return the veal to the pot, along with any juices that may have accumulated in the bowl, and bring back to a gentle simmer. The meat should be covered in liquid by two-thirds; add additional stock if necessary. Cover and place in the preheated oven. Braise in the oven until the meat is fork tender, about 2 to 2½ hours. Meanwhile, combine the ingredients in the gremolata.

6. When the veal is fork tender, transfer it from the pot to a serving platter. Cover loosely with foil to keep warm. Degrease the sauce and, if desired, reduce or thin. Taste and adjust seasonings. If the sauce is not thick enough, add a small amount of cornstarch or arrowroot slurry (page 26) and simmer until it thickens slightly.

7. Serve the veal with ¼ cup of the sauce ladled over the top of each serving. Sprinkle on the gremolata and serve. Or you can stir the gremolata into the sauce before you top the meat (I prefer the former).

SAUTÉED FILET MIGNON WITH MIXED CRACKED PEPPERCORNS

This contemporary Steak au Poivre is adapted from a recipe I learned from the California chef Wolfgang Puck. We served it with the Morel and Wild Mushroom Ragoût (page 227).

SERVES 6

> ¼ cup mixed black, white, green, and red peppercorns
>
> 6 filet mignons, about 6 ounces each, trimmed of excess fat
>
> Kosher salt to taste
>
> 2 tablespoons mild-flavored oil such as canola or safflower oil

1. Put the peppercorns in a plastic bag and coarsely crush them with a rolling pin. Or crush them in a mortar and pestle.

2. Put the cracked peppercorns on a plate. One by one, sprinkle both sides of each filet evenly with salt, and then press each side into the peppercorns to coat it. Set aside.

3. Over high heat, heat a heavy skillet or sauté pan large enough to hold the steaks comfortably (cook the steaks in batches if your pan is not big enough). Add the oil and, as soon as it ripples, carefully add the steaks. Cook the steaks undisturbed for 4 minutes, carefully turn them over, and cook 4 minutes more for medium-rare.

4. Remove from the heat and keep warm if not serving right away, or serve at once.

Side Dishes

BASIC RICE PILAF

Pilaf always begins on the top of the stove, usually by sautéing onion and garlic, and then the rice, in a little butter or oil. After the stock is added and the rice is brought to a boil, it can be finished in the oven or on top of the stove. The amount of liquid you use depends entirely on the type of rice called for. Here we're using 1¼ cups liquid for 1 cup of long-grain Carolina rice. You could use 2 cups liquid for slightly softer rice.

SERVES 6

1¾ to 2 cups Chicken Stock (page 142)
1 tablespoon butter or vegetable oil
3 tablespoons diced onion
1 clove garlic, minced
1 cup long-grain Carolina rice
¾ to 1 teaspoon salt, to taste
¼ teaspoon ground white pepper
1 bay leaf
1 thyme sprig

1. Bring the stock to a simmer in a heavy saucepan. If you plan to cook the rice in the oven, preheat the oven to 325°F.

2. Meanwhile, heat the butter or oil over medium heat in a medium-sized, heavy saucepan. Add the onion and garlic and cook, stirring, until the onion is translucent, 3 to 5 minutes. Add the rice and cook, stirring, until coated with oil or butter and heated through. Add the hot stock, salt, pepper, bay leaf, and thyme. Bring to a boil, stir once or twice to make sure the rice is not sticking to the bottom of the pan, reduce the heat, and cover tightly.

3. Place in the preheated oven or leave on the burner over very low heat. Cook until the rice is tender and the liquid is absorbed, 15 to 20 minutes. Remove from the heat and let stand undisturbed for 10 minutes. Remove the lid and cover the pot with a clean dish towel. Replace the lid and let sit for another 5 minutes. Uncover and, using a fork, gently separate the grains of rice and serve.

BOILED OR STEAMED POTATOES WITH PARSLEY

Chef Hinnerk was hilarious when he discussed this recipe with us: "I'm amazed by how many people can mess up boiled potatoes!" And he was right, as both times there were boiled potatoes on our menus, somebody messed them up. Chef Hinnerk is a German who grew up with properly boiled potatoes at just about every meal, so this must have been particularly painful for him.

You could take the time to make little potato balls with a melon baller if you want to for this dish, but who does that anymore? If you want to cut them, you'll retain more of the potato if you simply quarter them. Or you can simply peel them and leave them whole if they're not too big. Place them in a container of water as you work, to avoid discoloration. I like to use a waxy potato for this, such as fingerlings or new potatoes, as they maintain their shape better. You can steam or boil them, then hold them before finishing with butter and parsley.

SERVES 8

- 2 pounds potatoes, peeled and quartered if desired
- ¼ cup butter, at room temperature
- ¼ cup chopped fresh parsley
- 2 teaspoons salt (more or less to taste)
- ¼ teaspoon freshly ground black pepper (more or less to taste)

1. Put the potatoes into a pot and barely cover them with water. Add salt to taste to the water (about 1 tablespoon per gallon of water). Smear some oil along the inside of the pot above the surface of the water. This will prevent the water from boiling over.

2. Cover the pot and bring the water to a boil over high heat. As soon as the water comes to a boil, turn down the heat and boil gently for 20 to 30 minutes, until the potatoes are cooked through but maintain their shape.

3. When the potatoes are done, drain most of the water, leaving about ⅛ of an inch, and replace the lid.

4. Just before serving, add the butter, crank up the heat, and heat the potatoes through. Add the parsley, toss gently, and serve.

Variation: POTATOES WITH SAFFRON AND PARSLEY

Anyone who has eaten in a Parisian bistro has had these simple saffron-hued, boiled potatoes. They're a classic side dish with fish; on our menu they accompanied the Poached Fillet of Sole with White Wine Sauce (page 96).

Make the recipe through step 3. Heat the butter in a large, wide pan and add ¼ teaspoon powdered saffron or crushed saffron threads. Cook gently until the saffron releases its color into the butter, then add the potatoes and only 1 tablespoon parsley and toss to coat evenly. Taste, adjust seasoning, and serve.

BRAISED GREENS

Although I'm not usually a huge fan of long-cooked greens, there is a good reason for cooking them this way. The long cooking can liberate nutrients that aren't otherwise accessible. And with long cooking you get a rich-tasting, savory broth that is like a sauce. You could use a number of seasonal greens for this dish, including mustard greens, beet greens, collard greens, Swiss chard, or kale. In the traditional southern version, the greens would be cooked for longer than they are here.

SERVES 6

5 ounces bacon, diced (about 2 strips)

½ large onion, diced

2 pounds greens, stemmed and washed thoroughly

1 cup Chicken Stock (page 142) or Vegetable Stock (page 144)

1 teaspoon salt, or to taste

¼ teaspoon freshly ground black pepper, or to taste

1. Heat a large, lidded skillet or Dutch oven over medium-high heat and add the bacon. Cook, stirring often, until the bacon is crisp and has rendered its fat. Turn down the heat slightly, add the onion, and sauté until translucent, about 5 minutes.

2. Add the greens and the stock, salt, and pepper. Bring to a boil, reduce the heat, cover, and simmer until tender. The timing will depend on the type of greens used. Beet greens will be tender in about 3 minutes, chard in 5 to 8, whereas tougher greens such as collards, mustard greens, and kale will take longer—that means an hour in some kitchens, but in mine it means from 10 to 20 minutes.

3. Taste and adjust seasonings, and remove from the heat. (See photo on page 197.)

What the recipe doesn't know

` The type of greens you are cooking. This will determine the cooking time. This recipe is best with long-cooking greens such as mustard greens, collard greens, and kale. Chard will cook in less time but it's still good.

` What you have in your refrigerator. If you happen to have pancetta and no bacon, use pancetta for the recipe. The important thing is to use a cured pork product.

BRAISED RED CABBAGE

This braised cabbage has a fruity, sweet-and-sour flavor profile. Coming from Germany, Chef Hinnerk has strong ideas about braised cabbage. He prefers lard to the rendered bacon fat that was in the original recipe, and port to the red wine. He suggested adding red currant jelly to the mixture, or dried cranberries. He used a pot that was just big enough for all of the cabbage, noting that it would cook down (and he was right). Because he didn't want the cabbage to braise too much, he chose a pot that was higher than it was wide.

SERVES 6

- 1 strip bacon, diced, or 2 tablespoons lard
- ½ small onion, diced
- 2 pounds red cabbage (1 large head), cored and finely sliced (see sidebar)
- 1 tart apple, such as Granny Smith, peeled, cored, and diced
- 1 tablespoon honey
- 1 clove
- 1 small or ½ large bay leaf
- ½ cup red wine or port
- 2 tablespoons red currant jelly (optional)
- 2 tablespoons red wine vinegar
- 1 teaspoon salt, or to taste
- ¼ teaspoon freshly ground black pepper, or to taste

1. Heat a heavy pot, large enough to accommodate the cabbage, over medium-high heat and add the bacon or lard. Cook the bacon until it has rendered about half of its fat and is not yet crisp.

2. Add the onion and sauté until translucent, 3 to 5 minutes.

3. Add the red cabbage, apple, honey, clove, bay leaf, wine, jelly, vinegar, and salt and pepper, and bring to a simmer. Cover, reduce the heat, and simmer for 45 minutes to 1 hour, until the cabbage is very tender. Stir often so the cabbage doesn't cook too much on the bottom, or stick to the pan. Taste and adjust seasonings.

MAKING CABBAGE CHIFFONADE

Because the ribs of the cabbage are so much thicker than the leaves, it's a good idea to cut them out so that the cabbage cooks evenly. This is tedious, but the results can be worth it. Separate the leaves and cut out their ribs. Then stack several leaves, roll them up, and cut crosswise into thin strips.

BROCCOLI RABE WITH GARLIC AND OLIVE OIL

This is a classic Mediterranean way of preparing greens, and the recipe can be used for other greens besides broccoli rabe. Swiss chard, beet greens, kale, and spinach are all delicious prepared this way. Broccoli rabe is now widely available in supermarkets. Use it as a side dish, or toss the cooked greens with pasta.

SERVES 6

1½ pounds broccoli rabe
Salt
2 to 4 tablespoons olive oil (to taste)
4 garlic cloves, slivered
⅛ teaspoon freshly ground black pepper

1. Bring a large pot of water to a boil while you trim the broccoli rabe and coarsely chop it if you wish. Fill a large bowl with ice and water. Add a tablespoon of salt to the boiling water and add the broccoli rabe. Boil until tender-crisp, about 2 to 3 minutes. Transfer to the bowl of ice water, let cool in the water, and then drain well.

2. Heat the oil over medium-high heat in a large, wide skillet and add the garlic. Sauté until golden, about 1 minute, and stir in the broccoli rabe. Toss together until coated with oil. Add salt and pepper to taste. (See photo on page 178.)

Note: You can add a teaspoon of balsamic vinegar or lemon juice to the mixture just before serving. If you add it any sooner, the color of the greens will fade.

BUTTERED SUGAR SNAP PEAS

Sugar snap peas are like grown-up snow peas, the round sweet peas succulent inside their juicy, edible pods. Just make sure you remove the strings and stems before cooking. I sometimes find it easier, depending on the size of the snap peas, to remove the string that runs along the top of the pod before parboiling, and the bottom string afterward. This is a standard preparation for many green vegetables: first you parboil them in abundant salted water, then you shock them in ice water and drain. Shortly before serving you will reheat them by sautéing briefly in butter.

SERVES 4 TO 6

1 pound sugar snap peas, strings removed
2 tablespoons unsalted butter
Salt and freshly ground pepper to taste

1. Fill a large bowl with ice and water. Bring a large pot of generously salted water to a boil and add the peas. Boil 3 to 5 minutes, until just tender, and transfer to the bowl of ice water. Allow to cool in the water, then drain.

2. Just before serving, heat a large skillet over medium-high heat. Add the butter, and when it has melted and begun to foam, stir in the peas, salt, and pepper. Heat through and serve.

CARROT FLAN

We made this to accompany poached sole. It's delicate and rich, and very simple. You can use this formula for other types of vegetable timbales, such as cauliflower or spinach (though you would need to increase the amount of raw spinach to 1½ or 2 pounds). The cooked vegetable should be very flavorful when you puree it with the other ingredients, which is why the carrots are first sweated in butter and then cooked gradually in a small amount of seasoned liquid. Use a blender and not a food processor for this, to get the proper smooth texture. If you are making individual timbales, it helps to have the metal timbale molds that restaurants use. You can get them in restaurant supply stores. You can also use ramekins, or make one large flan in a baking dish.

SERVES 6

> 2 tablespoons butter
> ¾ pound carrots, peeled and sliced
> 1 cup chicken stock, as needed
> Oil or butter for the molds
> 6 chervil or parsley leaves
> 4 eggs
> ½ cup heavy cream
> ½ teaspoon salt
> ¼ teaspoon ground white pepper

1. Heat a wide sauté pan over medium heat and add the butter. When it foams, add the carrots and sweat gently until they become slightly tender. Add a small amount of stock and bring

Don't cook the timbales for too long or they'll curdle.

to a boil. Reduce the heat, cover, and simmer until the carrots are tender and the liquid has just about evaporated, 5 to 10 minutes. Drain any liquid remaining in the pan.

2. Meanwhile, preheat the oven to 325°F. Generously oil or butter 6 timbale molds or ramekins, or a 2-quart baking dish or soufflé dish. Place a chervil or parsley leaf, good side down, in the middle of each mold. Bring a kettle or pan of water to a boil.

3. Transfer the carrots to a blender and add the eggs, cream, salt, and pepper. Blend until smooth. Transfer to the greased molds and place in a baking pan.

4. Add enough simmering water to the baking dish so that the water goes halfway up the sides of the molds. Cover the pan with foil. Place in the oven and bake 25 minutes. Detach the foil and set loosely over the baking dish, and continue to bake until a skewer inserted near the center of the timbale comes out clean, about 5 to 10 more minutes.

5. Remove from the heat and keep warm. Unmold and serve.

Note: If you use oil instead of butter to lubricate the molds, they don't have to be hot when you unmold the timbales.

CORN BREAD

There was a Boot Camp corn bread recipe, but it was sweet and cake-like. None of the southerners in my class—and there were several—thought it was authentic. So the chef urged them to make their own recipe. This one is my version; it's moist and grainy, with only a hint of sweetness.

MAKES ONE 9-INCH SKILLET

1 cup stone-ground yellow cornmeal

½ cup all-purpose flour

¾ teaspoon salt

1 tablespoon baking powder

½ teaspoon baking soda

1 tablespoon sugar

2 large eggs

1½ cups buttermilk

3 tablespoons butter

1. Preheat the oven to 425°F.

2. Sift together the cornmeal, flour, salt, baking powder, baking soda, and sugar. In a separate, medium bowl, beat the eggs and beat in the buttermilk. Add to the cornmeal mixture and quickly beat together, taking care not to overwork the batter.

3. Place the butter in a 9-inch cast-iron skillet or a heavy 2-quart gratin dish, and place in the oven. Heat for 5 minutes, until the butter has melted and is beginning to bubble. Remove from the heat, brush the butter all over the sides of the pan, and pour out into the batter. Stir just until blended.

4. Scrape the batter into the hot pan. Place in the oven and turn the heat down to 400°F. Bake 30 to 40 minutes, until nicely browned and a toothpick inserted in the center comes out clean. Serve hot, or allow to cool in the pan and serve warm.

COOKING IN CAST IRON SKILLETS

Corn bread is a particular favorite of mine, and I've learned to make a fine version of my own. But I never make mine in a baking pan. I have found that the difference in texture and flavor when you use a cast iron skillet, or better yet, cornstick pans, is worth a little extra effort.

Put a liberally greased 10-inch cast iron skillet or some cast iron cornstick pans into the oven as it preheats and while you mix the batter. A very hot pan is critical for a crunchy, flavorful crust. When the oven is the right temperature, take the pan (or pans) out of the oven and wipe them out with a paper towel to remove any excess fat. Pour in the batter, and put the pan(s) into the oven to bake. Your corn bread may cook a little more quickly in a cast iron skillet than it does in a baking pan, so start checking it about 10 minutes earlier than the recipe says it will finish baking.

Served with Braised Greens (page 192) and Glazed Sweet Potatoes (page 201)

DEEP-FRIED PARSNIPS

Your guests will be surprised when they take a bite of what looks like a french fry and discover it's a sweet, moist parsnip. This goes well with just about anything. This is a good way to use up older, starchier parsnips.

SERVES 6

> 1½ pounds parsnips, peeled and cut in bâton-nets (see page 130)
> Flour as needed for dusting
> 2 to 4 eggs, as needed, beaten
> Salt and freshly ground pepper to taste
> About 1 quart vegetable or peanut oil for deep frying

1. Steam the parsnips or cook in salted boiling water until tender, about 5 minutes. Drain well, pat dry, and refrigerate until cold.

2. Begin heating about a quart of oil to 350°F in a deep fryer, a wok, or a wide pot. Season the parsnips with salt and pepper. Dust with flour and dip in the egg. When the oil has reached the correct temperature, deep-fry the parsnips to a golden brown. Remove from the oil with a spider and drain on racks. Add more salt and pepper if desired and serve hot.

FRENCH-FRIED POTATOES

I was thrilled that I got to make french fries at Boot Camp. Being a health-minded cook, this is not a dish I'm inclined to make at home, to the disappointment of my son, Liam. When I told him on the phone that night what I'd made, he said, "I wish you could bring one home." The trick to success with french fries is making sure they are thoroughly dry before you begin and using oil that is sufficiently hot but not too hot. You blanch them first in oil that is 275° to 300°F, to cook the starch on the insides. Then you drain them and finish them in 350°F oil to crisp the outsides.

SERVES 6

> 3 pounds Idaho potatoes, peeled and cut in bâtonnets or other desired shapes
> Vegetable oil as needed for deep-frying
> Salt to taste

1. Rinse the potatoes with cold water and dry thoroughly. Line sheet pans with racks. Heat the oil in a deep fryer or a large pan or wok to 275°F to 300°F. Add a batch of potatoes, being careful not to overcrowd the pan, and blanch in the hot oil for a couple of minutes, or until the exterior looks rough, like sandpaper (remove one and check; this indicates that the starch on the inside has been pushed to the surface of the potatoes; if you take them out too soon, they'll stick together). Drain well and transfer to the racks.

2. When all of the potatoes have been blanched in the oil, bring the temperature up to 350°F and add the potatoes in batches. Deep-fry until golden brown. Remove from the oil, shake off excess fat, and transfer to a sheet pan or a serving dish. Season while hot with salt, away from the oil to prevent flare-ups. Serve hot.

Things to watch

Make sure to salt the french fries away from the oil because salt falling into the hot oil can cause flare-ups, and flare-ups can cause kitchen fires.

GLAZED BEETS

Because beets are hard and dense, they should be cooked before you glaze them. They can be steamed, boiled, or (as I have always done) roasted at 425°F in a lidded baking dish with about ¼ inch of water on the bottom of the dish. After they're cooked, peel, quarter, and proceed with the recipe. Until Boot Camp, I just accepted red fingers as a by-product of working with beets. It never occurred to me to wear plastic gloves. This is one of those small things you learn at cooking school that can change your life in the kitchen.

SERVES 6

1½ pounds beets, scrubbed
2 tablespoons butter
1 tablespoon sugar
½ teaspoon minced fresh ginger (optional)
1 cup orange juice
¼ cup water
Salt and freshly ground pepper to taste

1. Cook the beets until tender, either by boiling in salted water, steaming, or roasting (see my description above). Remove from the heat and shock in ice water if desired, then peel and cut into 1½-inch wedges.

2. Heat the butter over medium heat in a large, lidded pan and add sugar, ginger, orange juice, and water. Bring to a simmer and add the beets. Cook, stirring often, until the liquid reduces and glazes the beets. If the glaze breaks, add a little more orange juice or water to the pan. Add salt and pepper to taste, and serve.

GLAZED CARROTS

This is a great technique for vegetables that are naturally sweet. Sweet potatoes, parsnips, turnips, and beets are all good candidates. Harder vegetables such as beets should be cooked first (see page 199), but carrots will do fine if you sweat them first and then finish the cooking with the glazing ingredients.

SERVES 6

2 tablespoons butter

1½ pounds baby carrots or regular carrots, cut oblique (see page 132) or sliced on the diagonal

2 tablespoons brown sugar or maple syrup

2 tablespoons orange or apple juice

¼ cup chicken stock

Salt to taste (up to 1 teaspoon)

Pinch of freshly ground black pepper

2 teaspoons minced fresh parsley

¼ teaspoon ground turmeric (optional)

¼ teaspoon ground toasted cardamom (optional)

¼ teaspoon ground toasted coriander (optional)

1 teaspoon fresh lemon or lime juice (optional)

Pinch of freshly grated nutmeg (optional)

1. Heat a large sauteuse over medium heat and add the butter. When the butter melts, add the carrots and cook until just beginning to be tender, about 3 minutes. Add the sugar or maple syrup, orange or apple juice, stock, and the salt. Add any of the optional ingredients and stir well with the carrots.

2. Bring to a boil, cover, and reduce the heat. Simmer until fork tender, about 8 minutes. Uncover and turn heat to high. When the liquid has just about evaporated and formed a glaze on the carrots, add the parsley and pepper. Taste, adjust salt, and serve. (See photo on page 186.)

IF THE GLAZE BREAKS...

This can happen before the vegetables are done if the liquid evaporates from the pan. If this occurs, add a little more liquid to the pan, stir, and continue to cook.

GLAZED SWEET POTATOES

These sweet, colorful, and buttery sweet potatoes go well with pork and with poultry. Glazes are best with vegetables that are naturally sweet, which is why sweet potatoes are a perfect candidate.

SERVES 6

> 6 tablespoons (¾ stick) butter
>
> 2 pounds sweet potatoes, peeled and diced or sliced
>
> 1 tablespoon light brown sugar
>
> ½ teaspoon salt
>
> ¼ teaspoon ground white pepper
>
> 1½ cups orange juice

1. Melt the butter over medium-high heat in a large lidded pan. Add the sweet potatoes, toss, and turn the heat to medium. Cover the pan and cook, shaking the pan often, until the potatoes are beginning to be tender but not brown, about 10 minutes.

2. Add the sugar, salt, pepper, and orange juice. Cover and simmer over low heat until the sweet potatoes are just about tender, about 20 minutes.

3. Remove the cover, turn up the heat, and cook until the liquid reduces to a glaze. If the glaze breaks, which will happen if all of the liquid evaporates, add a little more orange juice or water to the pan. Serve hot. (See photo on page 197.)

What the recipe doesn't know

` How you've cut your sweet potatoes. Are they cut into large or small dice, thick or thin slices? This will impact the cooking time and the heat at which you sweat them. However you do cut them, make sure they are uniform so they cook evenly.

` The size and thickness of your pan, and the heat your burner puts out. These also impact the cooking time and the degree of heat you will want to put under the pan. If the pan is thin, lower the heat. If it's not large enough to cook all of the sweet potatoes in a single layer, use two pans, or do the recipe in batches.

` How sweet your sweet potatoes are. Some are starchier and less sweet than others. You might want to use a little more sugar if this is the case.

Things to watch

` Make sure you cook the sweet potatoes long enough so they cook through.

` Don't let the pan dry out.

GNOCCHI WITH BASIL PESTO

Gnocchi, those wonderful Italian potato dumplings, were always daunting to me before I went to boot camp. The chef made them look pretty easy. They are still time-consuming, but they're luscious, especially with pesto. This pesto is a food processor version, but you can also make it in a mortar and pestle. Cook the potatoes following Chef Hinnerk's rules, page 191. You can serve these gnocchi as an appetizer or as a side dish.

SERVES 6

FOR THE GNOCCHI:

1 pound russet potatoes, peeled, washed, and halved or quartered

Salt and freshly ground pepper to taste

Nutmeg, to taste

1 egg, beaten

1 to 1 ⅓ cups bread flour or all-purpose flour, as needed

FOR THE PESTO:

4 garlic cloves

Leaves from 4 bunches basil, cleaned and dried

Leaves from 1 bunch Italian parsley, cleaned and dried

¼ cup toasted pine nuts

¼ cup freshly grated Parmesan

¼ cup freshly grated Pecorino

Olive oil as needed (⅓ to ½ cup)

Salt and freshly ground black pepper to taste

1. Make the gnocchi. Place the potatoes in a large pot, cover with water, add a teaspoon of salt, and bring to a boil. Reduce the heat and simmer until tender, about 25 minutes. Drain and return to the pot. Heat over low heat, stirring to prevent browning, until the potatoes are completely dry.

2. Mash the potatoes with a ricer or through a food mill and season to taste with salt, pepper, and a little nutmeg. Set aside to cool completely.

3. Add the egg to the potatoes, and gently mix in 1 cup of the flour. Do not overwork the dough or the gnocchi will be tough. If the dough is very sticky, gently stir in more flour. Taste and adjust seasonings.

4. Using your hands, roll out pieces of the dough into ropes about 1 inch in diameter. Cut the long cylinders into 2-inch pieces. With gentle pressure, roll the dough pieces over a gnocchi board, or over the tines of a fork, pressing and rocking the dumpling with your thumb, to achieve a ridged edge on one side and an indentation on the other. Set the gnocchi aside on parchment-covered baking sheets while you make the pesto.

5. Turn on a food processor fitted with the steel blade and drop in the garlic cloves. When they are chopped, scrape down the sides of the bowl. Add the basil, parsley, and pine nuts and process until finely chopped. Scrape down the sides of the bowl. Add the cheeses and process. With the machine running, slowly add olive oil, until you have achieved a smooth paste. Season to taste with salt and pepper. Scrape into a bowl.

6. Bring a pot or large saucepan full of generously salted water to a boil. Meanwhile, heat 6 heaping tablespoons of the pesto in a large frying pan over medium-low heat.

7. Drop the gnocchi into the boiling salted water and cook until they rise to the surface, about 2 to 3 minutes. Remove from the water with a slotted spoon and transfer to the frying pan, along with ¾ cup of the gnocchi cooking water. Coat the gnocchi with the pesto, transfer to warm plates or a platter, and serve immediately.

GREEN BEANS AND WALNUTS

Green beans and nuts always go well together. Almonds are a classic partner, but try this version, with walnuts. It has the added flavor bonus of walnut oil, which gives the dish a marvelously nutty flavor. You can parboil the beans ahead and finish them in the pan just before serving. Don't make the mistake our class made repeatedly with green vegetables: when you finish them in the oil or butter, you are just heating them through, not frying them.

SERVES 6

> 2 tablespoons walnuts
> 1½ pounds green beans, trimmed
> 1 tablespoon walnut oil
> 2 teaspoons minced shallots
> 1 teaspoon minced garlic
> Salt and freshly ground pepper to taste
> 2 teaspoons sliced chives

1. Heat a small sauté pan over medium high heat and add the walnuts. Cook, shaking the pan or stirring the nuts, until they begin to smell toasty, about 5 minutes. Transfer immediately to a bowl. Chop the nuts and set aside. Alternatively, toast the nuts in a 350°F oven for 10 minutes or until fragrant.

2. Fill a large pot with cold water and bring to a boil. Fill a large bowl with water and ice. When the water comes to a boil, add a generous amount of salt and the green beans. Cook 4 to 5 minutes, until tender, and transfer to the ice water. Allow to cool in the water for several minutes, and then drain well.

3. Heat the walnut oil over medium-high heat in a large, heavy sauté pan and add the shallots and garlic. Sauté until fragrant, a couple of minutes, and add the green beans. Toss until coated with oil and heated through. Season to taste with salt and pepper, stir in the walnuts and chives, and serve.

GREEN BEANS WITH BACON AND SHALLOTS

This is a nice combination that was new to me. Green beans with mushrooms is a classic combination, but I'd never thought about throwing bacon into the mix. The important thing to remember here is that you are cooking the beans when you parboil them, and simply reheating them with the bacon and mushrooms. In other words, don't overcook the beans!

SERVES 6

> 2 pounds green beans, trimmed
> 2 strips bacon, cut crosswise in julienne
> 2 shallots, quartered
> ½ pound mushrooms, trimmed and quartered
> Salt and freshly ground black pepper to taste

1. Bring a large pot of generously salted water to a boil and add the green beans. Meanwhile fill a bowl with ice and water. Cook the beans until tender, 4 to 5 minutes. Transfer to the ice water, leave for a few minutes, then drain.

2. Heat a large, heavy sauté pan over medium heat and add the bacon. Sauté until crisp. Remove from the pan and drain on racks.

3. Add the shallots to the bacon fat and sauté until tender, about 5 minutes. Add the mushrooms and continue to cook, stirring often or shaking the pan, until tender, 5 to 10 minutes. Season to taste with salt and pepper. Add the green beans and cook, stirring, until heated through. Adjust seasonings, sprinkle with the bacon, and serve immediately.

GRILLED ZUCCHINI

When you grill vegetables, you need to lubricate them first. You could use olive oil alone, but this mixture of olive oil, vinegar, garlic, herbs, and sugar is almost like a salad dressing that will infuse the inside of the zucchini and contrast nicely with the charred outside. The marinade here makes a nice formula for grilling other vegetables besides zucchini, such as eggplant, onions, and tomatoes. If you are grilling for a crowd, you can grill the squash ahead, and reheat on sheet trays in a medium oven before serving.

SERVES 6

½ cup olive oil

½ cup red or white wine vinegar

2 large garlic cloves, minced

1½ teaspoons chopped fresh thyme

1½ teaspoons chopped fresh oregano

1 teaspoon sugar

1½ pounds zucchini, cut on the bias into ½-inch slices

½ teaspoon salt

1. Prepare a hot fire in your grill. Mix together the olive oil, vinegar, garlic, thyme, oregano, and sugar. Stir until the sugar dissolves.

2. Pat the zucchini slices dry with paper towels and season generously with salt. Toss with the marinade, making sure that the zucchini is coated on both sides. Place on the grill and grill on each side until the zucchini is tender and marked with grill marks.

3. Transfer to a platter, drizzle on more of the marinade, and serve hot.

GRILLED YELLOW SQUASH

The method here is the same as that for grilled zucchini (at left), but this time the yellow squash is marinated in garlic-flavored olive oil rather than the mixture of vinegar and olive oil that is used for the zucchini. When grilling yellow squash or zucchini, cut long, thick slices on the diagonal, so that the pieces are big enough to stay on top of the grill rack and not fall through. The yellow is particularly pretty against the grill marks. You can grill these ahead and reheat on a sheet pan in the oven.

SERVES 6

¼ cup olive oil

2 cloves garlic, minced

1 teaspoon salt

¼ teaspoon freshly ground pepper

1½ pounds yellow squash, sliced on the bias into ½-inch thick slices

1. Prepare a hot grill. Meanwhile, mix together the olive oil, garlic, salt, and pepper. Toss with the yellow squash and let sit for 10 minutes.

2. Place the squash on the hot grill and grill the slices on both sides until tender, changing the angle of the slices once to create crosshatch marks if desired. Serve hot.

HARICOTS VERTS

Haricots verts are those elegant, thin green beans that cost a fortune at the farmers' market but are worth splurging on every now and then. They need nothing more than the butter, salt, and pepper called for here. Make this just before serving, or cook the beans ahead, shock, and reheat gently in the butter.

SERVES 6

- 3 quarts water
- 1 tablespoon salt, plus additional to taste
- 1½ pounds haricots verts, washed and trimmed
- 2 tablespoons butter
- Freshly ground black pepper to taste

Bring the water to a full boil. Add the tablespoon of salt and the haricots verts. Cook until crisp-tender, about 4 minutes, and drain. Toss with butter, salt, and pepper, and serve. (See photo on page 171.)

Things to watch

- Don't overcook the beans. They should be done in 4 to 5 minutes.

- If you cook them ahead, shock them and drain. Reheat gently in butter just before serving.

HOT AND SPICY MIXED VEGETABLES

Serve these spicy stir-fried vegetables with any simple main dish, such as roast chicken or pork, grilled fish or steak. Or feature it as part of a vegetarian plate, with grains and grilled tofu.

SERVES 6

- ¼ pound carrots, cut in medium dice
- ¼ pound daikon, peeled and cut in medium dice
- ½ teaspoon sugar
- 4 teaspoons tamari
- 3 tablespoons peanut oil
- ½ teaspoon minced fresh ginger
- ½ teaspoon minced garlic
- 1 teaspoon thinly sliced scallions
- ¾ teaspoon Asian chili sauce
- 1½ cups thinly sliced celery
- 2¼ cups thinly sliced zucchini
- 1 cup thinly sliced yellow squash
- 3 cups thinly sliced cabbage
- ½ teaspoon salt, or to taste
- 3 tablespoons dark sesame oil, or to taste

1. Bring a saucepan full of generously salted water to a boil and add the carrots and daikon. Blanch for a minute, shock in ice water, and drain.

2. Dissolve the sugar in the soy sauce and set aside. Heat the oil over medium-high heat in a large sauté pan or wok and add the ginger, garlic, scallions, and chili sauce. Stir-fry until fragrant, about 30 seconds, and add the vegetables one at a time, beginning with the celery and stir-frying each for a couple of minutes before adding the next. Add the blanched carrots and daikon last.

3. When the vegetables are crisp-tender, add the salt, sugar, tamari, and sesame oil, and mix together. Transfer to a large platter and serve.

Note: You can always use different vegetables in this dish, such as blanched cauliflower and/or broccoli, or try Napa cabbage instead of regular cabbage. You may have to cook the vegetables in batches to keep the pan very hot as you stir-fry.

OVEN-ROASTED VEGETABLES

When you roast a selection of vegetables, they should be cut in similar sizes, but complementary shapes. Blanch the drier, harder vegetables such as cauliflower and carrots before roasting, and use a double sheet pan so that the vegetables don't brown too much on the bottom.

SERVES 6

    4 carrots
    3 red onions
    ½ head cauliflower
    1 large red bell pepper
    1 large green bell pepper
    6 whole garlic cloves
    4 shallots, peeled and left whole
    1 tablespoon chopped fresh thyme
    2 teaspoons salt
    1 teaspoon freshly ground pepper, or to taste
    3 tablespoons olive oil, or to taste
    2 tablespoons butter (optional)

1. Peel the carrots and cut in 1-inch oblique cuts. Peel the onions and cut into wedges. Break or cut the cauliflower into florets. Cut the red and green peppers into 1-inch pieces.

2. Preheat the oven to 375°F. Prepare an ice bath. Bring a large pot of generously salted water to a boil and drop in the carrots and cauliflower. Boil 2 minutes and then shock in the ice bath. Drain thoroughly. Stack two sheet trays or roasting pans and oil the top one. Place in the oven.

3. Combine the carrots and cauliflower with all of the other vegetables in a large bowl. Season generously with thyme, ½ teaspoon salt, and ¼ teaspoon pepper. Add 1 tablespoon olive oil and mix together well.

4. Transfer the vegetables to the hot roasting pan or sheet and place in the oven. Roast, gently stirring the vegetables periodically to ensure even roasting, until the vegetables are lightly caramelized and tender, 30 to 40 minutes. Remove from the oven, dot with butter if desired, and serve.

MASHED POTATOES AND TURNIPS

A match made in heaven, this potato-turnip combo went very nicely with Poached Chicken Breast with Tarragon Sauce (page 170). Cook the potatoes and turnips separately, following Chef Hinnerk's rules for boiling potatoes (page 191).

SERVES 6

> 1 pound russet potatoes or Yukon Golds, peeled and quartered
>
> 1 pound turnips, peeled and quartered
>
> Salt to taste
>
> ¼ cup milk
>
> 2 tablespoons butter
>
> ¼ teaspoon freshly ground black pepper
>
> 2 tablespoons chopped Italian parsley

1. Put the potatoes into a pot and barely cover them with water. Add salt to taste to the water. Smear some oil along the inside of the pot above the surface of the water. This will prevent the water from boiling over.

2. Cover the pot and bring the water to a boil over high heat. As soon as the water comes to a boil, turn down the heat and boil gently for 20 to 30 minutes, until the potatoes are cooked through but maintain their shape. When the potatoes are done, drain most of the water, leaving about ⅛ of an inch, and replace the lid.

3. Cook the turnips following the directions for boiled potatoes. They will be done more quickly, in about 10 to 15 minutes. Drain and return to the pan, cover, and allow to dry for 5 minutes.

4. Purée the potatoes and turnips through a food mill while still very hot.

5. Heat the milk and butter until the butter melts, and add to the potatoes and turnips. Fold until smooth, and season generously with salt and pepper. Sprinkle with parsley and serve. (See photo on page 171.)

PARSNIP AND PEAR PUREE

It makes perfect sense that these two should marry so well. Parsnips are a sweet, earthy vegetable that never get enough attention. When you combine them with the pears, which contribute a fruity edge to the dish, everyone sits up and takes notice. At one of my Boot Camp sessions, however, people took notice because the mixture had a gummy, pasty consistency. The flavor was good, but… The parsnips were mature and starchy, and a food mill rather than a food processor should have been used to puree them. Rather than cooking the vegetables in a large pot of water, where the flavors would be lost, the parsnips and the pears are cooked in butter and a small amount of stock in a wide pan.

SERVES 6

> 2 tablespoons butter, plus additional as needed
>
> 1½ pounds parsnips, preferably tender young ones, peeled and finely chopped
>
> ¾ pound pears (Bartletts, Comice, or Anjou), peeled, cored, and finely chopped
>
> 1 cup Chicken Stock (page 142), Vegetable Stock (page 144), or water

Up to ½ cup heavy cream, as needed, heated to just below a simmer

Salt to taste

Ground white pepper to taste

1. Heat a large, wide skillet over medium heat and melt the butter. Add the parsnips and sweat in the butter until they begin to soften. Add the stock or water and cook, stirring often, until the parsnips are just about tender, about 5 minutes. Add the pears and continue to cook, stirring often, until the parsnips and pears are tender, about 5 to 10 minutes. Remove from the heat and drain off any liquid from the pan. Meanwhile, warm the cream in a small saucepan or in the microwave.

2. Puree the parsnips and pears together, while still warm, through the fine blade of a food mill or in a food processor fitted with the steel blade. With the machine running if using a food processor, slowly add the hot cream and blend the mixture to a smooth, light purée. Season to taste with salt and pepper.

3. Transfer the mixture to a serving dish and serve hot. If you are not serving this right away, keep hot in a covered bowl set over a pot of simmering water. If you like, before serving dot the top with butter, place briefly under the broiler, and lightly brown the top.

POLENTA

I loved the Boot Camp recipe for polenta; it combines milk and water, with onions and garlic as aromatics, for a rich, creamy version of this classic Italian cornmeal porridge. We made it on the day we made stews and braises. It always pairs well with rustic, saucy dishes, catching all of the gravy that isn't eaten with the meat. There are many ways to make polenta. Ours was begun in a tall stock pot and finished in the oven. I'd only made polenta using salted water before this, and that's good too, as long as you salt it sufficiently. You can also use stock. The important thing is to have a liquid that is well seasoned; so be sure to taste it before you add your polenta.

SERVES 6 AS A SIDE DISH

3 tablespoons butter or olive oil

½ large onion, finely chopped

2 garlic cloves, minced

2½ cups water

2½ cups milk

1¼ teaspoons salt, or to taste

1⅓ cups coarse Italian cornmeal (polenta)

1 cup freshly grated Parmesan cheese

1. Preheat the oven to 350°F. Heat a tall saucepan or stockpot over medium heat and add the butter or oil. Add the onion and cook, stirring, until translucent and tender, about 3 to 4 minutes. Add the garlic and continue to sauté until translucent and fragrant, another minute or two.

(continued)

2. Add the water and milk, and bring the mixture to a boil. Add the salt. Taste and add more if desired.

3. Gradually add the cornmeal to the boiling liquid, letting the grains slip through your fingers in a very slow stream. When all of the cornmeal has been added, boil it rapidly until the mixture begins to thicken, stirring constantly with a long-handled wooden spoon.

4. Scrape the mixture into a baking dish or gratin, cover, and place in the oven. Bake for 30 minutes without stirring. A light crust will form on the bottom of the pan. This is desirable.

5. Before serving, stir in half the cheese. Pass the remaining cheese at the table for guests to sprinkle on.

Note You can also cook polenta in the traditional Italian way, on top of the stove. You must stand by the pot and stir with a long-handled wooden spoon for 30 minutes, until the mixture is creamy and thick and you have a blister on your thumb from stirring. Scrape onto a platter when done, and serve.

POMMES DUCHESSE

You may have seen these on buffets: piped mashed potatoes, used as decorative borders and garnishes. They're classic, although I find them sort of dated. However, we learned to make them at Boot Camp, and I must say, it was fun to do. Just be sure not to brown them too far ahead of time, and to use very high heat, or they'll be leathery on the outside and dry in the middle. It's also very important to have your mise en place ready for mixing these. The potatoes need to be hot when they are mashed and especially when the egg yolks are mixed in, because the heat of the potatoes cooks the egg yolks.

SERVES 6

> 2½ pounds starchy potatoes, such as russets or Yukon Golds, peeled and quartered
>
> 3 egg yolks
>
> 6 tablespoons (¾ stick) butter, at room temperature
>
> 1 teaspoon salt (or to taste)
>
> ¼ teaspoon freshly ground white or black pepper
>
> ⅛ teaspoon ground nutmeg
>
> 1 egg beaten with 1 tablespoon water, for egg wash

1. Place the potatoes in a saucepan and cover with water. Add a generous pinch of salt and bring to a boil. Reduce the heat to medium and boil gently until the potatoes are tender all the way through when pierced with a fork, about 25 minutes. Drain and return the potatoes to the pan. Place over low heat and heat until all the steam has evaporated.

2. Remove the potatoes from the heat and puree while hot through a food mill or potato ricer. Immediately mix in the egg yolks. Stir in the butter and seasonings.

3. Line baking sheets with parchment paper and preheat the oven to 450°F, or preheat the broiler. Transfer the potato mixture to a pastry bag fitted with a large star tip and pipe into the desired shapes onto the parchment. Brush lightly with egg wash.

4. Brown in the hot oven or under the broiler until the edges are golden and the potatoes are heated through, 10 to 12 minutes. Do not bake for too long or the potatoes will dry out. Serve immediately. (See photo on page 63.)

Things to watch

- Make sure you cook your potatoes until they're tender and dry them out well in the pan.

- Make sure the potatoes are hot when you purée them and add the egg yolks.

- Don't forget the egg wash.

- Brown the piped potatoes briefly in a very hot oven or under a broiler.

POTATO PUREE

These rich mashed potatoes are great just the way they are, or they can be turned into Pommes Duchesse (page 214); so don't throw away the leftovers. We used a food mill to puree the potatoes. Never use a food processor, or you will have glue instead of mashed potatoes.

SERVES 6

2 pounds starchy potatoes, such as russets or Yukon Golds, peeled and cut in large dice

1 teaspoon salt (or to taste), plus salt for the cooking water

¼ cup heavy cream

2 tablespoons butter

¼ teaspoon freshly ground black pepper (or to taste)

1. Place the potatoes in a saucepan and cover with water. Season the water generously with salt and bring to a boil. Reduce the heat to medium and boil gently until the potatoes are tender all the way through when pierced with a fork, about 25 minutes. Drain and return the potatoes to the pan. Place over low heat and heat until all the steam has evaporated.

2. While the potatoes are cooking, heat the cream and butter together in a small saucepan until the butter has melted.

3. Remove the potatoes from the heat and puree while hot through a food mill. Add the hot cream and butter, and fold together until the mixture is smooth. Season to taste with salt and pepper. Serve hot. (See photo on page 173.)

SAFFRON RISOTTO WITH PORCINI MUSHROOMS AND BASIL

Although we made this risotto to accompany Ossobucco alla Milanese (page 188), it's so rich and delicious, I would serve it on its own as a starter or as a main dish.

SERVES 6 AS A SIDE DISH

- 1½ ounces (about 1½ cups) dried porcini mushrooms
- 1½ to 2 quarts Chicken Stock (page 142), as needed
- ¾ teaspoon saffron, crushed
- 1 tablespoon salt, or to taste
- 2 tablespoons olive oil
- ½ medium onion, minced
- 1½ cups Arborio rice
- ½ cup dry white wine, such as Sauvignon Blanc or Pinot Grigio
- 1 teaspoon freshly ground pepper, or to taste
- 2 ounces (½ stick) butter
- ½ cup freshly grated Parmesan
- 2 tablespoons basil chiffonade

1. Place the dried mushrooms in a bowl and cover with 2 cups boiling water or as needed. Let soak 15 to 30 minutes, until softened. Place a strainer lined with cheesecloth over a bowl and drain the mushrooms. Rinse off any sand in several changes of water. Add the soaking water to the chicken stock. Set aside.

2. Bring the stock to a simmer in a saucepan, add the saffron and salt.

3. Heat a large, heavy skillet over medium heat and add the olive oil. When it is hot, add the onions. Sauté until translucent, about 2–3 minutes, and add the rice. Stir to coat with oil for about 1 minute. Add the wine and stir the rice until the wine evaporates, about 1 minute. Ladle in enough of the simmering stock to barely cover the rice, and stir and simmer until most of the liquid has been absorbed. Ladle in more stock and continue to stir and simmer until the liquid has been absorbed. Continue to gradually add stock and cook, stirring, until the rice has been cooked al dente, slightly chewy.

4. Add the mushrooms, butter, cheese, and basil and fold in. Taste and add salt and pepper as desired. Serve at once. The risotto should be creamy and spread out on the plate. If it doesn't, add a little more liquid.

What the recipe doesn't know

How heavy and large your pan is, and how strong your heat source is. This will impact the cooking time, as well as the amount of liquid you'll need. If the risotto cooks fast, it will absorb liquid more quickly.

SAUTÉED MUSHROOMS

Mushrooms, I learned at Boot Camp, are 94 percent water, and if you don't cook them quickly over high heat, they will release their liquid and begin to stew before they have a chance to brown. So get the pan really hot first, then add the fat, and brown the mushrooms in batches in the hot fat. Then you can return them all to the pan with the other ingredients and cook until the mushrooms are tender and savory. Serve this garlicky dish with meat, fowl, or fish, stirred into a risotto, or even as the main event with a sturdy grain such as farro or with pasta. You can also use wild mushrooms for this recipe.

SERVES 4 TO 6

2 tablespoons olive oil

1½ pounds white mushrooms, wiped clean, trimmed, and quartered

1½ tablespoons minced garlic (about 3 cloves)

2½ teaspoons minced shallot

½ teaspoon fresh thyme leaves, or ¼ teaspoon dried

¼ cup dry white wine

1 tablespoon butter

Salt and freshly ground pepper to taste (about ½ teaspoon salt and ¼ teaspoon pepper)

1. Heat a large, heavy sauté pan over medium-high heat until it feels hot when you hold your hand above it. Add the oil, and as soon as you can see it ripple, add a batch of mushrooms, just enough to make a scant layer in the pan. Cook, stirring or shaking the pan, until the mushrooms brown, and transfer to a bowl. Repeat with the remaining mushrooms, until all have been caramelized.

2. Add the garlic and shallots to the pot and cook for a few minutes, then return the mushrooms and the remaining ingredients. Bring the wine to a boil and cook, moving the mushrooms in the pan from time to time, until most of the liquid has evaporated, about 10 minutes. Taste, adjust seasonings, and serve.

What the recipe doesn't know

` The size of your pan. That will tell you how many batches of mushrooms you will need to brown. There should be enough space in the pan for the mushrooms to move around freely; they shouldn't be crowded.

` How hot your stove is. That will affect how long it will take to brown the mushrooms. Use your eyes and your nose. If you have a professional stove, the mushrooms will brown quickly over the high heat. Regular stoves will require heating the pan for a longer time before adding the oil.

SAUTÉED RED AND YELLOW PEPPERS

This bright combination is one of my favorite side dishes, and it goes well with just about anything. The dish holds well, so you can sauté the peppers ahead of time if necessary and reheat.

SERVES 6

> 3 tablespoons olive oil
> 3 red peppers, cut in strips, dice, squares, or diamonds
> 3 yellow peppers, cut in strips, dice, squares, or diamonds
> Salt and freshly ground pepper to taste

Heat the olive oil over medium-high heat in a large, heavy sauté pan and add the peppers. Sauté until they reach the desired tenderness (I like them just tender, which takes about 8 minutes in my pan). Season with salt and pepper and remove from the heat.

What the recipe doesn't know

What's on your menu. The other foods on your plate should help you decide how to shape the peppers. If you are also serving green beans, for example, then cut the peppers into squares or diamonds for a contrasting shape on the plate.

SAUTÉED ZUCCHINI

The Boot Camp recipe for sautéed zucchini calls for cutting the vegetable into bâtonnets, and when Chef John showed us how to do this, he taught us to cut out and discard the middle part of the zucchini, where the seeds are. Chef Hinnerk prefers to cut his zucchini in half lengthwise, scoop out the seeds with a small spoon, and slice the halves on the bias, resulting in attractive crescent-shaped slices. This goes much more quickly than making bâtonnets, and the effect is the same as far as cooking is concerned. This attractive vegetable sauté makes a good accompaniment to just about any meat or fish dish, and since zucchini is available year-round, you can plan it for any seasonal menu.

SERVES 6

> 1½ pounds zucchini, trimmed (about 6 small)
> 4 tablespoons (½ stick) butter
> ½ small onion, minced
> 1 clove garlic, minced
> 1 teaspoon salt, or to taste
> ¼ teaspoon freshly ground pepper, or to taste
> 1 teaspoon basil chiffonade

1. Cut the zucchini into bâtonnets (page 130), or halve them lengthwise, scoop out the seeds, and cut crosswise on the bias into ¼-inch-thick slices. Heat the butter over medium-high heat in a large sauté pan, and when it begins to foam add the onion. Sauté until translucent, 3 to 5 minutes.

(continued)

2. Add the zucchini and sauté until crisp-tender, about 2–3 minutes. Add the garlic, salt, and pepper and continue to sauté until the zucchini is tender but still bright, another 2 to 3 minutes. Stir in the basil, adjust seasonings, and serve.

Note: The middle of the zucchini consists mostly of seeds and pulp, which become watery when cooked. So you're really not wasting anything if you cut this part away and discard, and your finished dish will have a pleasing, uniform texture.

SAUTÉED SNOW PEAS WITH SESAME SEEDS

If you blanch the snow peas in advance, you can finish them just before serving, which makes this colorful side dish a convenient one, and it's good with just about anything. Chef John had us cut out little triangles at each end of the snow peas—we stacked them first so that we could do a few at a time—but, frankly, I don't think anyone really noticed, and what a waste of time!

Just trim away the stems and strings and your prep work will be quickly done.

SERVES 6

- 1 pound snow peas, trimmed, strings removed
- 2 tablespoons olive oil or peanut oil
- 2 tablespoons toasted sesame seeds
- 1 teaspoon salt, or to taste
- ½ teaspoon freshly ground black pepper, or to taste

1. Bring a pot of generously salted water to a boil; meanwhile prepare an ice bath. When the water comes to a boil add the snow peas. Blanch for 1 minute and shock in the ice bath. Drain well.

2. Just before serving, heat a large sauté pan over medium-high heat and add the oil. Add the snow peas and heat through, stirring, until crisp-tender, just a minute or two. Stir in the sesame seeds, season to taste with salt and pepper, and serve. This step may need to be done in 2 batches, depending on the size of the pan.

STEAMED RICE

Our Boot Camp groups didn't have a way with rice. That's because we were never sure of what type we were getting, and if you don't know what kind you're using, you won't add the right amount of water. Asian rice, jasmine, or sushi rice, for example, takes very little water, whereas Carolina rice takes twice its volume. This recipe is for Asian rice. Very little water is called for. The steamed rice is chewy, all the grains separate and dry.

SERVES 4 TO 6

> 2 cups short-grain rice
> 1 teaspoon salt
> 2½ cups water

1. Rinse the rice under cold running water until the water runs clear. Drain.

2. Combine the rice, salt, and cold water in a saucepan and bring to a boil. Reduce the heat, cover, and simmer until all of the water is absorbed, about 15 minutes. Remove from the heat and leave undisturbed for 5 to 10 minutes before serving.

TOURNÉED ZUCCHINI AND CARROTS

The day that this was on the menu, the task of preparing the carrots and zucchini fell to me. I don't think I've come across many preparations that are more ridiculous than this arcane—and wasteful—way to present food, and even the CIA chefs will admit that they rarely do them. But it's a classic French way to prepare vegetables, so we learned how to cut the carrots and zucchini into uniform barrel or football shapes, each one with seven flat surfaces. Chef John himself admitted, as he demonstrated the tournés, that he was "better at fluting mushrooms."

SERVES 6

> 5 large carrots (8 to 10 inches long)
> 5 to 6 long zucchini (8 to 10 inches long)
> 1 teaspoon salt, plus more to taste
> 3 tablespoons butter
> ¼ teaspoon freshly ground black pepper

1. Peel the carrots and zucchini, and cut into 2-inch lengths. Using a paring knife or a special curved tourné knife, cut each piece into a football or barrel shape with seven smooth, evenly spaced faces and tapered ends.

2. Bring a large pot of generously salted water to a boil, and add the carrots. Parboil for 3 to 5 minutes, or until tender, transfer to a bowl of ice water, and drain.

3. Heat the butter over medium heat in a large sauté pan and add the zucchini. Sauté until tender, 5 to 10 minutes, and add the carrots. Sauté until heated through, season with salt and pepper, and serve. (See photo on page 172.)

SPAETZLE

Spaetzle are tiny little dumplings (the word means "little sparrows," and they do look a little like little sparrows, pointed at one end), and they are wonderful. They make a great side dish with meats such as veal or chicken, and a nice soup garnish as well. You don't have to have a spaetzler to make them—a colander will do the trick just fine. But I went right to the CIA store after class and bought one, as it's one of the few pieces of cooking equipment I didn't own. Although many spaetzle recipes, including the one we were given at Boot Camp, combine eggs, milk, and flour, Chef Hinnerk uses eggs and flour only, and his spaetzle are marvelous and easy. You can make the spaetzle ahead, shock and drain them, and hold them at room temperature for several hours.

SERVES 6

> 8 eggs
>
> 2 teaspoons salt (more or less to taste)
>
> 1 teaspoon freshly ground black pepper (more or less to taste)
>
> ¼ teaspoon freshly grated nutmeg (more or less to taste)
>
> 3½ cups all-purpose flour, or as needed
>
> Milk or water as needed
>
> ¼ cup (½ stick) butter, more to taste

1. Combine the eggs, salt, pepper, and nutmeg in a large stainless steel bowl or the bowl of a standing mixer fitted with the paddle and beat together well, about 1 minute.

2. Using the paddle attachment or by hand, work in the flour until you have a smooth batter, and "beat the living life out of it" (says Hinnerk) to aerate it and develop the gluten. The batter is ready when it blisters. Use milk or water to adjust the consistency, adding more or less as necessary. If large bubbles slowly come up to the surface and pop, the batter is the right consistency. If no bubbles occur, you need to add a little more flour. If bubbles appear but they can't rise, the batter is too stiff and needs some more liquid.

3. Let the batter rest for 10 minutes or longer. Meanwhile, bring 4 quarts of water to a boil in a large, wide saucepan or pot and add 4 teaspoons salt. Fill a large bowl with ice and water and set a strainer or colander in the water.

4. Put a few spoonfuls of batter at a time through a spaetzle maker or a colander into the pot and cook just until the spaetzle rises to the surface, about 30–45 seconds. Remove from the water with a spider or a slotted spoon and transfer directly to the ice water. When all of the spaetzle has been cooked and cooled, stir them in the ice bath, and drain well.

5. Just before serving, heat the butter over medium-high heat in a large, wide frying pan and add the spaetzle. Sauté for a few minutes, taste and add salt and pepper if desired, and serve.

SPINACH SPAETZLE WITH SAPSAGO CHEESE

I got to make this when I worked with Chef Hinnerk, the second time I went to Boot Camp. It was a revelation. Hinnerk makes his spaetzle with no added milk, and he doesn't even blanch the spinach in this version. All you need to do is blend the raw spinach with the eggs until smooth, then work in the flour and cheese. The resulting batter is bright green, the spaetzle marvelously herbal and savory. It's fine to use bagged baby spinach for this. Sapsago is a cone-shaped, light green, hard grating cheese from Switzerland. It has an herbal flavor—some would call it a strange flavor (as Chef Hinnerk said, you don't get up in the morning thinking, "Gee, I'd like some sapsago cheese")—resulting from the dried clover that gives it its green hue. If you can't get hold of it, substitute Parmesan or Gruyère.

SERVES 6

8 cups spinach, washed, stems trimmed

6 eggs

1½ to 2 teaspoons kosher salt, to taste

¼ teaspoon freshly ground black pepper, or to taste

Pinch of freshly grated nutmeg

1 cup grated sapsago cheese

3½ cups all-purpose flour, or as needed

6 tablespoons butter

1. Combine the spinach, eggs, salt, pepper, and nutmeg in a blender and blend until completely smooth. Transfer to a bowl or the bowl of a standing mixer fitted with the paddle, and stir in half the cheese. Using a large wooden spoon or the mixer, beat in the flour until you have a smooth, thick batter. Beat for 6–8 minutes to develop the gluten. (With the spinach version the dough will not develop bubbles as in the plain spaetzle on page 223.) Set aside and allow to rest for at least 10 minutes.

2. Bring a pot of salted water to a boil. Fill a large bowl with ice and water, and insert a strainer or perforated pot into the bowl. Using a spaetzle machine or a colander, drop small portions of the dough into the pot and cook until the spaetzle rises to the surface, about 30-45 seconds. Remove from the water with a spider or a slotted spoon and transfer directly to the ice water. Drain well.

3. Before serving, heat the butter over medium-high heat in a wide pan until light brown. Add the spaetzle, sauté until lightly browned, sprinkle with the remaining cheese, and serve.

SPINACH WITH BACON AND PINE NUTS

This is a classic combination, as familiar as a salad as it is as a cooked side dish. Make sure you don't overcook the spinach. Once the bacon has rendered its fat the dish should proceed very quickly.

SERVES 6

> 3 pounds spinach, stemmed and rinsed thoroughly
> 3 slices bacon, chopped
> ¼ cup olive oil
> 3 tablespoons finely chopped onion
> 2 garlic cloves, minced
> 1 teaspoon salt, or to taste
> ½ teaspoon freshly ground pepper, or to taste
> ½ cup toasted pine nuts

1. Wash spinach and remove all large stems. Bring a large pot of generously salted water to a boil and blanch the spinach for no more than 10 seconds. Shock in a bowl of ice water, then drain and squeeze dry. Chop coarsely if desired.

2. Heat a large sauté pan over low heat and add the bacon. Sauté until the bacon is crisp, and remove from the pan with a slotted spoon. Drain on paper towels.

3. Pour off most of the bacon fat from the pan and add the olive oil. Heat over medium heat and add the onion. Sauté until translucent and tender, about 5 minutes, and stir in the garlic. Cook, stirring, until fragrant, about 1 minute, and add the spinach. Don't crowd the pan; cook in batches if necessary. Sauté while turn-ing the spinach constantly until it is just barely wilted, about 2 minutes. Heat through, stirring, season with salt and pepper, stir in the pine nuts and bacon, and remove from the heat. Serve hot.

WARM COLESLAW

This spicy coleslaw, steamed in its own vinaigrette, was one of my favorite Boot Camp recipes. It was, unsurprisingly, on the barbecued ribs menu. You can make this on top of the stove or in the oven.

SERVES 6

> FOR THE VINAIGRETTE:
> ¼ cup cider vinegar
> ¼ cup sugar
> ¾ to 1 teaspoon salt (or to taste)
> 2 to 3 teaspoons freshly ground black pepper (to taste)
> 1 tablespoon powdered mustard (like Coleman's)
> 1½ teaspoons caraway seeds
> 1 teaspoon ground celery seeds
> ¾ cup vegetable oil
>
> FOR THE SALAD:
> 1½ pounds Savoy cabbage, shredded
> ½ medium red onion, thinly sliced
> 6 ounces red cabbage, ribs removed, shredded

1. Preheat the oven to 350°F (if using the oven). Whisk together the ingredients for the vinaigrette in a small saucepan and bring to a boil.

2. If using the oven, combine the Savoy cabbage and red onions in a roasting pan. Pour on the hot vinaigrette and toss together. Bake in the preheated oven until wilted, about 10 minutes. If cooking on top of the stove, place the cabbage mixture in a large saucepan and pour on the hot vinaigrette. Place over low heat and simmer for 10 minutes, until wilted.

3. Add the red cabbage, toss, and bake or simmer another 10 minutes. Serve warm.

What the recipe doesn't know

Whether you are turning on your oven for something else. Then you might want to use the oven to wilt the cabbage. Otherwise, you can cook this on top of the stove.

MOREL AND WILD MUSHROOM RAGOÛT

This was the ragoût we made to accompany our steaks for our final examination. The dish stands well alone and also makes a great sauce, not just for a steak, but also for a roast turkey or chicken, or even a chicken breast.

SERVES 6

1 ounce dried morels

1 cup Brown Veal Stock (page 140)

1 cup mushroom broth (from the dried mushrooms)

2 teaspoons arrowroot

2 tablespoons Madeira

2 tablespoons olive oil

2 shallots, finely chopped

2 cloves garlic, finely chopped

2 teaspoons tomato paste

1 pound mixed dried mushrooms, thickly sliced if large

1 pound button mushrooms, quartered if small, thickly sliced if large

1 cup red wine

Salt and freshly ground black pepper to taste

2 tablespoons cold butter, cut into small pieces

1 tablespoon chopped fresh tarragon

1. Place the dried morels in a bowl or a Pyrex measuring cup and pour on 2 cups boiling water. Allow to soak for 30 minutes while you prepare the other ingredients. Line a strainer with cheesecloth, place over a bowl and drain the mushrooms. Squeeze the morels over the strainer, rinse, squeeze again, and set aside. Measure out 1 cup of the broth and set aside.

(continued)

2. Combine the veal stock and mushroom broth in a small saucepan. Bring to a boil and reduce by half. Taste, adjust seasonings, and if desired (for a stronger flavor), reduce a little more. Turn down the heat and keep at a simmer.

3. Dissolve the arrowroot in the Madeira and stir into the broth. As soon as the mixture thickens, remove from the heat and set aside.

4. Heat a large sautoir or saucepan over medium-high heat and add the olive oil. When it is hot, add the shallots. Sauté until tender but not brown. Add the garlic, stir-fry for 30 seconds, until fragrant, and stir in the tomato paste. Cook for a minute or so, until it begins to smell toasty, and add the fresh mushrooms. Sauté until tender, about 10 minutes, moving them in the pan frequently. Season to taste with salt and pepper, and add the red wine. Turn up the heat, bring to a boil, and reduce the red wine by half. Stir in the thickened brown sauce, taste, and adjust seasonings. Remove from the heat and whisk or stir in the butter a little at a time, until the sauce is silky. Just before serving, stir in the tarragon.

GRATIN DAUPHINOIS

This decadent potato dish is the soul of simplicity, although it does require a bit of patience. Baking the dish very slowly in a hot water bath gives the potatoes plenty of time to thoroughly absorb every drop of cream. Chef Hinnerk suggested a potato with a bit of "waxiness" like Yukon golds so that the gratin is easy to slice and serve.

MAKES 6 SERVINGS

> 1 tablespoon unsalted butter
> 1½ pounds red or Yukon gold potatoes
> 1 clove garlic, minced
> Salt and freshly ground white pepper
> 1½ cups heavy cream, or as needed

1. Preheat the oven to 325°F. Grease an 8 x 8-inch baking pan with the butter. Peel the potatoes and use a slicer or mandoline to cut them into 1/8-inch-thick slices.

2. Scatter the garlic in the prepared pan, then layer in the potatoes, seasoning each layer with salt and pepper and drizzling with cream. Pour the last of the cream over the top and press into an even layer so that the cream just covers the top of the potatoes.

3. Cover with aluminum foil and bake in a hot water bath for 45 minutes. Remove the foil. With the back of a large spoon, press on the potatoes to bring any juices and cream to the top. Bake, uncovered, until the potatoes are lightly browned on top and tender when pierced with a fork, 20–25 minutes more.

4. Let the gratin rest for about 10 minutes before serving.

Reflections on Culinary French

Each Boot Camp day brought new key terms into our kitchen vocabulary. Much of it is the language of classical French cuisine. The language of restaurant cooking, like the language of dance, is French. Just as dancers, no matter where their origins, will continue to do pliés and jetés and tours jetés, cooks on a line, mother tongues notwithstanding, will sauté suprêmes in their sauteuses, put bouquet garnis in their soups, and cut bâtonnets and chiffonades. They will make their pan sauces from the fond left in the pan after cooking their meat and will use the bouillon resulting from simmering chicken bones for their stocks.

Kitchen French is intriguing to me, a French-speaker, because it's inconsistent. Why is my skinned, seeded, finely chopped tomato a tomato concassé and not a *tomate concassée*? The language is really Franglais, a mix of French and English; if it is French, it is ungrammatical French. My sauce is *nappé* when it coats the spoon, yet in French the term would refer to the spoon, the thing coated. *Sauté* is a participle in French, an active verb in English. Why do some French terms stick while others are translated? Why, for example, when the gravy is made with flour, stock, and drippings, is it a pan gravy, but when the gravy is simply meat juices thickened with a slurry, it's a jus de viande, or simply a jus? Why is my egg and cream thickener a liaison but my cornstarch thickener a slurry? Why is the liquid that remains after you poach something a cuisson, but the liquid that results from simmering a chicken and vegetables for some time a broth?

These questions don't really need answers. Kitchen French is not French; it is from French, like our words *rendezvous* and *Chardonnay, entrée* (which is the first course in France, not the main dish) and *hors d'oeuvre*. France has given us one of the great cuisines of the world, and with that cuisine comes a common culinary language that allows cooks from all over the world to run polyglot kitchens.

Every word that follows is a word we used and grew to understand during our week at Boot Camp. Along with the cooking instruction, we got a Berlitz course in kitchen French.

BARBECUE To cook food by grilling it over a wood or charcoal fire.

BASKET METHOD A method for deep frying in which the food is placed in fryer baskets, which are then immersed in the fat. The preferred deep-frying method for breaded items and many small items such as french fries. Sometimes foods are immersed a second time (double basket method).

BÂTONNET Item cut into small sticks, about ¼ by ¼ inch by 1 to 2 inches.

BÉCHAMEL One of the "grand sauces," a white sauce made with milk and thickened with a roux. The CIA defines béchamel as flavored with onion, but I have seen and made many a béchamel without.

BEURRE MANIÉ A mixture of equal parts by weight of whole butter and flour, used to thicken gravies and sauces. The literal translation is "kneaded butter."

BISQUE A thick, creamy soup based on crustaceans or a vegetable purée.

BLANCH To cook an item briefly in boiling water or hot fat before finishing or storing it. Blanched food is usually cooled, or "shocked," immediately after cooking in an ice-water bath.

BOUILLON Broth.

BOUQUET GARNI A small bundle of herbs tied with a string and used to flavor stocks, braises, and other preparations. It usually contains a bay leaf and a few sprigs of parsley and thyme, but it can also include other aromatics such as the dark green portion of a leek.

BRAISE A cooking method in which the main item, usually meat, is seared in fat, then simmered in stock or another liquid in a covered vessel. The cooking liquid is then reduced and used as the basis of a sauce.

BRIGADE A team of cooks organized in the French system instituted by George-Auguste Escoffier. Each cook works in a designated station and has specific responsibilities.

BROIL To cook by means of a radiant heat source placed above the food.

BROTH A flavorful, aromatic liquid made by simmering water or stock with meat, vegetables, and/or spices and herbs. Vegetable broths are made without meat.

BROWN SAUCE A sauce made from a brown stock and aromatics and thickened by a roux, a pure starch slurry, and/or a reduction.

BROWN STOCK An amber liquid made by simmering browned bones and meat (usually veal or beef) with vegetables and aromatics that include caramelized mirepoix.

BRUNOISE Small dice, about ⅛ inch on a side. Fine brunoise are ¹⁄₁₆-inch dice. Brunoise are made by first cutting julienne, then cutting crosswise.

CARAMELIZE To cook an item until the sugars in it brown. The temperature range in which sugar caramelizes is 320°F to 360°F.

CARRYOVER COOKING The process by which heat retained in cooked foods allows them to continue cooking even after removal from the cooking medium. This is especially important to know about when you roast foods, so that you don't overcook them.

CARTOUCHE A piece of parchment, cut the size of a pan, used to cover food that is being poached.

CHIFFONADE Leafy vegetables or herbs cut into fine shreds. Often used as a garnish.

CLARIFY, CLARIFICATION The process of removing solid impurities from a liquid (such as butter or stock). Clarification also refers to a mixture of ground meat, egg whites, mirepoix, tomato purée, herbs, and spices used to clarify broth for consommé.

CONCASSÉ Tomatoes that have been peeled, seeded, and chopped. The French verb *concasser* means to pound or chop coarsely.

CONSOMMÉ Broth that has been clarified using a mixture of ground meat and/or egg whites and other ingredients that trap impurities.

COULIS A thick purée, usually of vegetables but also of fruit.

COURT BOUILLON A quickly made, aromatic vegetable broth that usually includes an acidic ingredient, such as wine or vinegar. Most commonly used for poaching fish.

CUISSON Poaching liquid, including stock, fumet, court bouillon, or other liquid, which may be reduced and used as a base for the poached item's sauce.

DEEP FRYING Cooking food by immersion in hot fat. Deep-fried foods are often first coated in a batter or in bread crumbs before being cooked.

DEGLAZE To use a liquid, such as wine, water, or stock, to dissolve food particles and/or caramelized drippings left in a pan after roasting or sautéing.

DEGREASE To skim the fat off the surface of a liquid, such as a stock or a sauce.

DEMIGLACE A mixture of equal proportions of brown stock and brown sauce that has been reduced by half to a very concentrated mixture. One of the grand sauces.

DICE A knife cut that produces a uniform, cube-shaped product. Fine dice (brunoise) are ⅛ inch on a side, derived from julienne cuts. Small dice are ¼ inch cubes, derived from bâtonnet cuts. Medium dice are ⅓ inch on a side, derived from large bâtonnets. Large dice are ¾-inch cubes. Cubes are anything larger than ¾ inch dice.

FOND Stock. The term also refers to the solids left in a pan after cooking an item, which are deglazed with a liquid.

FOND DE VEAU (OR VOLAILLE) LIÉ An enjus of veal or chicken. This is a flavorful reduced sauce that is naturally low in fat, due to the use of slurry (as opposed to a roux) for thickening. It begins with the browned solids (fond) in the pan after cooking a meat, and serves as a base sauce for various preparations.

GRILL To cook food over a radiant heat source placed below the food. Also, the piece of equipment on which grilling is done.

JULIENNE Vegetables, potatoes, or other items cut into thin strips. The standard julienne cut is ⅛ inch by ⅛ inch by 1 to 2 inches. A fine julienne is 1/16 inch by 1/16 inch by 1 to 2 inches.

JUS Juice. Jus de viande is meat gravy. Meat served au jus is served with its own juice or jus lié.

JUS LIÉ Meat juice thickened lightly with arrowroot or cornstarch.

LIAISON A mixture of egg yolks and cream used to thicken and enrich sauces. Can be loosely applied to any thickener.

MARINADE An ingredient or mixture of ingredients used before cooking to flavor and moisten foods. Marinades may be liquid, in which case they usually contain an acidic ingredient such as wine, lemon juice, or vinegar, or they may be dry, in which case they are usually based on salt and herbs or spices.

MINCE To chop into very small pieces.

MIREPOIX A combination of chopped aromatic vegetables used to flavor stocks, soups, braises, and stews. The usual combination is two parts onion, one part carrot, and one part celery. A white mirepoix does not include carrots and may include mushroom trimmings. It is used for pale or white sauces and stocks.

MISE EN PLACE The preparation and assembly of ingredients, pans, utensils, and serving pieces needed for a particular dish or service period. The literal translation is "put in place."

NAPPÉ When something is coated with sauce, it is nappé. The word has come to describe the thickness of a sauce that can coat an item. A sauce that is nappé will coat the front and back of a wooden spoon.

OBLIQUE CUT (ROLL CUT) A knife cut used with long, cylindrical vegetables, in which the item is cut on a diagonal, rolled 90 degrees, then cut on the same diagonal, producing a piece with two angled edges.

OIGNON BRÛLÉ A peeled, halved onion seared on top of the stove and used to enhance the color of stock and consommé.

OIGNON PIQUÉ A whole peeled onion to which a bay leaf is attached, using a clove as a tack. Used to flavor béchamel sauce and some soups.

PAN FRYING Cooking food in a deep fat in a skillet. The method involves more fat than sautéing or stir frying, and less fat than deep frying.

PAN STEAMING A method of cooking in which food is cooked in a very small amount of liquid in a covered pan over direct heat.

PARBOIL To rapidly boil a food (usually a vegetable) to minimize cooking time and retain color and texture. An item is never parboiled longer than 7 minutes. Parboiled vegetables are usually shocked in ice water and held to be finished before service.

PAUPIETTES A fillet or scallop of fish or meat that is rolled up, often around a stuffing, and poached or braised.

PINCÉ A tomato product that has been caramelized by sautéing.

POACH To cook gently in simmering liquid that is 160°F to 185°F. Shallow poaching is gentle cooking in a shallow pan of simmering liquid. The liquid is often reduced and used for the sauce. Deep poaching is gentle cooking in which the food is completely submerged.

PRESSURE STEAMING A method of cooking using a pressure cooker, in which food is cooked in water that is heated under pressure in a sealed compartment, allowing it to reach temperatures higher than boiling. The food is placed in the sealed chamber and is not removed until the pressure is released.

PUREE To process food by mashing, straining, or chopping it very finely in order to transform it to a smooth paste. Also refers to the product produced using this technique.

RAFT A mixture of ingredients used to clarify a consommé. The ingredients rise to the surface and form a floating mass.

RECOVERY TIME The time it takes oil to come back up to the right temperature for deep frying between batches.

REDUCE To reduce the volume of a liquid by simmering or boiling. It is done to concentrate flavors and provide a thicker consistency.

REDUCTION The product that results when a liquid is reduced.

RONDELLES Rondelles are made by cutting long cylindrical vegetables crosswise. They can be varied by cutting on the diagonal to produce ovals, by cutting the vegetable in half lengthwise first to produce half-moons, or by scoring the surface with channels to produce flowers.

ROUX A thickening agent made with flour and fat (usually butter) and cooked to varying degrees (white, blond, brown), depending on its intended use. Used to thicken liquids. The standard ratio of flour to fat is (by volume) 2½ parts flour to 1 part fat or (by weight) 60 percent flour and 40 percent fat.

SACHET D'ÉPICES Aromatic ingredients, encased in cheesecloth, that are used to flavor stocks and other liquids. A standard sachet contains parsley stems, cracked peppercorns, dried thyme, and a bay leaf.

SAUTÉ To cook quickly in a small amount of fat in a pan on top of the stove.

SAUTEUSE A shallow skillet with sloping sides and a single, long handle, used for sautéing. Referred to generically as a sauté pan.

SAUTOIR A shallow skillet with straight sides and a single, long handle, used for sautéing. Referred to generically as a sauté pan.

SEAR To brown the surface of food in fat over high heat before finishing by another method (for example, braising or roasting) in order to add flavor.

SHOCK To quickly cool down a cooked item in an ice-water bath.

SLURRY A starch such as arrowroot, cornstarch, or potato starch dispersed in a small amount of cold liquid to prevent it from lumping when added to a hot liquid as a thickener.

SMOKE POINT The temperature at which a fat begins to break down when heated.

SMOKE ROASTING A method for roasting in which items are placed on a rack in a pan containing wood chips that smolder, emitting smoke, when the pan is placed in the oven or on the range top.

SPIT ROASTING A method for cooking an item in which the food is placed on a large skewer or spit over or in front of an open flame or other radiant heat source.

STATION The place a person works in a professional kitchen.

STEAMING A cooking method in which food is cooked in a vapor bath created by boiling water or other liquid.

STIR FRYING A top-of-the-stove method of cooking similar to sautéing, in which items are cooked over very high heat, using little fat. In Asia this is done in a wok, and the food is kept moving constantly.

SUPRÊME The breast fillet and wing of chicken or other poultry.

SWEAT To cook something in a small amount of fat over moderate heat without browning.

SWIMMING METHOD A method of deep frying in which the product is placed directly in the hot fat. The food will be agitated and removed with a spider. This is preferable for battered items.

TIMBALE A small pail-shaped mold used to shape rice, custards, mousselines, and other dishes. Also, a preparation made in such a mold.

TOURNÉ A decorative cut usually used for garnishes. The shape of "turned" vegetables is similar to a barrel or football.

VELOUTÉ A sauce made with white stock (chicken, veal, seafood) thickened with white roux. One of the grand sauces. Also a cream soup made with a velouté sauce base and flavorings, usually finished with a liaison.

WHITE STOCK A light-colored stock made with bones that have not been browned.

Index

A

Aglianico del Vulture, 105
Allumettes, 130
American Bounty Restaurant, 77–79
Amish-Style Chicken and Corn Soup, 163–164
Appellation d'Origine Controlée (AOC), 74–76
Appetizers:
  Beef Satay, 150
  Bruschetta with Oven-Roasted Tomatoes and Fontina Cheese, 151
  Chicken and Fennel Bandilleros with Tomato and Roasted Pepper Coulis, 154
  Coconut Shrimp with Sweet and Sour Sauce, 155
  Crab and Cod Cakes, 160–161
  Goat Cheese in Phyllo with Roasted Pepper Salad, 152
  Mozzarella Roulade, 157
  Pork and Corn Dumplings in Cilantro Cream Sauce, 158–159
  Steamed Mussels with Chorizo, Peppers, and Tomatoes, 161
Apples, cutting, 135
Aromatics:
  for braising, 88
  for soups, 34–35
  for steaming, 91
  for stocks, 12
Arrowroot, 26
Asian Kitchen, 39, 49
Asian rice, 222
Asian-Style Barbecue Sauce, Pork Ribs with, 185
Avocados, cutting, 134

B

Baby back ribs, grilling, 185
Balance, in plating, 110
Barbecue, 65, 230
Barbecue Sauce, Asian-Style, Pork Ribs with, 185
Basic Rice Pilaf, 190
Basil Pesto, Gnocchi with, 202–203

Basket method (deep frying), 47–48, 230
Bâtonnets, 129–130, 230
Béchamel Sauce, 15, 16, 230
Beef:
  Filet Mignon, Sautéed, with Mixed Cracked Peppercorns, 189
  Rainbow, 176
  Roast Sirloin of, with Jus Lié, 184
  Satay, 150
  stock, 13
  Swiss Steak, 175
  Wellington, 115
  Yankee Pot Roast, 174–175
Beets, Glazed, 199
Bell peppers, cutting, 134
Bench scrapers, 127
Beurre blanc, 16, 147
  Pommery Mustard, Grilled Pork Chops with, 187
Beurre manié, 24, 230
Bisques, 34
  defined, 230
  Lobster, 38
  making, 36–37
  Shrimp, 169
Blanching, 97
  defined, 230
  for french fries, 198
  pineapple, 136
  tomatoes, 133
Blocking lamb shanks, 173
Blond roux, 24
Boiled or Steamed Potatoes with Parsley, 191
Boiling, 97
Boning knife, 127
Bordeaux, 76
Bordelaise Sauce, 15
Bouillons, 34, 35
  court, 231
  defined, 230
Bouquet garni, 230
Braised Fennel with Parmesan Cheese, 90
Braised Greens, 192

Braised Lamb Shanks, 173–174
Braised Red Cabbage, 193
Braising, 84–90
  accompaniments for, 87
  basic procedure for, 85, 88–89
  defined, 230
  ingredients for, 85–87
Bread, Corn, 196
Breading, for pan-frying, 40–41
Brigade, 230
Brine (for tenderizing), 60
Broccoli Rabe with Garlic and Olive Oil, 194
Broiling, 65–67
  basic procedure for, 65
  defined, 230
  grilling vs., 65
Bromelain, 136
Broths, 34, 35
  Chicken, 162
  defined, 230
  stocks vs., 162
Brown Chicken Stock, 142
Brown roux, 24
Brown sauce, 15, 16, 230
Brown stocks, 13
  defined, 230
  ingredients/procedures for, 14
  Veal, 140–141
Brunoise, 129, 230
Bruschetta with Oven-Roasted Tomatoes and Fontina Cheese, 151
"Building a raft," 164, 165
Buttered Sugar Snap Peas, 194

C

Cabernet Sauvignons, 74, 76
Caramelize, 230
Caraway Orange Glaze, Grilled Salmon with, 70
Carolina rice, 222
Carrot(s):
  cutting, 132
  Flan, 195
  Glazed, 200
  Tournéed Zucchini and, 222

Carryover cooking, 61, 230
Cartouche, 93, 231
Carving fork, 127
Cast iron skillets, cooking in, 196
Catsups, 16
Celery, cutting, 132–133
Chardonnays, 73, 76
Chasseur Sauce, 16
Chefs, status of, 32
Chef's knife, 126, 127
Chicken:
    Breast, Provençal, 22–23
    Broth, 162
    Consommé, 164–165
    and Fennel Bandilleros, with
        Tomato and Roasted Pepper
        Coulis, 154
    Pan-Fried Breast of, with Prosciutto
        and Mozzarella, 179–180
    Pan-Fried Buttermilk, with Coun-
        try-Style Gravy, 180–181
    Poached Breast, with Tarragon
        Sauce, 170
    Roast, with Pan Gravy, 64
    roasting, 62–63
    sautéing, 18–21
    Soup, Amish-Style Corn and,
        163–164
    Stock, 13, 142
    Stock, Brown, 142
    trussing, 137
    Velouté, 144–145
Chiffonade, 130, 193, 231
Chile peppers, cutting, 134
Chopping, 129
Chutneys, 16
CIA, see Culinary Institute of America
Cilantro Cream Sauce, Pork and Corn
    Dumplings with, 158–159
Citrus fruit, cutting, 135
Citrus suprêmes, 135
Clarify/clarification:
    of consommé, 165
    defined, 231
Cleanliness in cooking, 126
Clear soups, 34–35
Coatings:
    for deep frying, 47
    for pan-frying, 40–41
Coconut Shrimp with Sweet and Sour
    Sauce, 155
Cod and Crab Cakes, 160–161
Colavita Center for Italian Food and
    Wine, 103

Cold soups, 34
Coleslaw, Warm, 226–227
Color:
    in menu planning, 98
    in plating, 110, 113
Combination cooking methods, 84
Concassé:
    defined, 231
    Tomato, 133, 148–149, 234
Consommés, 34–35
    Chicken, 164–165
    clarifying, 165
    defined, 231
Contemporary sauces, 16
Cook to color, 18, 44
Corked wines, 76
Corn Bread, 196
Cornstarch, 26
Coulis, 16
    defined, 231
    Tomato, 149
    Tomato, Deep-Fried Flounder with,
        182
    Tomato and Roasted Pepper,
        Chicken and Fennel Bandilleros
        with, 154
    Tomato and Roasted Red Pepper, 148
Country-Style Gravy, Pan-Fried Butter-
    milk Chicken with, 180–181
Court bouillon, 231
Crab and Cod Cakes, 160–161
Cream of Mushroom Soup, 167
Cream soups, 34. See also Velouté(s)
    base for, 144
    bisques, 36–37
    Lobster Bisque, 38
    Mushroom, 167
    Shrimp Bisque, 169
Creole mustard, 146
Cross-contamination, 126
Crudo di Tonno alla Battuta, 100, 104
Crus, 75
Cuisines of Asia, 49
Cuisson, 95, 231
Culinary Boot Camp, 5
Culinary French, 9, 229–234
Culinary Institute of America (CIA):
    American Bounty Restaurant,
        77–79
    Asian Kitchen, 39, 49
    courses offered by, 9
    Escoffier Restaurant, 53–55
    fabrication rooms/storerooms/walk-
        ins, 33, 49–52

    ingredients used by, 49
    meat room, 52
    Ristorante Caterina de' Medici, 100,
        103–105
    Roth Hall, 4, 49
    St. Andrew's Café, 27–29
    Seafood ID & Fabrication Kitchen,
        49, 51
    skills kitchens, 9–10
Cuts, 24, 128–137
    for fruits, 135–137
    precision, 129–130
    rough, 129
    for vegetables, 131–135

D

Dashi, 12, 34
Deep-Fried Flounder with Tomato
    Coulis, 182
Deep-Fried Parsley Sprigs, 183
Deep-Fried Parsnips, 198
Deep frying, 47–49
    basket method for, 47–48
    defined, 231
    recovery time, 233
    swimming method for, 48
Deep poaching, 93
Deglazing, 19, 21, 231
Degreasing, 14–15, 231
Demiglace, 15, 16, 231
Demonstrations, in skills kitchens, 9
Dépouiller, 13
DeShetler, John, 5–7
    on barbecue, 65
    on bisques, 36, 37
    blocking lamb shank demo, 173
    cutting steak demo, 150
    on cutting zucchini, 219
    on demiglace, 16
    on dicing, 129
    on draining pan-fried foods, 42
    on mise en place, 125
    mozzarella-making demo, 157
    on peeling and cutting, 133–137
    on poaching fish, 94
    on presentation, 119
    on stir-frying, 39
    stir-frying demo, 176
    on tourné cuts, 222
    on trussing poultry, 137
Dice, 129, 231
Dogfish, 51
Doneness test:
    "by hand," 18

for meats, 18, 23
for pan-frying, 45
for roasted meats, 62
Dry heat cooking, 58 70
    broiling, 65–67
    carryover cooking with, 61
    grilling, 65–70
    roasting, 59–64
Dumplings:
    Gnocchi with Basil Pesto, *202–203*
    Pork and Corn, with Cilantro
        Cream Sauce, *158–159*
    Spaetzle, *223*
    Spaetzle, Spinach, with Sapsago
        Cheese, *224*

E

Eggs, poaching, 92
Emulsions, 16
Enjus, 231
Entrées:
    Braised Lamb Shanks, *173–174*
    Chicken Breast Provençal, *22–23*
    Deep-Fried Flounder with Tomato
        Coulis, *182*
    Grilled Pork Chops with Pommery
        Mustard Beurre Blanc, *187*
    Grilled Salmon with Caraway
        Orange Glaze, *70*
    Ossobuco alla Milanese, *188–189*
    Pan-Fried Breast of Chicken with
        Prosciutto and Mozzarella,
        179–180
    Pan-Fried Buttermilk Chicken with
        Country-Style Gravy, *180–181*
    Pan-Fried Pork Loin with Herb
        Sauce, *46–47*
    Poached Chicken Breast with
        Tarragon Sauce, *170*
    Poached Fillet of Sole with White
        Wine Sauce, *96*
    Pork Ribs with Asian-Style Barbecue
        Sauce, *185*
    Rainbow Beef, *176*
    Roast Chicken with Pan Gravy, *64*
    Roast Sirloin of Beef with Jus Lié,
        184
    Sautéed Fillet Mignon with Mixed
        Cracked Peppercorns, *189*
    Yankee Pot Roast, *174–175*
Escoffier, Auguste, 15, 22
Escoffier Restaurant, 53–55
Espagnole Sauce, 15
Essences, 13

F

Fabrication rooms, CIA, 49, 51
Fats, cooking with, 39–49
    deep frying, 47 49
    pan frying, 40–47
    sautéing, 16–25
    stir frying, 39–40
Fennel:
    Braised, with Parmesan Cheese, *90*
    and Chicken Bandilleros, with
        Tomato and Roasted Pepper
        Coulis, *154*
Fermiere cut, 131
Filleting tomatoes, 133
Fillet knife, 127
Filet Mignon, Sautéed, with Mixed
    Cracked Peppercorns, *189*
Final exam:
    food order lists for, 33
    menu development, 32–34
    presentation, 119–120
    production, 33, 114–117
Fine brunoise, 129
Fine julienne, 130
Fish:
    Crab and Cod Cakes, *160–161*
    Flounder, Deep-Fried, with Tomato
        Coulis, *182*
    Fumet, *143*
    grilling, 68–69
    poaching, 92, 94–95
    Salmon, Grilled, with Carraway
        Orange Glaze, *70*
    Sole, Poached Fillet of, with White
        Wine Sauce, *96*
    for steaming, 91
    Stock, 13, *143*
Flan, Carrot, *195*
Flatfish, 51
Flavor:
    in menu planning, 98
    in plating, 113
Flavored butters, 16
Flounder, Deep-Fried, with Tomato
    Coulis, *182*
Flow (in plating), 110–111
Fond de cuisine (fond), 12
    defined, 231
    as sauce base, 18
Fond de veau (volaille) lié, 231
Fontina Cheese, Bruschetta with
    Oven-Roasted Tomatoes and, *151*
Food selection, in plating, 110
French cooking terms, 7, 9, 229–234

French-Fried Potatoes, *198–199*
Fruits:
    cutting, 135–137
    for poaching, 92
    for steaming, 91
Fumets, 13
    Fish, *143*
Functional garnishes, 108, 110

G

Garlic, cutting, 132
Garnishes, 108, 110
Gaufrettes, 130
Ginger, cutting, 133
Glaze, Caraway Orange, Grilled
    Salmon with, *70*
Glazed Beets, *199*
Glazed Carrots, *200*
Glazed Sweet Potatoes, *201*
Glutamic acid, 12, 144
Gnocchi with Basil Pesto, *202–203*
Goat Cheese in Phyllo with Roasted
    Pepper Salad, *152*
Graduation (from Boot Camp), 120
Grand sauces, 15–16
Grapes (for wines), 72
Gratin Dauphinois, *228*
Gratins, 89
Greens, Braised, *192*
Green Beans:
    with Bacon and Shallots, *204–205*
    Haricots Verts, *208*
    and Walnuts, *204*
Grilled Pork Chops with Pommery
    Mustard Beurre Blanc, *187*
Grilled Salmon with Caraway Orange
    Glaze, *70*
Grilled Yellow Squash, *207*
Grilled Zucchini, *207*
Grilling, 65–70
    basic procedure for, 65
    broiling vs., 65
    defined, 232
    fish, 68–69
    marinades for, 66
    salmon, 68–69
    sauces for, 66, 68
    vegetables, 207
Guiding hand, when cutting, 128
Guilfoyle, Bill, 74

H

Haricots Verts, *208*
Height:
    in menu planning, 98
    in plating, 110, 113
Hollandaise Sauce, 15, 16
Hot and Spicy Mixed Vegetables, *208–209*
Housekeeping issues, 7
Hydrogenated fats, 41

I

Ingredients, organizing, 126
Items:
    in menu planning, 98
    in plating, 113

J

Jasmine rice, 222
Julienne, 129–130, 232
Jus, 232
Jus Lié:
    defined, 232
    Roast Sirloin of Beef with, *184*

K

Kiwis, cutting, 137
Knife kit, 126–127
Knife skills, 24, 124. *See also* Cuts

L

Lamb Shanks:
    blocking, 173
    Braised, *173–174*
Large dice, 129
Leeks, cutting, 133
Liaison, 24, 232
Lobster Bisque, *38*
Lozenge cut, 131

M

Mahi, 51
Maillard reaction, 60
Maltese Sauce, 16
Mangos, cutting, 136
Marinades:
    for braising, 88
    defined, 232
    for grilling/broiling, 66
    for roasting and grilling, 60
Marinara sauce, 149
Mashed Potatoes and Turnips, *212*

Matchsticks, 130
Mayonnaise, 16
Measuring spoons, 127
Meats:
    blanching, 97
    for braising/stewing, 84–86
    carryover cooking in, 61
    cooking to color, 18
    doneness test for, 18, 23
    for pan-frying, 40
    for poaching, 92
    roasting, 59–63
    for sautés, 17
    for soups, 35
    for steaming, 91
    for stir-frying, 39
    tenderizing, 60
Meat room, CIA, 52
Medium dice, 129
Melon ballers, 127
Menu development:
    for final exam, 32–34
    S.C.H.I.F.T. procedure for, 98–99
Menu Development Worksheets, 98
Merlots, 74
Metal spatula, 127
Mincing, 129, 232
Minestrone, 34
Mirepoix:
    for braising, 88
    defined, 232
    for stocks, 12
Mise en place, 125–126
    defined, 6, 232
    for stir-frying, 39–40
    work area organization, 125–126
Mixed Vegetables, Hot and Spicy, *208–209*
Moist heat cooking, 82–97
    boiling, 97
    braising, 85–90
    poaching, 91–96
    simmering, 97
    steaming, 91
    stewing, 84–85
Molecular splashover, 49
Morel and Wild Mushroom Ragoût, *227–228*
Mornay Sauce, 16
"Mother sauces," 15
Mousseline Sauce, 16
Mozzarella Roulade, 157

Mushrooms:
    Porcini, Saffron Risotto with Basil and, *217*
    Ragoût, Morel and Wild Mushroom, *227–228*
    Sautéed, *218*
    Soup, Cream of, *167*
Mussels, Steamed, with Chorizo, Peppers, and Tomatoes, *161*
Mustard Tartar Sauce, *146*

N

Nappé, 18, 232
Nonfunctional garnishes (NFGs), 108, 110

O

Oblique cuts, 130, 232
Oignon brûlé, 232
Oignon piqué, 232
Oils, for deep frying, 48–49
Onions, cutting, 131–132
Organization of work area, 126
Ossobuco alla Milanese, *188–189*
Oven-Roasted Vegetables, *211*

P

Pale roux, 24, 25
Pans:
    for braising/stewing, 86
    organizing, 126
    for pan-frying, 41
    for poaching, 93
    for sautés, 17–18
    for stir-frying, 39
Pan-Fried Breast of Chicken with Prosciutto and Mozzarella, *179–180*
Pan-Fried Buttermilk Chicken with Country-Style Gravy, *180–181*
Pan-Fried Pork Loin with Herb Sauce, *46–47*
Pan frying, 40–47
    basic procedure for, 44–45
    breading procedure for, 40–41
    defined, 232
    fats for, 41
    foods for, 40
    pans for, 41
    sauces for, 42
Pan Gravy, Roast Chicken with, *64*
Pan sauces, 16, 19, 21
Pan steaming, 232

Parboiling, 97
    defined, 232
    of vegetables, 194
Paring knife, 126
Parisian scoops, 127
Parsley Sprigs, Deep-Fried, *183*
Parsnips:
    cutting, 132
    Deep-Fried, *198*
    and Pear Purée, *212–213*
Pasta, simmering, 97
Paupiettes, 233
Paysanne cut, 131
Peanut Sauce, *146*
Pear and Parsnip Purée, *212–213*
Peelers, 126, 127
Peppers, cutting, 134
Pinçage, 36
Pincé:
    defined, 233
    tomato, 141
Pineapples, cutting, 136
Pinot Noirs, 74, 76
Plating, 108–113
    choosing plates for, 111
    components of, 110–111
    for final exam, 119–120
    garnishes, 108, 110
    of sautéed chicken, 21
    S.C.H.I.F.T. checklist for, 113
Poached Chicken Breast with Tarragon
    Sauce, *170*
Poached Fillet of Sole with White
    Wine Sauce, *96*
Poaching, 91–96
    deep, 93
    defined, 233
    shallow, 92–95
    temperatures for, 92, 93
Polenta, *213–214*
Pommery Mustard Beurre Blanc, *147*
    Grilled Pork Chops with, *187*
Pommes Duchesse, *214–215*
Pork:
    Chops, Grilled, with Pommery Mus-
        tard Beurre Blanc, *187*
    and Corn Dumplings, with Cilantro
        Cream Sauce, *158–159*
    Loin, Pan-Fried, with Herb Sauce,
        46–47
    Ribs, with Asian-Style Barbecue
        Sauce, *185*

Portioning cuts, 129
Potato(es):
    Boiled or Steamed, with Parsley, *191*
    French-Fried, *198–199*
    Mashed, Turnips and, *212*
    Pommes Duchesse, *214–215*
    Puree, *215*
    with Saffron and Parsley, *191*
Potato starch, 26
Pot Roast, 84
    Yankee, *174–175*
Poultry:
    boning, 124
    for poaching, 92
    roasting, 62–64
    stock, 13
    trussing, 137
Precision cuts, 129–130
Presentation:
    for final exam, 119–120
    plating, 108–113
Pressure steaming, 233
Production:
    defined, 32
    for final exam, 114–117
Proteins:
    building dishes around, 100, 102
    exposed to heat, 59–60
Puck, Wolfgang, 99, 189
Purees, 16, 34
    defined, 233
    Parsnip and Pear, *212–213*
    Potato, *215*
Pure starches, 26

R

Raft:
    building, 164, 165
    defined, 233
Rainbow Beef, *176*
Raw tuna appetizer, 100, 104
Recipe development, 100–102
Recovery time (deep frying), 48, 233
Red and Yellow Peppers, Sautéed, *219*
Red Cabbage, Braised, *193*
Reduce, defined, 233
Reduction, defined, 233
Relishes, 16
Restaurants:
    American Bounty Restaurant,
        77–79
    Escoffier Restaurant, 53–55

Ristorante Caterina de' Medici, 100,
    103–105
    St. Andrew's Café, 27–29
Ribbons (cut), 130
Rice:
    amounts of water for, 222
    Pilaf, Basic, *190*
    Saffron Risotto with Porcini Mush-
        rooms and Basil, *217*
    Steamed, 222
Rieslings, 73
Ripple cuts, 130
Risotto, Saffron, with Porcini Mush-
    rooms and Basil, *217*
Ristorante Caterina de' Medici, 100,
    103–105
Roast Chicken with Pan Gravy, *64*
Roasted Pepper Salad, Goat Cheese in
    Phyllo with, *152*
Roasting, 59–64
    carryover cooking with, 61
    chicken, 62–63
    internal temperatures for, 60, 61
    protein behavior during, 59–60
    smoke, 234
    spit, 234
    steps in, 61
    vegetables, 211
Roast Sirloin of Beef with Jus Lié, *184*
Roll cuts, 130, 232
Rondelles, 130–131, 233
Roth Hall, 4, 49
Rough cuts, 129
Roux, 24–25
    defined, 24, 233
    making, 24–25
    ratio of fat to starch for, 24
    ratio of roux to recipe ingredients, 25
    slurries vs., 173
Rubber spatula, 127

S

Sachet d'épices, 142, 233
Saffron Risotto with Porcini Mush-
    rooms and Basil, *217*
St. Andrew's Café, 27–29
Salmon, 51
    Grilled, with Caraway Orange
        Glaze, *70*
    grilling, 68–69
Salsas, 16
Sancerres, 76

Sante Fe Chili Soup, *168*
Sauces, 15–16
    Barbecue, Asian-Style, Pork Ribs
        with, *185*
    Béchamel, 15, 230
    beurre blanc, 16, 147
    Bordelaise, 15
    brown, 15, 16, 230
    Chasseur, 16
    Chicken Velouté, *144–145*
    Cilantro Cream, Pork and Corn
        Dumplings with, *158–159*
    contemporary, 16
    defined, 15
    Espagnole, 15
    fond as base for, 18
    grand, 15–16
    for grilling/broiling, 66, 68
    Herb, Pan-Fried Pork Loin with,
        46–47
    Hollandaise, 15, 16
    Maltese, 16
    marinara, 149
    Mornay, 16
    Mousseline, 16
    Mustard Tartar, *146*
    for pan-fried items, 42
    Peanut, *146*
    for poached foods, 92, 93, 95
    Pommery Mustard Beurre Blanc, *147*
    with roasted meats, 63
    for sautéed chicken, 19, 21
    with sautés, 16
    Soubise, 16
    for stir-frying, 40
    Sweet and Sour, Coconut Shrimp
        with, *155*
    Tarragon, Poached Chicken Breast
        with, *170*
    thickening, 173
    Tomato, 15
    Tomato and Roasted Red Pepper
        Coulis, *148*
    Tomato Concassé, *148–149*
    Tomato Coulis, *149*
    Velouté, 15
    White Wine, Poached Fillet of Sole
        with, *96*
Sauté, defined, *233*
Sautéed Filet Mignon with Mixed
    Cracked Peppercorns, *189*
Sautéed Mushrooms, *218*
Sautéed Red and Yellow Peppers, *219*

Sautéed Snow Peas with Sesame
    Seeds, *220*
Sautéed Zucchini, *219–220*
Sautéing, 16–23
    defined, 16
    making pan sauce, 19
    pans for, 17–18
    procedure for, 19
Sauteuse, 17, 233
Sautoirs, 17, 41, 93, 233
Sauvignon Blancs, 73
S.C.H.I.F.T. checklist, 98–99, 113
Seafood:
    bisques, 36–37
    Crab and Cod Cakes, *160–161*
    Lobster Bisque, *38*
    Mussels, Steamed, with Chorizo,
        Peppers, and Tomatoes, *161*
    for pan-frying, 40
    for poaching, 92
    raw tuna appetizer, 100, 104
    for sautés, 17
    Shrimp, Coconut, with Sweet and
        Sour Sauce, *155*
    Shrimp Bisque, *169*
    simmering, 97
    for steaming, 91
    in stews, 86
    for stir-frying, 39
Seafood ID & Fabrication Kitchen, 49,
    51
Searing, 18
    defined, 234
    prior to roasting, 60
Sequencing, 21
Serrated knife, 126, 127
Shallots, cutting, 132
Shallow poaching, 92–95
Shape:
    in menu planning, 98
    in plating, 110, 113
Sharpening stone, 127
Shock, 234
Shortening, 41
Shrimp, Coconut, with Sweet and
    Sour Sauce, *155*
Shrimp Bisque, *169*
Side dishes:
    Basic Rice Pilaf, *190*
    Boiled or Steamed Potatoes with
        Parsley, *191*
    Braised Fennel with Parmesan
        Cheese, *90*

    Braised Greens, *192*
    Braised Red Cabbage, *193*
    Broccoli Rabe with Garlic and Olive
        Oil, *194*
    Buttered Sugar Snap Peas, *194*
    Carrot Flan, *195*
    Corn Bread, *196*
    Deep-Fried Parsnips, *198*
    French-Fried Potatoes, *198–199*
    Glazed Beets, *199*
    Glazed Carrots, *200*
    Glazed Sweet Potatoes, *201*
    Gnocchi with Basil Pesto, *202–203*
    Gratin Dauphinois, *228*
    Green Beans and Walnuts, *204*
    Green Beans with Bacon and Shal-
        lots, *204–205*
    Grilled Yellow Squash, *207*
    Grilled Zucchini, *207*
    Haricots Verts, *208*
    Hot and Spicy Mixed Vegetables,
        208–209
    Mashed Potatoes and Turnips, *212*
    Morel and Wild Mushroom Ragoût,
        227–228
    Oven-Roasted Vegetables, *211*
    Parsnip and Pear Purée, *212–213*
    Polenta, *213–214*
    Pommes Duchesse, *214–215*
    Potato Puree, *215*
    Saffron Risotto with Porcini Mush-
        rooms and Basil, *217*
    Sautéed Mushrooms, *218*
    Sautéed Red and Yellow Peppers, *219*
    Sautéed Snow Peas with Sesame
        Seeds, *220*
    Sautéed Zucchini, *219–220*
    Spaetzle, *223*
    Spinach Spaetzle with Sapsago
        Cheese, *224*
    Spinach with Bacon and Pine Nuts,
        226
    Steamed Rice, *222*
    Tournéed Zucchini and Carrots, *222*
    Warm Coleslaw, *226–227*
Simmering, 84, 97
Singer (singe), 167
Skills kitchens, 9–10
Skimming stock, 13–14
Slurries, 26
    defined, 24, 234
    roux vs., 173
Small dice, 129

Smith, Brian, 72–74, 77, 78
Smoke point, 234
Smoke roasting, 234
Snow Peas, Sautéed, with Sesame
    Seeds, 220
Sole, Poached Fillet of, with White
    Wine Sauce, 96
Soubise, 16
Soups, 34–38
    Amish-Style Chicken and Corn,
        163–164
    aromatics for, 34, 35
    bisques, 36–37, 230
    Chicken Broth, 162
    Chicken Consommé, 164–165
    clear, 34–35
    cooking technique for, 34
    Cream of Mushroom, 167
    Lobster Bisque, 38
    major components of, 34–35
    Sante Fe Chili, 168
    Shrimp Bisque, 169
    thick, 34
Spaetzle, 223, 224
Spatula, 127
Specialty soups, 34
Spinach:
    with Bacon and Pine Nuts, 226
    Spaetzle, with Sapsago Cheese, 224
Spit roasting, 234
Squaring off, 129
Starches:
    with braises/stews, 87
    pan-frying, 40
    for thickening, 26
Station, 234
Steamed Mussels with Chorizo, Pep-
    pers, and Tomatoes, 161
Steamed Rice, 222
Steaming, 91
    defined, 234
    pan, 232
    pressure, 233
Steel, sharpening, 127
"Stepped-up" dishes, 100, 115
Stewing, 84–85
    accompaniments for, 87
    basic procedure for, 85
Stir frying, 39–40, 234
Stocks, 12–15
    basic ratio for, 12
    broths vs., 162
    brown, 230

Brown Chicken, 142
Brown Veal, 140–141
Chicken, 142
defined, 12
degreasing, 14–15
Fish, 143
quality of, 12
simmering times for, 13
skimming, 13–14
straining, 15
Vegetable, 144
white, 234
Storerooms, CIA, 33, 49–52
Sugar Snap Peas, Buttered, 194
Suprême, 234
Sushi rice, 222
Sweat, 234
Sweet and Sour Sauce, Coconut
    Shrimp with, 155
Sweet Potatoes, Glazed, 201
Swimming method (deep frying), 48,
    234
Swiss Steak, 84, 175
Swivel-bladed peeler, 126, 127
Syrahs, 74

T
Tannins (in wine), 72
Tarragon Sauce, Poached Chicken
    Breast with, 170
Tasting foods, importance of, 9
Tenderizing meats, 60
Terroir, 74, 75
Texture:
    in menu planning, 98
    in plating, 113
Thermometers, 127
Thickened soups, 34–37
Thickeners, 24–26
    for braising, 88
    for contemporary sauces, 16
    roux, 24–25
    for sauces, 173
    slurries, 26
Timbale, 234
Tomato(es):
    Concassé, 133, 148–149, 234
    Coulis, 149
    Coulis, Deep-Fried Flounder with,
        182
    cutting, 133
    Oven-Roasted, Bruschetta with
        Fontina Cheese and, 151

paste, 12
pincé, 141
and Roasted Pepper Coulis, Chicken
    and Fennel Bandilleros with, 154
and Roasted Red Pepper Coulis, 148
Sauce, 15
Tomato product, 141
Tongs, 127
Tournés, 130, 131, 234
Tournéed Zucchini and Carrots, 222
Trans fats, 41
Trussing poultry, 137
Tuna cake, 29
Turnips, Mashed Potatoes and, 212

U
Unity (in plating), 110
Utility knife, 126, 127

V
Valpolicella, 105
Veal:
    Ossobuco alla Milanese, 188–189
    stock, 13, 140–141
Vegetable(s):
    blanching, 97
    for braising/stewing, 87, 88
    cutting, 131–135
    grilling, 207
    Mixed, Hot and Spicy, 208–209
    Oven-Roasted, 211
    for pan-frying, 40
    parboiling, 97, 194
    for poaching, 92
    roasting, 211
    for sautés, 17
    soups, 34, 35
    for steaming, 91
    for stir-frying, 39
    Stock, 13, 144
Velouté(s), 34
    Chicken, 144–145
    defined, 234
    Sauce, 15
Vinaigrette, 16
Viogniers, 73, 74
von Bargen, Hinnerk, 5, 7, 9
    on beurre blanc, 147
    on boiled potatoes, 191
    on braised cabbage, 193
    on chicken stock, 142
    coaching by, 115
    on cutting tournés, 130

on cutting zucchini, 219
on deep frying, 49
on final exam assignments, 33–34
on fish stock, 143
on grilling, 65, 66
on meats for sautés, 17
on pan-frying, 40–42
on plating, 108
on poaching, 91–93
on pot roast, 84
on proteins exposed to heat,
    59–60
on recipe development, 100
on roux for velouté, 147
on sachet d'épices, 142
on sauces, 16
on sautéing chicken, 18, 19
on skimming stock, 13
spaetzle made by, 100, 223, 224
on steaming, 91

on stir-frying, 39
on thickening agents, 26
on trussing poultry, 137

W

Waffle cuts, 130
Walk-ins, CIA, 33, 49–52
Warm Coleslaw, *226–227*
Whisk, 127
White roux, 24, 25
White stocks, 14, 234
White Wine Sauce, Poached Fillet of
    Sole with, *96*
Wines, 72–76
    AOC of, 74–76
    corked, 76
    grapes for, 72
    qualities of, 72–74
    and *terroir,* 74
Wine tool, 127

Woks, 39, 49
Wooden spoon, 127
Work area, 125–126
Work surfaces, 126

Y

Yankee Pot Roast, *174–175*
Yellow Squash, Grilled, *207*

Z

Zest, citrus, 135
Zones (grilling), 69
Zucchini:
    cutting, 134–135
    Grilled, *207*
    Sautéed, *219–220*
    Tournéed Carrots and, *222*

Benefactors Acknowledgments

Many of the educational facilities at The Culinary Institute of America are made possible by the generous financial support of the friends and benefactors of the college. We wish to acknowledge and thank the following individuals and companies who have made the facilities pictured in "Culinary Boot Camp" available:

Dr. Lewis J. and Ruth E. Minor for the Dr. Lewis J. and Ruth E. Minor Skills I and Skills II Kitchens in the J. Willard Marriott Continuing Education Center (ii, iii, vi, viii, 2, 3, 5, 30, 31, 33, 56, 57, 68, 69, 71, 80, 81, 83, 97, 109, 111, 114, 121, 138, 139); North American Companies/ABC Affiliated Distributors/Sherman Memorial Fund for the North American Companies/ABC Affiliated Distributors/Sherman Memorial Fund Lecture Hall in the J. Willard Marriott Continuing Education Center (xiii, 106, 107, 118, 122, 123); Pollio Italian Cheese Company and Victoria Packing Corporation for the Pollio Pizza Station and Victoria Packing Corporation Antipasto Bar in the Colavita Center for Italian Food and Wine (103); Franz W. Sichel for the Hilde Potter Room in the American Bounty Restaurant (79); Ed Hartley Benenson for the Escoffier Restaurant (55); H. Jerome Berns for the Martha Berns Reading Room in the Conrad N. Hilton Library (xi); Basic American Foods for the Basic American Foods Production Kitchen in the Student Recreation Center (67); H.J. Heinz Corporation for the Storeroom in Roth Hall (50); Banfi Vintners for the Banfi Vintners Dining Room in the J. Willard Marriott Continuing Education Center (xv); John and Clara Farquharson for Farquharson Hall in Roth Hall (8).